CREATIVE WRITING FOR SOCIAL RESEARCH
A Practical Guide

Richard Phillips and Helen Kara

First published in Great Britain in 2021 by

Policy Press, an imprint of
Bristol University Press
University of Bristol
1–9 Old Park Hill
Bristol BS2 8BB
UK
t: +44 (0)117 954 5940
e: bup-info@bristol.ac.uk

Details of international sales and distribution partners are available at
policy.bristoluniversitypress.co.uk

Cover design by Qube Design Associates, Bristol
Front cover: image kindly supplied by iStock/flickr.com
Printed and bound in Great Britain by CMP, Poole
Bristol University Press use environmentally responsible print partners

To Richard's mother, Elizabeth Phillips, for curiosity and creativity, and

To Helen's father, Mark Miller, for a lifetime of writerly inspiration.

Contents

Creative writing in practice

List of figures

Acknowledgements

The adventure began with a two-day workshop on creative writing in social research, in Sheffield, in November 2018. The workshop was co-ordinated by this book's authors and attended by its contributors and others. Each person attending had the opportunity to give a short performative presentation and to participate in the ensuing discussions. Their responses were inspirational and took many forms – from facilitated exercises to stand-up comedy, and from academic reflections on creative writing to creatively written stories and songs, performed in the workshop. We wanted to work together and to share and encourage others to explore the possibilities of creative writing in social research, and this book is the outcome of our collaboration during and after the workshop. Those who attended the workshop and contributed to this book are credited elsewhere for their individual writing, but here we want to acknowledge them in a broader sense: for their part in a collective project, which they entered with generosity, creativity and fun. They are: Alke Gröppel-Wegener, Andrew McMillan, Hayden Lorimer, Hester Parr, Julia Molinari, Kate Fox, Katherine Collins, Kay Inckle, Kitrina Douglas, Kristina Diprose, Mary Evans, Nafhesa Ali, Rowan Jaines, Ruth Raynor, Sarah McNicol and Stacy Bias. We also wish to acknowledge co-authors, who contributed to the finished contributions in this book: Ruth Olden and David Carless. Other participants in the workshop, who contributed to this collective adventure, included Brendan Stone, Safina Mazhar, Kirit Patel and Michal Kupis.

We are also grateful to others who have supported and encouraged us in this project: Kate Pahl, Cate Watson, Ben Clayton, Claire Chambers, Alistair Roy, Afshan D'souza-Lodhi, Les Back, Jennifer Mason, Nick Sousanis, Susie Weller, Chris Bailey, Sarah de Leeuw and Maggie O'Neill.

At Policy Press, Catherine Gray helped to shape this book from the outset, and Philippa Grand supported its completion. Thank you both.

The workshop was supported by the Arts and Humanities Research Council (AHRC) through funding for a project entitled Storying Relationships (AH/N003926/1).

Finally, we would like to acknowledge our learning from the students we have been fortunate to work with – Richard at the University of Sheffield, and Helen through her workshops in universities worldwide. Creative writing for social research blurs the boundaries between students, teachers, researchers and participants: we learn from each other, share ideas and create together.

Preface

This book provides a resource for people who are interested in learning more about creative writing and its applications for social research. Social researchers come in many forms: undergraduate and postgraduate students and academics across a range of disciplines, community and professional researchers, and others too. The book is for you if you are intrigued by the possibilities of using creative writing in social research, but are not sure where, when or how this can be done. It is also for you if you are interested in exploring – and forming critical readings of – ways in which other social researchers are working with creative writing.

Our book distinguishes and explores three main ways in which social researchers engage with creative writing:

- bringing creative writing into the practice – the doing – of social research;
- using creative writing to work with participants and generate data;
- using creative writing to analyse data and communicate findings.

This is the first book of its kind: part introduction, part practical guide to the interface between creative writing and social research. It complements some related literatures:

- Manuals and textbooks on creative and arts–based research (ABR) methods more generally.
- Books about the research activities of creative writing departments, which now exist in many universities and colleges, delivering degrees and diplomas in creative writing practice.
- Books and manuals about creative writing as an end in itself. There are many excellent books on the market for those who are learning the craft of creative writing. We introduce and recommend some of these in Chapter 1. Though it is not a manual, this book does include practical hints and tips – including 'Try This' sections to help you put ideas into practice – and explains how principles of creative writing can be applied to social research.

This book:

- shows how social researchers can, and do, work with creative writing;
- suggests how social researchers who are new to this can get started and develop skills in creative writing, expanding their own writing practices in particular within data collection, analysis and dissemination;
- offers 'permission' and ideas for researchers who would like to work with creative writing.

Just as there are different forms of creative writing, and different ways of engaging with writing, there are different ways of writing about creative writing. It is therefore essential that we find space within this book for different forms of writing and for different voices. Appropriately, then, this book is polyvocal or, to be more precise, polygraphical or polytextual. The format includes two main approaches:

1. Substantive sections, written by Richard Phillips and Helen Kara. These provide an explanatory narrative, with examples from a wide range of researchers and writers. These sections quote some accomplished and inspiring writers and offer practical suggestions for how to get started or improve the creative writing you do in your own social research (or your students do in theirs).
2. 'Creative writing in practice' contributions by researchers. Some write creatively about creative writing, in keeping with the 'show don't tell' traditions of creative writing, which we explain in the course of this book. Others bring their experience to bear upon creative writing for social research through the reflections and insights they share. One, Alke Gröppel-Wegener, doesn't write at all, but draws a number of 'inspiration dolls', inspired by and introducing the writing of the other contributors.

Polygraphical as it is – created by two authors with different voices and styles, and by 15 other contributors – this text has a messy quality, which we have resisted the temptation to smooth over and edit out (Law 2004). Messiness, we think, is something to hold on to, to tolerate and celebrate, as it underpins our broader project: to 'queer writing'. Queer, in this sense, means to trouble, to unsettle, to destabilise, to see afresh. To queer our writing is to trouble and unsettle the ways in which we write and, through this writing, the ways in which we see: playfully, critically, transgressively, insightfully.

 Further resources to support readers in exploring the themes of this book can be found on the companion website at: https://policy. bristoluniversitypress.co.uk/creative-writing-for-social-research/ companion-website.

Introduction

Sociology is anathema to poetry. (Linton Kwesi Johnson, BBC 2018)

Poetry … allows me to be a better social scientist. (Sandra Faulkner, 2019: 222)

Linton Kwesi Johnson read sociology at the University of London before making his name as the inventor of dub poetry. Reflecting on his life and work in the radio interview quoted here, he seems to dismiss his studies as a way of passing the time until he found his real calling: a performance art that brings together words and music.

While Johnson seems to insist that poetry has nothing to do with the study of society, others are not so sure. Sandra Faulkner, a researcher in the field of communication, suggests the opposite: that poetry allows her 'to be a better social scientist' (Faulkner 2019:222). Zygmunt Bauman, the influential sociologist, said he had 'personally learned more about the society we live in from Balzac, Zola, Kafka, Musil, Frisch, Perec, Kundera, Beckett … than, say, from Parsons' and others who are routinely cited in his academic field (Blackshaw 2002:2; see also Jacobsen and Marshman 2008). Johnson contradicts himself, in any case; he has never stopped examining society, analytically and critically. His poetry speaks of race and racism, class and inequality, and it narrates and explores social conflicts and crises: from police brutality to struggles over public housing. These are the preoccupations of many social researchers, extending far beyond the discipline of sociology to include human geography, anthropology, cultural and religious studies and more, within and beyond universities and academic enquiry.

If poetry and other forms of creative writing were once seen as anathema to social research – and it is a big if – this is no longer true. In the course of this book, we will turn to work that shows how creative writing and social enquiry can complement and enhance each other. This engagement with a particular form of creative practice can be located within a wider creative turn – or, as Harriet Hawkins (2018:963) puts it, acknowledging some important foundational work in the past, 'creative (re)turn' – which has energised and diversified research across the social sciences.

Some researchers have turned to creative writing because they came up against the limits of its more conventional academic counterparts. As a student, Bruce Chatwin struggled with a thesis on nomadism, which was becoming increasingly unwieldy; it refused to say what he wanted it to say. Chatwin eventually abandoned the original, conventionally academic manuscript and approached the problem from another angle: writing a fictionalised travel narrative, which was eventually published as *The Songlines* (1987). In this innovative work, several characters allow Chatwin to speak in different voices and explore different perspectives: among others, those of the author/narrator, the protagonist (a version of Bruce Chatwin), and a fictional anthropologist. Chatwin felt he had found the right medium to say what he needed to, in a way that would hold readers' attention and reach a wide audience. He let go of his tentative academic career and reinvented himself as a novelist and travel writer (see King and Wyndham 1993).

Other researchers, frustrated by the limitations of academic writing, have also experimented with fiction, but unlike Chatwin they have done so within the scope of their ongoing academic careers (Banks and Banks 1998). Patricia Leavy dismissed 'traditional methods for carrying out research and then sharing that research' as 'sterile, jargon-filled, and formulaic' (Leavy 2015:1). This assessment of the state of the art – or rather the artlessness – of academic writing led Leavy to some productive experiments with new ways of getting her ideas and findings across. This included 'an arts-based novel titled *Low-Fat Love*' that enabled her (she claims) 'to deliver the content, layer more themes, portray composite characters sensitively, create empathetic understandings, promote self-reflection in readers, create longer-lasting learning experiences for readers, and most important, get the work out to the public' (Leavy 2015:2). Leavy also founded a book series, *Social Fictions*, which has published social research in the form of novels, plays and other fictions. Notable titles in the series include *October Birds*, subtitled *A Novel about Pandemic Influenza, Infection Control, and First Responders*, by Jessica Smartt Gullion (2014), and Toni Bruce's *Terra Ludus* (2016), also a novel, which explores media, gender and sport.

There are also ethical grounds for fictionalising findings. By 'selecting representative elements from the data set and composing a new original that is not traceable back to the originals' (Markham 2012:342), it is possible to make composite quotations and case studies, which conceal participants' identities and preserve their anonymity. These ethical advantages apply not only to work about others, but also to autobiographical and autoethnographic research, in which self-revelation might expose the author to risk or compromise their privacy (Delamont 2004).

This work – exploring and disseminating ideas through the novel and other forms of fiction – has some distinguished ancestors, including philosophers and public intellectuals from Jean-Paul Sartre to Iris Murdoch. There are also precedents for the use of published fiction in both research and teaching. Svend Brinkmann reads the French writer Michel Houellebecq as a source on 'contemporary human lives, experiences, and sufferings' (Brinkmann 2009:1376). Whether or not we agree with Brinkmann's flattering depiction of Houellebecq as a 'lyrical sociologist' – his subject is wilfully objectionable, courting controversy through his depictions of contemporary Islam, and his provocatively misogynistic depictions of women – this writer does throw some light on what Brinkmann (2009:1379) calls 'contemporary social life'. His reading of Houellebecq may be situated within a broader recognition that fiction and non-fiction offer complementary insights (Batty and Taylor 2019:390), opening doors to different kinds of truth and to different experiences (Pickering and Kara 2017:299). And, while some social researchers are now writing and working with fiction, others are exploring the possibilities of creative non-fiction. Donna Lee Brien (2013:50), a specialist in this field based in Queensland, reflects that creative non-fiction 'draws its power from the truths it tells' and earns popularity through 'the compelling and engaging ways it relays those truths'.

So it is not only on the fringes of social research that we find creative writing. Leading figures in the field, past and present, have also been creative writers. Bauman's 'methodological stance' has been described as 'somewhere between social science and literature' (Jacobsen and Marshman 2008:798), Bauman himself as 'a sociologist with a certain poetic or literary edge' (Jacobsen and Marshman 2008:801; see also Brown 1977). Leading anthropologists such as Clifford Geertz and Claude Levi-Strauss were also fine writers. The craft of writing is equally central to geography, a word comprised of two terms: *geo* and *graphein*, earth and writing (Barnes and Duncan 2013 [1992]:1). Social scientists in other fields including sociolegal and management studies have also brought writing into focus, experimenting with ways of writing and with textual interpretation (Fish 1980; Gabriel 2000).

The engagement between creative writing and social research remains a work-in-progress, with plenty of space for innovation and contribution (DeLyser and Sui 2014:297). Its open-endedness presents challenges and opportunities, which can be exciting and inclusive. But its unfolding status means it is not always as assured and accepted as its canonised counterparts (Denzin 2010/2016:90–2). In other words, the place of creative writing in social research is contested and controversial. Some advocates of arts-based research (ABR) and scholars who write experimentally accuse their conventional counterparts of using 'the all-knowing, all-powerful voice of the academy' (Richardson 1997:2) and privileging work that is 'highly abstract, jargonistic, difficult to read' (hooks 1991:4). Fighting the opposite corner, some social researchers and writers are resistant to ABR methods, which they may see as gimmicky and un-social-scientific (Gergen and Gergen 2012:50; see also Jackson 2017). Dydia DeLyser and Daniel Sui (2014:294) warn researchers not to be distracted by methodological novelties, to the exclusion or neglect of tried-and-tested methods such as interviews. (Taking their point, we should also remember that some established methods have short histories, questionnaires reaching back only into the 19th century, research interviews into the 20th.) Drawing these points together, we can identify opportunities and risks across the spectrum of creative and conventional academic writing. There is space for different ways of writing, and more generally for methodological pluralism, within social research (DeLyser and Sui 2014:297).

So we advocate engagement with creative writing where appropriate, rather than everywhere. Reasons for working with creative writing include:

- complementary insights: 'what is known in prose might be known differently in poetry' (Patrick 2016:385);
- reaching larger and more diverse audiences than conventional research writing (Banks and Banks 1998);
- reaching readers emotionally, affecting them in ways that formal academic writing cannot (Eshun and Madge 2012).

Here, we develop the case that social researchers can and should do more to explore the possibilities for creative writing and for the spoken and written word that does not 'fit into social scientific conventions' (Gandolfo and Ochoa 2017:187). We have much to gain from reaching outside these conventions, and paying attention to the ways in which people use words when they tell their stories and reflect upon their lives (Gandolfo and Ochoa 2017). Doing so, we wish to share skills and offer 'permission' to researchers seeking to work with creative writing. With such permission, their work may gain credibility and respect, taking its place within the sphere of recognised and respected social research methodologies.

Definitions

We have begun to refer to 'social research', 'creativity' and 'writing' without having defined any of these key terms. It will be useful to venture preliminary definitions, not to artificially tie down language that is delightfully, frustratingly, productively slippery, but to provide points of departure for this book. What, then, do we and others mean by social research, by creativity and creative, and by writing and creative writing? What are the synergies between creative writing and social research?

Social research

Since this book is aimed primarily at social researchers who are interested in learning more about creative writing, most readers will already have an understanding of social research. So we will be brief in our presentation of an approach to social research that advances inclusivity and highlights potential synergies with creativity.

Social research begins with questions about people and society, typically from a social science perspective, before considering methods through which to answer these questions. So, when social researchers engage with creative writing, they approach it as a means to an end. There is an important distinction between the application of creative writing methods to social research – our focus here – and the research component of creative writing as an academic discipline. Both attempt 'research through, and in, creative writing' (Harper 2013:133), though they come at this from different directions and with different priorities. Graham Mort explains that the study of creative writing, as it exists within universities, 'is a practice-led discipline' which may be theoretically engaged and is often socially curious, but is fundamentally 'compositional', implying the 'primacy of linguistic/literary mark-making' (Mort 2013:207). Notwithstanding his own work and teaching in cross-cultural creative writing, and the social and cultural insights this has brought, Mort identifies his approach as writing first, research second. Here, Mort speaks for many of his colleagues in university creative writing programmes (see: Kroll and Harper 2013; Harper 2019). Social research – our focus here – is the opposite.

Social research occurs in many different places. In schools and universities, social researchers are found within and between social science and humanities disciplines such as sociology, anthropology, human geography, and religious, cultural, women's, gender and sexuality studies. But, as Linton Kwesi Johnson stressed, learning and enquiry take place in many other settings too. For social researchers, these may include government research departments, corporate R&D units, commercial research companies, and community organisations. It follows that social research is best defined broadly: as a form of inquiry into a topic concerning society.

Social research also takes many different forms, some of which reach well beyond conventionally social scientific methods (Kara 2017:41). Researchers are borrowing and adapting methods from other disciplines in the social sciences, humanities, arts and natural sciences too, and exploring the possibilities of innovative, diverse methodologies. We are working with a wide range of arts and crafts including painting, drawing, theatre, film, animation, dance, storytelling and – the focus of this book – creative writing.

Creativity and creative

Creativity is notoriously difficult to define (Pope 2005:52; Walsh, Anders and Hancock 2013:21). Harriet Hawkins observes that creativity has descended into 'an anything goes term that applies to everything and so nothing' (Hawkins 2017:1–2). That said, attempts have been made to pin down this term. Existing definitions tend to focus on what it does and how it operates rather than what it is (Kara 2020:13). Defined this way, creativity will do one or more of the following:

- produce something entirely new (Runco and Jaeger 2012:92, citing Stein (1953) and Barron (1955));
- combine existing elements in a new way (Kara 2020:15);
- resist categorical or binary thinking (Jones and Leavy 2014:1);
- cross-disciplinary, social, professional and other boundaries (Kara 2020:6).

For all these reasons, creativity is associated with possibilities. It tends to be idealised, seen as intrinsically positive. We argue for a more measured understanding, which recognises potential benefits but also develops a critical perspective, remembering to ask searching questions: Who gets to be creative?

Whose creativity is recognised? What is creativity? Finally, to paraphrase cultural geographer Oli Mould (2018): What is creativity for, who or what does it serve, and when is it a good thing?

These questions will not be resolved within this book, but they have been useful to acknowledge because they both complicate the definitions of creativity that we have begun to put forward and place creativity in its social context.

First, creativity is a social rather than a 'natural' practice. Graeme Harper's assertion that 'human beings are by nature creative creatures' (Harper 2013:142) makes intuitive sense because creativity is often seen as innate: universal in humans, some more than others, simply waiting to be cultivated. And yet, creativity is understood differently in different times and places. As such, differently creative dispositions and practices are taught and learned, encouraged and tolerated. Understandings and definitions of this term must be equally flexible.

Second, as a social practice, creativity is relational, something people do together – or at least with others in mind – rather than in isolation. This challenges another common assumption about creativity: that it is the province of individuals (Sawyer 2010). Howard Becker – a sociologist celebrated for his creativity – unsettled the individualistic picture of the creative artist, that great mythical figure, insisting that 'art emerges from a collective effort' (McNally 2018:344, citing Becker 1976). This means that, though the creative process has a psychological dimension in which 'ideas hatch and develop beyond our conscious control or awareness' (Neale 2006a:68), creativity is never a purely individual matter.

These observations apply to writing, including creative writing. People often think of writing as an individual activity. But all sorts of people and organisations may be involved with a piece of academic writing: imagined and implied readers plus editors, reviewers, designers, typesetters and proofreaders, printers, distributors – the list is long. It is longer still in academic settings, where writing also involves tutors and supervisors, examiners, colleagues, research participants, ethical reviewers, peer reviewers, universities and publishers. A writer may not be aware of all these people, structures and relationships as they write, but they are likely to be aware of some, and of the consenting and 'non-consenting others' they write about (Mannay 2016:122).

Third, since creativity is socially produced and relationally performed, its power relations need to be acknowledged. Monica Reuter (2015) argues that creativity is not democratic because powerful gatekeepers – including cultural critics, government advisors and administrators, and business leaders – decide what sorts of creativity are valued and endorsed.

Recognising that creativity is fundamentally social, rather than some mysterious and preformed sphere, we can also see that is it contested and contestable. It follows that we are not limited to importing definitions of creativity; we can decide what we want this term to mean. Hawkins argues for a critical approach to creativity – as both the object and also the methodology for social and cultural research – and challenges us to ask 'how exactly' creative scholarship is 'critical and creative, and for whom?' (Hawkins 2015:249).

The creativity we advocate and practise in this book is inclusive. This includes things we do alone and together, things we can learn to do for the first time or to do differently, and in our own ways. Inclusive creativity is present in everyday acts of 'getting by', and thus in practical acts as much as artistic gestures (Kersting 2003; Richards 2007). There is space here for amateurs: makers of home movies (Nicholson 1997), musicians (Finnegan 2007) and, of course, amateur creative writers. There is space, too, for those with artistic ambitions, but also for those who write for its own sake, or for pleasure, therapy, self-discovery, or countless other reasons. These writers are not necessarily motivated by the criteria with which we initially defined creativity – producing something entirely new, resisting established ways of thinking, crossing boundaries – but their work still belongs within the understanding of creativity we have moved towards here, one which is expanded and more inclusive.

Writing and creative writing

Writing isn't as easy to define as it might seem. Writing is both a verb and a noun: I am writing; that is my writing. The boundary between writing and drawing is not always clear, such as with Egyptian hieroglyphs and Japanese kanji. Nevertheless we think we can formulate a single working definition of 'writing' that will serve for this book: writing is a method of communicating between people using symbols marked on an artefact such as paper or a screen.

What, then, is creative writing? On first inspection, this term is self-explanatory, telling us 'all we need to know' (Harper 2019:2). Graeme Harper observes that attempts to define creative writing tend to revolve around the circular claim that creative writing is 'writing that is creative' and to draw upon 'synonyms for creativity, words such as invention, novelty, originality, innovation, vision' (Harper 2019:1). Some forms and genres – or, a term favoured by Patricia Leavy (2015:2), 'shapes' of writing – fit this definition more comfortably than others. Shapes typically seen as creative, and used to explore and narrate human lives, include short stories, novels and other fiction, poetry, scripts for screen and stage, comics and graphic novels (Weiner and Syma 2013), animation, blog and social media posts (Peacock and Holland 1993; Somers 1994). These genres and shapes provide starting points, which can orient both creative writers and readers. Writers may then go on to transgress these categories. Indeed, as Derek Neale (2006a) explains, doing so can be an important part of creativity.

But, on closer inspection, the term creative writing is not self-explanatory. It is culturally specific and historically recent, a modern and western term, said to have been coined as recently as the 1930s (Pope 2005:198). Pushing for a more illuminating understanding of this term and field of practice, Harper argues that creative writing is distinctive in its 'unique' combination of 'imaginative' and 'analytical' capacities and components 'in and through writing' and because it 'creates or … *brings into being*' through writing (Harper 2019:12, original emphasis). This definition is dynamic, reaching beyond what creative writing is to what it does: to the processes and effects of writing. This distinction echoes our earlier definition of creativity and anticipates much of what follows in this book in terms of the processes (not just the products) of creative writing, and the significance of those processes upon writers and readers alike (Law 2004). This distinction between process and product may be traced to Donald M. Murray (1972), the Pulitzer Prize-winning writer, who advocated attention to process. That priority is reflected in this book, and more generally in the place of creative writing within social research.

Creative writing, defined in this way, opens up particular ways of doing social research. These potential contributions stand to complement more conventional approaches in which the place of writing tends to be limited to 'writing up' – done once the real research is complete. Writing, as we see it, belongs at the heart of social research; it is part of research; a research method in its own right; a means of enquiry, exploration and articulation.

Synergies between creative writing and social research

The differences between creative writing and social scientific writing are often overstated. For example, when Graham Mort (2013:218) asserts that '[t]he creative writer is unlikely to be able to create new knowledge in the way that a scientist can – based upon new and observable phenomena', we think he draws too sharp a contrast between creative writing and social research, and understates the synergies and overlaps between them.

The conventional distinction between creative and academic writing places emphasis on two different and seemingly opposing areas: showing and telling. Creative writers are told to 'show' rather than 'tell' whereas academic researchers are taught the opposite, leading with distilled claims and abstract insights (Neale 2006b:127). This distinction is a little too bold. There is a place for telling in creative writing and for showing in academic/research writing (Sword 2012:99–111). Creative writers and academic researchers must each decide what and how much to show and tell. Unsettling Harper's argument that creative writing is a 'unique' cocktail of the imaginative and the analytical, it is easy to find examples of imaginative and imaginatively written social research. While Harper (2019:20) credits creative writers with constantly tacking 'between the recognized systems of our written language and types of novelty and of originality', social scientists and other academics often do the same, and not only in their writing. Novelty and originality are key criteria for research assessment and governance, for example in the UK's Research Excellence Framework (Phillips 2010).

On closer inspection, the boundaries between creative writing and social research are blurred. Leavy is too categorical, we think, when she dismisses mainstream social science writing as 'loaded with jargon' and 'in all ways inaccessible' (Leavy 2015:56). Similarly, Jon Cook (2012:100) overstates the distinction between social research and creative writing when he identifies a 'lack of fit between prevailing ideas about what it means to do research in a university and what it is like to write a novel, or a collection of poems or a script'. And, while Harper (2019:xiv–xv) is no doubt right to say that creative writers bring 'distinctive ways of thinking, as well as ways of responding to the world, and ways of interpreting facts, and ways of moving between the intellect and the imagination, often fluidly, seamlessly', this doesn't mean creative writers are categorically different from others who observe and interpret the social world around them. Rather than seeing creative writing and social research as separate spheres, it may be more accurate and useful to speak, as Beck et al (2011) do, of a 'continuum' of research and the creative arts. Between the extremes of this continuum, research and creativity blend into each other, coexisting and cross-fertilising (Richardson 1997; Henderson and Taimina 2001; Phillips and Johns 2012; Chilton and Leavy 2014; Leavy 2015; Harron 2016; Hawkins 2017; Finley 2019; Kara 2020).

To explain why some of the best social researchers are already interested in creative writing, we shall now turn to some overlaps, intersections and synergies between these spheres, which we revisit and develop in the course of this book. These revolve around human curiosity: about others and oneself (Phillips 2016). Advice offered to creative writing students is equally applicable to social research: 'Try to cultivate an attitude of curiosity' (Anderson 2006:21); and pursue a 'sense of discovery or revelation' (Neale 2006a:58). Like these aspiring creative writers, social researchers wonder about people, observe and talk to them, listen to what they have to say, and explore all these things through the written word (as well as through other representational forms, including numbers and images).

Another thing they have in common is that creative writers and social researchers both have to make choices around *how* they write about others. This involves choices about authorial perspective and point of view. Again, there are broad differences between researchers and contemporary creative writers – the former typically being more comfortable than the latter to assume the perspective of the omniscient or all-seeing narrator (Baldick 2015) – though once again this distinction is a matter of degree, not categorical. Both creative writers and social researchers make choices about perspective and point of view, and both experiment with these choices. Doing so is fundamental to their empathetic curiosity: their interest in other people.

Creative writing handbooks offer many exercises in empathy, which begin speculatively, with exercises in wondering and guessing about other people's experiences and writing from their imagined points of view, and sometimes follow through with more informed empathy: finding out about and learning to listen to others. Linda Anderson (2006:114–15) suggests the following exercise:

> Recall an argument you have had with someone. Write about the quarrel from your opponent's point of view, using third-person limited omniscience. The objective here is to practise empathy with points of view that antagonise you in reality. Empathy is not always easy to attain but it expands the fiction writer's imaginative range like nothing else.

ABR researcher Ronald Pelias (2019:143) proposes a more sustained exercise along the same lines: 'Calling upon your empathetic self':

1. Write an essay where you call upon a spiral of shifting perspectives. Start with your own point of view and then shift to another person's perspective. Keep the spiral going: I think … I think you think …, I think you think, I think … Allow yourself to shift topics, but continue the structure of shifting perspectives.
2. Think of a person or group of people with whom you have had or currently have a disagreement or conflict. Imagine all the things you would like to say to them. See them sitting across from you. Say what you would like to say to them. Then, exchange places, and let them speak back to you from their perspective. Write a piece where you account for both perspectives.

These ideas have much to offer social researchers, as we explain in Chapter 2, where we adapt and develop empathetic writing exercises with social researchers in mind.

In writing, as in research, speculative empathy is just the start. Creative writers typically go beyond guesswork that might lead them to write about social types, even stereotypes Harper (2019:6) argues that 'creative writing is frequently a response to something or someone' and is 'borne on personal perception'. It can also be informed by more systematic research, which may inform the development of characters and stories (de Freitas 2003). Of course, this is the focus of social research. Interest in the lives of others is a point of contact between creative writing and social research.

Creative writers also write about *themselves*; so do social researchers, who increasingly bring their own stories into their work. Doing so, they reflect on their own lives and their relationships, consider what they have in common with others, and ponder how their lives and experiences converge and diverge. Self-reflection and social exploration intersect. Think, for example of the worker-writer groups, which formed in Britain in the 1960s and 1970s, and 'encouraged ordinary people to write memoirs, stories and poems' that 'consciously highlighted the voices (recorded and written) of working men and women, and people from immigrant/ethnic, other cultural, communities' (Wandor 2012:53). Writing from experience, it is possible to explore and to 'learn about social phenomena' (Ellis and Adams 2014:263), broaching subjects as varied as violence, kindness, prejudice, tolerance, illness, healing, ageing, eating, embodiment and, on a more abstract level, sexuality, gender, race and class (Thompson-Lee 2017). There are many different ways of writing from experience: autobiography or memoir, of course, but others too, including autoethnography, the essay, diary, blog and other forms of first-person narrative. We explore these and other ways of writing creatively in the context of social research in Chapter 2.

As an introduction and practical guide to creative writing for social research, this book overlaps with two other kinds of book – on the techniques of creative writing and on writing for researchers – and on the intersections between these: on creative writing for research. We expect many readers of this book will also want to consult books on these topics so we include some suggestions here. First, on creative writing techniques, we recommend Linda Anderson's *Creative Writing: A Workbook with Readings* (2006) and Derek Neale's *A Creative Writing Handbook: Developing Dramatic Technique, Individual Style and Voice* (2009). We also point you to specialised introductions and handbooks on practical exercises in writing (Goldberg 1991), screenwriting (McKee 1999), graphic storytelling (McCloud 2006) and the first principles of writing (Moran 2019). You may also be interested in another set of handbooks and monographs, which we refer to throughout this book, which explore the possibilities of academic and non-fiction writing (for example, Richardson 1997; Elbow 1998; Elbow 2000; King 2000; Davis, Senechal and Zwicky 2008; Luey 2010; Nygaard 2015; Kara 2017; Pandian and McLean 2017; Sword 2017; Leavy 2019; Pelias 2019). Full details are of course in the References.

What follows

With many different voices and styles of writing, this book is polyvocal or, more precisely, polygraphical. It includes substantive sections in which Richard and Helen explain how creative writing can be used in the course of social research. In Chapter 2, we explore ways in which social researchers can do creative writing, and we show how particular genres or shapes of writing can be used as means of questioning and collecting data. Chapter 3 explores creative writing as a participatory research method, and explains how we can use creative writing to explore experiences that we may miss when we use more direct and conventional research methods. In Chapter 4, we focus upon the use of creative writing in data analysis and dissemination. These discussions are interspersed with contributions by researchers, who provide sustained expositions and illustrations of particular forms of creative writing.

Throughout the book we draw out the shapes of writing with the help of Alke Gröppel-Wegener, the creator of a series of drawn 'inspiration dolls', which you will find throughout this book. Each 'doll' was inspired by one of the contributor pieces and appears with that piece. The dolls are designed to help us visualise the enabling but blurred genres that we necessarily work with, and to remind us that the boundary between writing and drawing is also blurred. They are intended not only to decorate this text but also to trouble and inspire us as writers; they are an unruly pack of genre-bending figures.

With two main authors and 15 other contributors, and with quotations from many more, this book has a messiness, which we have been careful to respect and to preserve. We have taken inspiration from John Law's argument that social researchers are wrong to fixate on methods geared towards clarity and precision when the worlds we are describing (and shaping) are fluid, elusive, unclear, vague and multiple (Law 2004). Rather than smoothing out and polishing this text, we have embraced a strategic scruffiness, which revolves around queer writing, and the queering of writing for social research. Queer is a complex and contested term, but historian David Halperin provides an introductory definition, which it is useful to quote here and develop later: 'whatever is at odds with the normal, the legitimate, the dominant' (Halperin 1990:62). Queering means unsettling orthodoxies, troubling certainties, challenging the intellectual order and power relations of the status quo, and thereby opening new ways of seeing and new possibilities for understanding. Queer writing is necessarily inclusive, fluid and open-ended. Practically, this means that we resist the temptation to over-polish our writing and that of the contributors. Though we are proud to include some beautiful writing in this book, we have not set out in search of decorative creative writing, or writing with great literary pretensions; nor have we banished 'bad poems' or inelegant prose, where such writing fosters a searching, transgressive and creative approach to social research. Queer writing, we find, is in the spirit of critical social research: questioning; finding out; collecting and analysing data; analysing and sharing findings; advancing understandings.

CREATIVE WRITING IN PRACTICE

Some questions about being creative *by Mary Evans*[1]

Mary Evans is Emeritus Leverhulme Professor in Gender Studies at the LSE. Creative writing is central to her investigations of how we learn and acquire our social identities. Mary's works on this subject include a study of detective fiction entitled *Detecting the Social* (Evans et al 2018). Here, she reflects on what it means to think critically about creativity.

Contemporary validations of higher education often endorse the idea that this experience encourages students to think 'critically' and to be able to 'assess objectively different theories'. Whether or not this actually occurs is of course a matter of speculation; what is more important is the way in which these expectations often suggest that it is entirely positive to marginalise the 'subjective'. Even though many of the social sciences have seen, in recent decades, what are described as 'turns' to the cultural and more recently the 'affective' we still have to think through, and about, the extent to which our own, individual, experiences have a place in both the documentation and the understanding of the social world (on the cultural and affective turns, see: Barrett 1992; Ahmed 2004). The distinction between the general and the

Figure 1.1: Inspiration doll by Alke Gröppel-Wegener, created in response to this piece by Mary Evans. Inspiration dolls comment on and play with genres of creative writing.

personal is crucial, since the mantra that commands social scientists never to generalise from a single instance is one that constitutes a fundamental lesson. Even if fictional and non-fictional cases from those of a disturbed young man (Hamlet) to an equally disturbed young woman (Freud's patient, Dora) have informed endless speculations about the human condition, we are nevertheless wary of where this might take us. Indeed, in the early decades of the 21st century we have reason to be suspicious given

---

[1] This contribution should be cited as follows: Evans, M. (2021) 'Some questions about being creative'. In Phillips, R. and Kara, H. *Creative Writing for Social Research*. Bristol: Policy Press.

that entire political regimes and policies are increasingly being built on instances of the single benefit cheat or the criminal immigrant.

So it would appear that encouraging the idea of creative writing, writing that emerges from the individual case or the individual circumstance, is something that we should be careful about. But I want to argue here that truly creative writing, while placed around the single case, can nevertheless be properly constructed through some processes which we need to consider, define and integrate into our work. The point, therefore, is not to assume that in creative writing we are using individual cases and experiences as unproblematic locations for generalisations about the social world but that we could have at our command a general method through which we might investigate that more conventional social space of the collective. The first of the rules of engagement which I would suggest is that creativity, and creative writing, has to involve the imagination. This might sound obvious – we might assume that 'creative' work implicitly involves the imagination – but I suggest that we have to be creative about what we take for granted: the 'everyday' language of the social sciences. So we have to allow ourselves space to re-think some of the basic assumptions and categories of social science. Here I would offer as instances of this fundamental need for imaginative thinking those two basic concepts of the social sciences: social class and social mobility. In the case of social class, the questions that we have to ask are not just about how we define it, but how we go on making and producing it in ourselves. English canonical fiction is replete with examples of people determined both to keep and to improve their class: the imagination of writers of fiction has shown how fragile our location within the class structure can be. At the same time, fiction has also shown the power which owning, maintaining and living a classed identity can exercise over individuals. For example, William Thackeray understood with absolute clarity the way in which class is 'made'; in the 20th century writers as disparate as Kingsley Amis, George Orwell and P.D. James have shown how frantic is the human pursuit of social definition through class. One of the most powerful crime novels of the 20th century, Ruth Rendell's *A Judgement in Stone* (1977), is about what Richard Sennett and Jonathan Cobb (1972) called the 'hidden injuries' of class. In Rendell's novel the injury is that of illiteracy and the murderous class hatred it triggers. All these writers have recognised the psychic world of class; precisely the energy which fuels that intense competition for upward social mobility, about which the social historian Selina Todd (2014) has written with such perception. Creativity in creative writing involves this same process of constant re-thinking and asking what we mean when we use terms which we so easily take for granted. In the UK in 2020, in the case of the specific instance of the meaning of 'class', we have to ask exactly what a term such as 'middle class' actually means, and if such an apparently secure social generalisation can accurately encompass the social range which it encompasses. In this context, thinking creatively might also ask us to think less about the result of social processes but rather more about both the workings of the processes and the possibility that the making of 'class' is never a completed process. This demands the recognition that we are all prismatic, have different parts to our lives, parts to which terms such as 'work' or 'class' can scarcely do justice. Anyone who has read autobiography will know that many writers omit significant aspects of their lives; a point which must make us wary of regarding a personal record as anything other than an imperfect interpretation of self. At the same time, we have to recognise the social mirror into which writers of autobiography are gazing: not simply the gaze on a person, but the extent to which a person wishes to meet the demands of the gaze (debates about the gendered gaze were sparked by Berger 1972).

So imagination is first. But then two reservations: the first is about judgement. I am sure that many of us have collected our children's art. We might also have looked at it in terms of Picasso's comment that 'it took me four years to paint like Raphael, but a lifetime to paint like a child'. Remembering this might have also led us to consider the difference between the artwork pinned to our kitchen walls and works by Picasso hanging on the walls of the world's art galleries. This is the paradox which perhaps lies in many of our efforts to integrate the untutored, the spontaneous expressions by those who we regard as the unheard. Performance, engagement, participation are all parts of any education worth the name, but we also have to be able to assess, to assess the ways in which an object, a comment, a story contributed by others can help us to understand both those individuals and the world in which they live. Yet here we meet some of the straitjackets on the imagination, predominant among which are those of cliché. Our children today learn phrases about 'being there for you' and 'understanding your pain' but clichés, however well meaning, might not always be more than recent framings of what used to be articulated as 'sincere condolences'. It is not up to us to dismiss diverse or unfamiliar voices. Yet it is up to us – and very much in the light of the third comment to be made here – that we consider how to assess, to review, to judge. This involves an understanding of our individual and collective relationship to forms of power.

Thus the third comment is about power. The early years of the 21st century have endorsed ideas about democratisation and 'the people' at the same time as concentrations of power beyond any kind of democratic control have also been recognised and often deplored. Further fractures of our times are between the individual and the collective, in the sense that various forms of institutional life further and encourage competition between individuals while at the same time questioning the legitimacy of collective forms of social intervention and support. These shifts – albeit contested and always with considerable historical roots and allegiances – are such that individual cases can be used to illustrate general themes, just as the individual might be blamed for failing to recognise collective norms. Self-awareness, the ability to see oneself in a context, the understanding of our own *habitus*, are real aspects of power: in any exchange between individuals these should be fundamental to our understanding. When we view the work of another individual it is often difficult to remember that we are also an individual. But just as much as the person or the object which we are studying, we are also a person with a collectively constructed history from which our creativity, be it critical or otherwise, is drawn. Given that historians have identified the concept of 'possessive individualism' as existing in England from the 17th century it is hasty to argue that individualism is an invention of the late 20th or early 21st centuries, but it is certainly possible to show that we are encouraged in our everyday lives to nurture those tastes and habits which support our sense of the individual self (on the long history of individualism, see: Macfarlane 1978).

My final point is that we should always be alive to the complexities of what the art historian Robert Hughes (1991) has described as the 'shock' of the new and what in the history of science Thomas Kuhn (1962) has named as a 'paradigm shift'. A paradigm shift is of course the holy grail of intellectual achievement: the discovery of an aspect of the world which transforms previous theories. But alongside these recognitions of the unarguably transformative moments in intellectual life we must note that we live in a social world much involved with the sensational. Much of the world, and its political economy, actually acquires its dynamic from the new, the 'sensational', be it in an art form or fashions in clothing. In his *Sensational Subjects* John Jervis (2015) points out that we have come to 'dramatise "sensation" in modern culture; events, people, forms of dress, which can shock become something more: they become sensational'. Jervis's study of sensation is hugely important in exploring the way that we regard and assess creative work, in that it asks us to examine the motives underlying creative energy. It is about recognising the fragile, insecure and tentative boundaries between the wish to explore or develop as much as those needs to attract attention or attempt to heal those absences we feel in ourselves.

The above asks that in being and in encouraging the creative we also think creatively about what we are producing. Without diminishing the possibilities of the 'new', it remains our responsibility to see the hidden and unspoken creativity of the past, both as memory and as an ongoing part of the present. In recent weeks I have read various accounts of dealing with people who are living with dementia and other forms of mental impairment. It is suggested that a new way of treating these human beings should be to engage with and not necessarily interrupt their accounts of the world. This, in its turn, has been hailed as novel. Yet back in 1848 Thackeray, in *Vanity Fair*, presents us with a daughter allowing and engaging with her elderly father's view of the present, a view which is in the strictest empirical terms incorrect. In this we have to see that although we have long known the possibilities of the disparate, we are less good at maintaining its presence. Looking for those places where we have failed to value individual acts of the creative is a central part of the creative imagination.

2

Doing creative writing

Introduction

Social researchers of all stripes are, of necessity, also writers. We write research proposals, funding bids, ethics applications; research reports, journal articles, book chapters; theses, dissertations and books; newspaper articles, blog posts and emails; the list goes on. We choose words to put together into sentences and paragraphs that nobody else has written. Whether or not we are specifically using creative writing techniques, this is a creative process. That said, some social researchers write more creatively than others; some social research is more creatively written. Some forms, genres, ways or shapes of writing accord more closely to definitions of creative writing, including Harper's broad definition that includes writing with both 'imaginative' and 'analytical' capacities and components (Harper 2019:12).

Writing (more) creatively means looking beyond the orthodox and canonical forms of writing which most of us have learned in study skills and research training courses. It means exploring all the possibilities that are open to us as writers, and resisting the pressure to conform unthinkingly to the default mode. And it means recognising that writing is more than a means of communicating; it is a resource, which remains to be fully tapped. Helen's teaching is particularly relevant here. In her creative thesis workshops for doctoral students, she has conceptualised writing as teacher, therapist and friend. Like a good teacher, the act of writing helps writers to explore and articulate their ideas (Colyar 2009:425–6). Writing can help us to explore experiences and identify and express emotions, as one might with a therapist. As Pelias (2019:26) puts it, 'writing allows disorder to find some order; chaos to settle into manageable form'. In this way creative writing can also be a reliable source of pleasure, perhaps of comfort, like a friend – though, like a friend, it can also be annoying and disappointing at times!

Different social science disciplines and social research practitioners have different writing conventions, but all of these tend to revolve around formal prose, with no clichés, slang or text-speak. The passive voice has typically been used, in part to reflect the then-prevailing theory that researchers were neutral observers who had no effect on the phenomena they were observing. This convention has been discredited, notably by feminist critics, who have insisted upon the importance of the positionality of researchers, and argued that this must be made explicit (Rose 1997). Nowadays, the active voice is increasingly common, adopted by leading journals such as *Nature*, *Science* and the *British Medical Journal*. This is linked to greater openness, not only in the social sciences and humanities but also within science, technology, engineering and mathematics (STEM) subjects, towards a broader range of written expression with scope for the overtly creative (Ahearn 2006:117; Harron 2016). There is an ethical dimension to the embrace of the active voice, in particular, since this enables the writer to say who did what, rather than only being able to say what was done. The increased use of the active voice is linked to another shift, also led by feminist scholars, towards writing in the first person and otherwise challenging orthodox forms of writing (we substantiate and illustrate these claims in the following section on writing in the first person).

Another aspect of this shift involves centring the researcher's positionality, which is made up of one or more locations. How you define 'location' depends on many interacting complex factors around the needs of the research and your own needs, but it may include professional, personal, geographic, temporal, and/ or other locations. Identifying the relevant locations for your current research, and being open about your positionality in your writing, offers readers another dimension to help them in assessing the quality of your work.

But, as we have said, it is possible to write creatively, even if one continues to work within more conventional forms. One way to write more creatively – within any genre or shape of writing, from the overtly creative to the formal and orthodox – is to become more conscious of the act of writing, what one is doing as a writer, the choices one is making, and the possibilities that remain. This is why, in this chapter, we explore a series of contrasting ways of writing and make suggestions for getting started: first steps within these different approaches.

Though we have tried to write as accessibly as possible, suggesting first steps in unfamiliar ways of writing, we recognise that this may take many of us out of our comfort zones and areas of expertise. Jane Piirto, the American poet and writer, reminds doctoral students and professional researchers that their training and skills lie in research, not writing. If they are to use creative writing techniques effectively, she advises, they must gain skills in creative writing commensurate with those they gain in research (Piirto 2009:97). Piirto's argument is about quality, and this is understandable, because there are still people who think that the use of arts techniques in non-arts subjects reduces the quality of work produced. Nevertheless, our view is more akin to those of Kitrina Douglas and Mary and Ken Gergen, who believe that people can learn to use arts techniques while they conduct research (Douglas 2012:529; Gergen and Gergen 2012:163). We should read and judge this work as social research, and not by the standards of fine art (see also Tracy 2010).

Jane Piirto's words of warning illustrate one of a number of barriers which might deter some social researchers from attempting to write creatively. Other barriers include:

- lack of confidence
- impostor syndrome (Clance and Imes 1978)
- uninterested or discouraging colleagues/peers/superiors
- institutional inertia

- conservatism in the regulation and governance of research
- lack of precedents and relevant literature

These are common problems. Even hugely successful creative writers, such as the novelist and poet Maya Angelou and the novelist, screenwriter and comics writer Neil Gaiman, have spoken of experiencing impostor syndrome. As with lack of confidence, writers experiencing this problem need to carry on regardless. Fortunately, those who persist in writing creatively also find they benefit from enablers, which include:

- supportive colleagues/peers/superiors
- conducive institutional or departmental culture
- precedents and relevant literature

We begin and end Chapter 2 with some tips on stepping out of comfort zones, and exploring different forms of creative writing. We devote much of this chapter to a series of short sections, each outlining and illustrating a genre, form, shape or – our preferred term – *way* of writing. Here, we have had to be selective: from all the possible ways of writing in social research we could have discussed, we focus upon the following, overlapping examples: first-person writing; observation and description; story and storying; essays and lists; and, how to follow through and do creative writing yourself. Other ways of writing, explored elsewhere in the book, include scriptwriting for stage and screen, animation, visual writing and poetry. We end each of the short sections here with suggestions for getting started: 'try this' exercises.

CREATIVE WRITING IN PRACTICE

Playing with #acwri: a play on academic writing *by Julia Molinari*[1]

Julia Molinari teaches and researches academic writing in the School of Education at the University of Nottingham. Her piece uses scriptwriting to discuss contested aspects of academic writing and changing academic practices. She draws on data generated from ethically sanctioned research in the form of interviews she conducted with her students.[2]

Dramatis personae (in order of speaking)
Narrator [framing #acwri instruction as drama]
Quintiliana [academic writing tutor; traditionalist and conventionalist with a penchant for Quintilian Aristotelian rhetoric. Also an IELTS examiner]
Tyana [earnest international millennial student with multimodal and multilingual literacies. In Year 1 of an EdD (Education Doctorate) at a British university. Caught between literacy conventions and agentic creativity]
Master Ponty [Tyana's reflexive and creative conscience, akin to Pinocchio's wise cricket. Inclined towards Phenomenology and Critical Realism. Can see beyond the horizon, where #acwri forms are changing and afford diverse epistemological representations]

Figure 2.1: Inspiration doll by Alke Gröppel-Wegener, created in response to this piece by Julia Molinari. Inspiration dolls comment on and play with genres of creative writing.

---

[1]   This contribution should be cited as follows: Molinari, J. (2021) 'Playing with #acwri: a play on academic writing'. In Phillips, R. and Kara, H. *Creative Writing for Social Research*. Bristol: Policy Press.

[2]   In the spirit of creative writing, I have not weighed down the script with academic references; I use brief footnotes instead. This play draws upon findings from my research and reflects on writing, education and the tensions between creativity and pedagogical norms and standards (see: Collier 1994; Merleau-Ponty 2002; Tan 2017).

Scene I – On Rules

[Narrator: Quintiliana and Tyana, in a tutorial]

Act 1 – Learn the rules before you break them
Quintiliana: ... argument. Good academic writing is all about argument! It must be linear, clear, complex, logical, balanced, formal, objective and above all, precise! This is what will make your writing persuasive!
Tyana: [taking notes] ... logical ... objective ... persuasive ...
Quintiliana: a good argument must unfold across five stages: the *exordium*, then the *narration* ...
Tyana: ... the *nation*?
Quintiliana: [peeved by the interruption] *NARR*ATION ... a good argument has 5 stages: an *introduction*, a main body made up of *claims*, *arguments* and *counter-arguments*, and finally a *conclusion*
Tyana: ... like IELTS Writing Task? The five paragraphs?
Quinitiliana: [vexed by the crude analogy] ... erm, I suppose so, but much more sophisticated. You must avoid repetitions and emotional language, your writing must be objective, polished, clean and pristine but also critical; never plagiarise and above all, never use Wikipedia as a reference.
Tyana: until I came to UK, my writing was uncritical and repetitive. I did not think in a logical way. Very talk-talk, not precise thinking
Quintiliana: indeed. But follow these rules, Tyana, and you will write with the transparency of Orwell, not the turgidity of Spivak
Tyana : yes, I will follow the rule ... topic sentence ... but if necessary, I will change, I'm still traditional, I'll stick to the traditional way, I can learn fixed phrases, not a pleasure, but an efficient way. I have to follow the style of my supervisors. I have to make the passage clearly understood, it's the first step, and maybe next I will use metaphor and other figures of speech
Quintiliana: that's right. Once you have mastered the rules, then you can break them

[Narrator: discussion around Tyana's literature review]

Act 2 – Which rules? Whose rules?
Tyana: If I have a clear idea and a clear structure, then I will become more confident [...] sometimes I want to write creative, I want to make it more logical, to have my own ideas, sometimes I use someone else's outline, e.g. a literature review, I follow their structure, but then I try to forget it, but then I think 'are my ideas right?', I compare it with their ideas, I feel trapped by their structures [...][3]

---

[3] The digital age is providing opportunities and prompts to reimagine the dissertation (Andrews et al 2012).

Quintiliana: having a plan, a structure is good, an introduction, main body, conclusion, avoid contractions and personal pronouns, your writing must be objective ... these rules will make you confident ...

Tyana: If I can use the first person 'I' to communicate with my readers ... just like in person, talk-talk, I think it would be better, I would prefer that kind of style ... I don't think I can do that because I have to follow the style of my supervisor, I don't think they like this style [laughs]

Quintiliana: indeed

Tyana: I have read some articles by my supervisor, he is a professor, he didn't use that, so I don't think he will accept it [...] I don't think I express myself best in words, I express myself best by doing things, not by speaking [...] for me at present, I have to express myself clearly and logically in English. That's the first step. And when I feel confident at this one, maybe I will try to use the other skills such as metaphors [laughs]

Quintiliana: yes! Clarity first, then creativity

Tyana: but, sometimes in English academic writing, writers have flexibility, we can choose our writing styles [...] you can do that [be more flexible] but you can't have it published. I remember in her writing she used some of her native language, also comics, emotions, music, even ...

Quintiliana: ... but these are one-off exceptions, Tyana, not standard rules. Academic writing should be precise, it should avoid emotion. It is not a novel! It is not a poem! As Cardinal Newman said, it should not be full of 'slang and personal sentiments' or 'decked in conceits, fancies, and prettiness'![4]

CURTAIN
Scene II – On Possibilities

[Narrator: Tyana reflects alone with her conscience, Master Ponty]

Act 1 – Mobile writing landscapes

Tyana: I would like my readers to find their voices through my writing [...]. I like to write through my experience, I think experience is very important for writing, I like to be very authentic ... experience ... it's really a conflict, sometimes you want to use metaphors but what you tried is not the same as what you want to convey. If I want to write something in a serious way, I should investigate it at first, then I can get some conclusions, then maybe I can add some imagination, but without facts, imagination is nonsense in research

Master Ponty: "add imagination"? Like an ingredient, like salt and pepper?

Tyana: yes

Master Ponty: but you said you want to be authentic. To be authentic, imagination is not an added ingredient, it is what makes the dish. Les Back argues that when we write, we need to 'take our reader there', make them feel what we are seeing, showing

---

4   This conversation echoes wider debates about pedagogy (Le Ha 2009).

them, not telling them. That requires imagination, finding ways to help your reader *see* it like you do

Tyana: But how? Experience is personal, I need to be logical, objective, balanced. But methods are messy, not neat or linear, how do I take my reader there? Why should I? Where do I put my feelings? In a blog? In my thesis? My problem is I know *about* these rules, but how and when do I use them? Why do supervisors have different rules? I am researching migrant children and their parents' literacies, so how do I make their words vivid, real? They are not formal or objective. Do I transcribe and translate or keep the original audio? What is gained and what is lost in transduction? How can I be authentic? It's paradoxical, I write to be a writer, sometimes I am embedded in my writing, I like this kind of feeling, but sometimes it's a wrestle. My tutor says I have too many ideas and they aren't really connected to the main question. I also don't really know what a paragraph is or how long it should be and what should go in the introduction and conclusion? Is the conclusion just a summary? I just don't know where to start now. I want to do it right, but I don't know how. How do you write academically? How is it different to what they taught me before?

Master Ponty: you are beginning to notice that academic writings are open systems. They are part of structures with histories and traditions and influences that shape and change them. But it is humans who create these structures. This makes them contingent, part of a mobile global landscape. Which means they can change. And this means that even emotions matter in academic writing because these can be understood as 'commentaries on our human concerns'. The topic of your EdD is a *very* human concern, *your* concern, the *children's* concern

Tyana: but I need to do it critically and objectively, not emotionally, not personally!

Master Ponty: what makes you think these are mutually exclusive? When people say that critical thinking is something only the 'West' does, they are mistaken. Ask yourself, Tyana, what do people mean by this thing called 'critical thinking'? In Confucianism, for example, critical judgment is expressed through experience, through the *dao*. Established norms and procedures are there for us to interpret, for us to take a stand within a collective where we help ourselves and others reach their goals. It is human beings who are able to broaden *dao*, not *dao* that broadens human beings. You are a twenty-first century academic *human* writer, Tyana – your experience, your emotions, your imagination, your judgments matter

[Narrator: weeks later, Quintiliana discusses Tyana's draft]

Act 2 – Academic writing is contested and emergent
Quintiliana: What is this? This is not what we agreed
Tyana: do you like it?
Quintiliana: [concerned] well, I am not sure what to make of it? Instead of an *introduction*, which should clearly signal your aims, you have told me a story about a migrant child who is bullied; instead of a series of *claims*, which should describe the event in question, you have drawn a spiral sequence of cartoon panels – evocative, I admit, but ambiguous; the *argument* is, erm, yes, well-written, your claims clear ...,

but your *refutatio* ... erm, I mean, your *counter-argument*, is an animation! And one voiced by the children themselves! It ... it kind of makes sense, as a whole ... and, finally, your *conclusion*, yes, it is concise, it brings together your research vividly ...

Tyana: [hopeful] so you are persuaded?

Quintiliana: I ... well, I guess I am, yes ... it is well-researched, methodologically sound, compelling, evidence-based, theory-informed, your stance is clear but ...

Tyana: but?

Quintiliana: [anxious] but where are the paragraphs and topic sentences? The nominalisations? The formal academic jargon? You've even used Wikipedia as one of your references! Where do I even start with feedback on this? What criteria do I use to assess it?

Tyana: but my research does not fit into your five-paragraph structure. I looked at how academics write, and they take risks, they use Wikipedia, they use more than language to argue! They even say that academic writing has to be fit for the modern world, for modern academic practices. How can I do it?

Quintiliana [out of her comfort zone]: Tyana, you are perceiving a reality that I am blind to. But maybe you are right, it is a reality that is out there, one that has changed since my time as an IELTS examiner. Maybe the future university is indeed more creative, more imaginative[5] ... for students like you, global millennials whose literacies afford far greater possibilities

CURTAIN

---

[5]   This dialogue references debates about academic writing and the future of the university (Newman et al 1996; Barnett 2013; Besley and Peters 2013; Paré 2019).

Doing it yourself: getting started

We frame this chapter with some broad suggestions and tips for getting started in creative writing, wherever you may be in your profession or your life. Some of these tips are taken from experience: both authors of this book have not only led but have also participated in creative writing workshops; and we have both used creative writing in our own research. Other tips, passed on here, are generic: distilled from manuals and handbooks of creative writing, of which there are many in print, and learned from specialists in creative writing per se. We try to avoid passing on too much generic advice about the doing of creative writing; we defer to specialists in the field for that, and refer readers to their publications (in Chapter 1 we recommended a number of these, including Anderson 2006 and Neale 2009). We are also careful to keep this discussion focused on creative writing for social research; we distinguish this from manuals and handbooks on writing for academic purposes, including writing dissertations and theses and writing research reports (for example, Davis at al 2008; Luey 2010; Nygaard 2015; Kara 2017). Our distinctive contribution, here, will be to bring that creative writing practice to social research, and it is in this spirit that we open Chapter 2 with broad suggestions for researchers wishing to write creatively, perhaps for their first time.

Reading for writing

Creative writing begins with reading. There is a synergy between reading and writing (Goodson 2017:237). Accordingly, rather than plucking writing exercises out of thin air, we begin this section with readings of creative writing, across a series of ways or shapes of writing. Once we have surveyed each of these ways of writing, by reading others, we are in a better position to write.

Reading other people's work goes hand in hand with writing. Often you will need to turn to relevant literature to check a fact, find inspiration, or increase your knowledge of a field. Reading comes in handy in other ways too. For example, if you get stuck with your writing, a spot of reading can help you get going again. Try it and see.

There are risks here, though. If we read too much, we can find ourselves parroting others. And, as we all know, more reading can be an excuse for procrastination. So it is important for each of us to find our own balance between reading and writing (Elbow 2000:281; Foss and Waters 2016:417).

Small steps and time frames

In the following sections we propose a series of exercises to help you take first steps in creative writing or to develop your work if you already have some experience, working within and across a series of ways or shapes of writing.

First, choose a medium: something to write with. Some people prefer to write longhand, some digitally, and some have no choice because of ability or resource constraints. If you can use a pen, smart pens are great for spanning the boundary between longhand and digital, enabling you to create a hard copy and a digital copy at the same time. You may also need other resources, such as voice recognition software if you find the physical act of writing difficult. Some people find it possible to write differently in different media, and benefit from switching between media. So try writing longhand if you usually use a keyboard and on your phone if you are used to a laptop. Those who can do both often choose to write in longhand then type up their notes and edit digitally, or write digitally then edit on printouts. Switching can help writers gain the necessary distance from their work to facilitate good editing.

It is important, when stepping outside one's comfort zone and trying something new, to work within 'bite-size' chunks of time. This has the effect of 'containing' potentially intimidating activities. It is best not to be too ambitious, at first, so start with short time frames for writing exercises. Later on, different writers arrive at different habits, though many still like to work within limited blocks of time. This may be half an hour first thing in the day, 45 minutes at lunchtime, or 300 words after dinner in the evening. Others can write any time, or don't have a routine life so can't create a routine writing habit. Whichever kind of writer you are, you may benefit from a short pre-writing ritual (Sword 2017:53). This could involve making a particular drink or arranging your analogue or digital desktop into its 'writing' configuration. This can help to prepare you for writing in the same way that a bedtime routine can help to prepare you for sleep.

Experienced creative writers advise you to be strategic in how you use your writing time. Rowena Murray uses the metaphors of 'snack' and 'feast' writing (Murray 2009:72). These denote short periods of intensive writing versus longer periods when the words flow so smoothly you don't want to stop. Most effective writing is made up of regular snacks. This seems counterintuitive: surely if you had more time you could do more writing, right? Wrong. As Murray explains, you will be more productive if you write little and often.

Warm-up exercises

Even if you are writing in snacks, warm-up exercises can be helpful. A few minutes of freewriting (which we explain in more detail in Chapter 3) can be a worthwhile investment in getting you going. Some writers like to do more formalised warm-up exercises. If you want to try this, choose one from this list or devise your own:

- Write about your research from the point of view of a character in a novel, a film, or comic strip.

- Write about your research from the point of view of an inanimate object connected with you or your work, such as: something you use for personal grooming, something you use at work, or something you always carry with you.
- Write a short poem, such as a haiku or limerick or a short free verse, about the next stage of your research.
- Put on some random music – from a selection on shuffle, or whatever a radio station happens to be playing. Write a few sentences about how the music makes you feel and think, then write about how that might link with your research.
- Write an email or letter, to someone connected with your research, about anything you like.
- If there's something bugging you about your research, write about that. Your language can be as ranty or rude as you please!
- Write a fictional diary entry about an ideal day of research work.

Don't spend too much time on a warm-up exercise. Between three and five minutes is about right, depending on how much writing time you have allocated altogether. The idea is to get your writing muscles going and then launch into what you really need to write. Also, your warm-up writing is entirely confidential; if you want to, you can delete or destroy it as soon as it's done.

Putting yourself in the picture

The conventional adherence to the passive voice within social research is challenged through experiments in writing using the active voice. This means the researcher-writer assumes a more immediate and greater presence within the text. In this section, we explore the active voice, initially through a broad discussion of first-person writing, subsequently through a specific way of writing in the first person: the diary. We continue to explore first-person writing later in other ways, including autoethnography and the essay.

Writing in the first person

How can we unlearn the habit of writing in the passive voice? How and when can we, as social researchers, put ourselves in the picture?

These questions introduce two sets of demands. The first involves knowing how and what to say about ourselves as authors, and having the confidence to hold ourselves accountable (Nygaard 2015:52). The second involves telling a story, writing engagingly, while also pushing theoretical ideas. This means writing in such a way as to 'pull readers into the world [we] are creating' through our words (Pelias 2019:147).

To learn these skills, it helps to turn to an influential social researcher who worked in this way, and asserted the theoretical significance of doing so: bell hooks. Here is an extract from *Belonging: A Culture of Place*:

Riding in the car, away from the town, riding in the country we were surrounded by fields and fields of tobacco. Growing up in Kentucky I learned the reverence for the tobacco plant that had been handed down from generation to generation. In those days tobacco was not demonized. Tobacco was a sacred plant, cherished and deemed precious by the old folks who knew its properties and its potentialities.

I cannot recall any time in my childhood when tobacco did not have meaning and presence. Whether it came from watching Big Mama smoke her pipe, or emptying the coffee cans that were used to spit out chewing tobacco, or watching mama's mother Baba braid tobacco leaves for use to ward off bugs ... .

The history of black folks and the history of tobacco like braided leaves were once deeply intertwined. (hooks 2009:106)

Here, hooks writes about Kentucky and, through Kentucky, she develops broader theoretical points about place and belonging, race and class.

Another writer who responds to the two challenges we have identified – finding the right way to put oneself in the picture; and crafting a story that is at once engaging and theoretically searching – is the geographer Ann Varley. Writing about herself and her father's dementia, Varley (2008) develops a series of ideas about home and the self:

Home care workers found my father, Maurice, on the floor by his bed when they went in to make his breakfast one morning in September 2004. No formal diagnosis was made, but we suspected that he had probably had a stroke. That made sense, since Dad had angina as well as the dementia with which he'd been diagnosed three years earlier. Whatever the cause, there was no doubt that his cognitive abilities had also been affected. His performance on diagnostic tests had plummeted. The conclusion was predictable: he could no longer live safely on his own.

When we moved him into a specialist home, the staff asked me to make up a 'memory box' for my father. Something to contain family photographs and other small objects that might trigger memories and help to keep his mind active. So my husband helped me get down the boxes stored in the loft of the bungalow that my parents had bought, newly built, in the 1950s, and I started to look for photographs that would mean something to my father – and to me. There were pictures that I was particularly keen to find: some of me as a baby in the bath and one of my mother standing over a window. Taken from behind, it showed her looking at the world outside. (Varley 2008:47)

This first-person point of view feels uncomfortable at times, moving at others. It raises ethical questions about the consequences of speaking about others when speaking about oneself, particularly if they are 'non-consenting others' (Mannay 2016:122). The author navigates these mixed feelings and ethical questions and, through this first-person account, she develops theoretical positions on geographies of home.

It should be clear from these readings of hooks and Varley that it is possible to speak in the first person without putting oneself at the centre of the story. Varley speaks of 'we' and 'I' in order to explore the ways in which positionality and perspective shape the story.

A writer who showed how it is possible to work to great effect in the first person without becoming the story was Doreen Massey. Massey was a captivating speaker, but it was largely through the written word that she reached audiences around the world. Massey wrote simply and directly, without literary pretensions, distilling complex ideas in immediate and accessible prose, which reached audiences that formal academic writing could not. One of her best-known articles, 'A global sense of place', includes a first-person description of Massey's neighbourhood:

> Take, for instance, a walk down Kilburn High Road, my local shopping centre. It is a pretty ordinary place, north-west of the centre of London.
>
> In two shops I notice this week's lottery ticket winners: in one the name is Teresa Gleeson, in the other, Chouman Hassan.
>
> Overhead there is always at least one aeroplane – we seem to live on a flight-path to Heathrow and by the time they're over Kilburn you can see them clearly enough to tell the airline and wonder as you struggle with your shopping where they're coming from. (Massey 1991:27)

But Massey does not privilege her own perspective of this place. As she puts it elsewhere, in an essay about a journey from one city to another, '[t]he voyager is not the only active one. Origin and destination have lives of their own' (Massey 2003). The pedestrian in Kilburn High Road or the passenger on a train from Manchester to Liverpool 'is travelling not across space-as-surface but across a multitude of stories', transecting 'a million ongoing histories' (Massey 2003). Here, the personal meets the social.

Another option when writing in the first person is to create a fictionalised other. This is a common practice for novelists and short story writers, who choose the first person for a more immediate and personal form of communication. In the first paragraph of the novel *Incendiary* by Chris Cleave (2009:3), the protagonist is addressing Osama bin Laden, the founder and former head of the militant organisation, Al-Qaeda:

> Dear Osama they want you dead or alive so the terror will stop. Well I wouldn't know about that I mean rock n roll didn't stop when Elvis died on the khazi it just got worse. Next thing you know there was Sonny & Cher and Dexy's Midnight Runners. I'll come to them

later. My point is it's easier to start these things than to finish them.
I suppose you thought of that did you?

These 75 words give us a strong initial sense of a person. In the next paragraph we find out that the protagonist is a working–class woman whose husband and son were killed in a bomb attack attributed to Al-Qaeda. She is writing to Osama bin Laden to ask him to stop these attacks. It is as if we are reading her letter, and the intimacy is compelling.

As we saw in Chapter 1, there are good reasons for researchers to consider the use of fictionalisation at times. We would also suggest that there are good reasons for a researcher to consider combining fictionalisation with first-person writing, when drawing their readers into a close relationship with a single character would be a good way to communicate their message.

 Try this

The examples we have quoted in the section on writing in the first person have all revolved around experiences of home and place, albeit on different scales and in different voices. All three of these researcher-writers are women and their accounts are both feminist and gendered (see: England 1994; Rose 1997). This presents us each with a practical challenge and intellectual opportunity.

Here is one way of taking up this challenge: describe a place you lived in during your childhood, twice. First, write as objectively as you can, without first-person pronouns. Then describe the place again, but put yourself in the picture, writing in the first-person singular and/or plural: as 'I' or 'we'. Now, compare your two descriptions. Is the first as neutral as it seems? Or is there a hidden point of view? (This may be a function of your gender, class, race, ethnicity, religion, or some other aspect of your positionality.) Finally, turning to your second description, what does the more explicitly personal point of view reveal?

Diaries and journals

A diary is a daily record; a form of observational writing, organised around dated entries, which are usually chronological. A journal is a similar but less frequent or regular record. Diaries and journals comprise 'a regular, personal and contemporaneous record' (Alaszewski 2006:1). These assume a number of forms, which we expand upon here (Kara 2020:172):

- personal diary, intended solely for the writer's own private purposes;
- reflective diary, for thinking critically about experiences related to work or study in order to help improve professional skills (Alaszewski 2006:12; Phillips and Johns 2012:38);
- field journal, for descriptions of 'the people, places, and events you observe in the field' (Phillips and Johns 2012:38);
- arts-based journal, such as one based on poetry (Slotnick and Janesick 2011:1353) or comic strips;
- photo-journal including personal photographs and other images as well as some explanatory text;
- online journal, often in the form of a blog, which can include text, images, audio, video, hyperlinks and so on.

Diaries and journals have a great deal of potential for creative use in social research. Diaries and journals can be: written by researchers or participants or both; freeform or structured; used as a record, for reference, or as data in their own right. They are attuned to social research because they 'lie at the cusp between private and public worlds' (Neale 2006d:330). Keeping a diary can enable the writer to 'see the everyday from a new angle' (Neale 2006d:338). Most diarists are interested in other people. For some, this means friends, family members, and others they meet in their daily lives. Well-known diarists range from Alan Bennett, whose daily chronicles have been published in the *London Review of Books*, to Helen Fielding, whose fictionalised diary of friends and boyfriends formed her bestselling 1996 novel, *Bridget Jones's Diary*. Some diarists inform public understandings of places and times, politics and societies: Anne Frank left a detailed picture of Nazi-occupied Amsterdam, Samuel Pepys of 17th-century London. Alongside these great writers, we find – and can aspire to join – researchers whose diaries of everyday life build up smaller pictures of culture and society. These researcher-diarists include fieldworkers, keeping copious notes about the people and places, things and happenings they observe in the field. Traditionally, these field diaries have been the raw material for more polished dissertations and publications. Recently, though, some of these diarists have begun to publish their diaries as they write, online in the form of blogs.

Like other published diaries, blogs may be edited and polished before they are shared, and unlike private diaries these observational diaries tend to be written with an eye to publication. Some writers use their blogs to find and refine their voice and build up an audience. This is how Kevin Boniface, an artist and postal delivery worker, came to publish *Round About Town* (2018), a book about the streets and houses he observed on his postal round. His blog is a form of creative social research in its own right, with qualities – including immediacy (enhanced through use of the present tense, writing about a day as it happens), digestible segments and temporal rhythms – that tend to be missing from more sustained and refined books. Here are some illustrative extracts from his blog:

Friday, 16 August 2019
It starts to rain heavily and a thick petrichor scent fugs up from the busily embellished gardens of the cluttered over-60s retirement village; an eerie 1970s time machine of moorland park homes. The ambient scent around here is more usually best described as a blend of damp Players No.6 infused Austin Maxi upholstery and stewing steak. The perms and the glasses are big around here and the dogs are small. There are owl themed knick-knacks on the windowsills and chintzy cane furniture in the conservatories. Bookshelves are stuffed with faded spines: Giles, Thelwell, Richard Adams, Willie Carson, Jimmy Greaves, a Haynes Car Manual for a Fiat Strada… Gravel paths are sewn with couch grass, dandelions and bent old poppy heads. Even the bird life is vintage, there are sparrows and chaffinches instead of the long tailed tit and goldfinch interlopers that have taken over further down the valley. I glimpse an old wood veneer box-shaped TV on a swirly patterned carpet and half expect to see Ken Cooper there reading the news in his Purdy cut and wide lapels; another gruesome Ripper slaying followed by a fundraising flatbed parade organised by some church pensioners in Kettlewell. (www.themostdifficultthingever. com/, last accessed 22 August 2019)

These observations resonate with Derek Neale's (2006d:338) vision for the diary, as a way of seeing 'the everyday from a new angle'. Boniface reflects that his blog helped him to see his life and his round in a new light. What began as coping, and staving off 'a small nervous breakdown', reached towards something more positive. 'I was picking away at the ordinary and what began to unravel was extraordinary' (Boniface 2019:236).

Among social researchers, the blog is sometimes but not always a medium for overtly creative writing. Some researchers use personal and institutional blogs as shop windows for conventional academic writing, spaces for dissemination and discussion rather than innovation (Carrigan 2020). Well-regarded examples include Sara Ahmed's feministkilljoys.com and *The Sociological Review*'s blog (www.thesociologicalreview.com/category/structure/blog/). In contrast, Les Back exemplifies the experimental possibilities of the research diary. When Back, a sociologist at Goldsmiths, University of London, decided to write about 'why higher education still matters', and to explore the creative and disruptive possibilities of education, he chose to write in an appropriately experimental form.

Back's *Academic Diary* (2016) is composed of entries, listed by date and location or theme, arranged under subheadings including Autumn Term, Spring Term, and The Summer. An entry for '25 September: Goldsmiths and its District' consists of notes about the history and location of Goldsmiths (Back 2016:26–8). This is not a conventional diary – in the form of specific observations of the happenings of a particular day – though it is not unprecedented either. Like Derek Jarman's *Modern Nature* (1992), for example, Back's *Academic Diary* does not simply record what happens on a particular date; he describes selectively, interprets, makes connections with other days and times, and with ideas he has come across elsewhere, and may be in the process of distilling and developing. The creativity of this writing lies in its detail, though, and in the eccentricity of the observations, such as the entry for '27 September: Ratology':

> The shriek of the first-year student – whom I had just had the pleasure of teaching – drew my attention. I scurried up the street to see the evidence for myself. The vertically challenged beast was a pretty unpleasant sight. The stain on the road gave weight – if not depth – to the urban myth that these monsters are among us at every turn. (Back 2016:29)

Back goes on to explain how he sought and found a shovel, then removed the offending rodent. This leads him to remember Georges Perec's assertion that: 'To live is to move from one space to another, while trying as far as possible to avoid bumping into anything'. The lesson for staff and students in British higher education (Perec 1997, quoted by Back 2016:31) is one of 'avoiding stepping on anything unspeakable'. Like Kevin Boniface, Les Back resists the temptation to draw grand conclusions from small observations, or to construct a coherent narrative arc from fragmentary experiences. The rhythms and revelations of his diary, like those of academic life, are stop–start and cyclical; they revolve around days, weeks, terms and years. In the stop–start rhythms of his diary, as in Boniface's postal diary, extraordinary things and experiences emerge.

Try this

Start a diary … today! Put the date, time and place of writing at the top of the page. Derek Neale, writing in a handbook of creative writing, introduces the diary as an 'attempt to be a daily record of your life', and advises that 'entries should be more than a chronicle (a list of events), and more too than a calendar (a list of appointments)' (Neale 2006d:331). Neale recommends writing about events and experiences in chronological order, but adds that there are few rules beyond that. 'You may wish to record what you've done previously today, who you met with, the weather, your impressions of a person or place – anything and everything' (Neale 2006d:331–2). You can include whatever you like: things you eat, conversations you overhear, memories triggered by your experiences. This is a form of freewriting (a topic we explain in Chapter 3), in which you write about what sticks in your mind, and what makes an impression on you. After you have been writing your diary for some weeks or months, read back over it, and look for themes, phrases and words that appeal to you. Thinking about how to continue your diary, you may decide to focus some of your ongoing research upon the themes that stand out to you as promising or insightful.

Observation and description

While many social researchers are now writing in the first person, they are doing so in different ways which merit detailed attention. In this section, we explore a form of first-person writing known as autoethnography, which comprises observations and descriptions in which the researcher is part of the picture. This first-person writing is increasingly mainstream; so much so, that the possibilities and practices of third-person and other more self-effacing writing may be forgotten. Accordingly, after exploring autoethnographic writing, we stop to consider its counterpoint: observational writing in which the observer is implied rather than explicitly present.

Autoethnography

Autoethnography revolves around observations and descriptions of the researcher's behaviours, thoughts and experiences, typically related in the first person, and in their cultural and social context (Ellis and Bochner 2000; Bochner and Ellis 2016). This ultimate focus – upon culture and society rather than the author and the individual life – is what distinguishes autoethnography from its sibling, autobiography (Plummer 2012). In autoethnography, 'a personal story' (Wall 2008:39) informs a sociological understanding (Sparkes 2000).

Autoethnographic writing takes time to learn and refine. This writing confronts challenging 'issues of representation, "objectivity," data quality, legitimacy, and ethics' (Wall 2008:39). Writing about the self can feel unnatural to students and researchers who, as we have explained, are trained to be self-effacing. Autoethnographers face the risks and possible embarrassment of self-exposure, and make judgement calls about what and how much it is appropriate and ethical to say. In writing through oneself, one also has to navigate the dangers of seeming or becoming too self-absorbed and self-obsessed; it is not uncommon for peer reviewers to accuse autoethnographic writers of navel gazing.

Catherine Thompson-Lee (2017) draws a distinction between evocative and analytical autoethnography, in which the former relies more heavily upon the researcher's own experiences, and his or her ability to describe or evoke them, whereas the latter triangulates these experiences with more sustained use of secondary sources and other research data.

Examples of evocative and analytical autoethnography include a sickness story or diary by Ken Plummer and a study of homophobia by Thompson-Lee. Plummer was 'taken seriously ill and diagnosed with end stage alcoholic related liver disease' (Plummer 2012). His sickness story tells of specific experiences and reaches towards broader insights into the disruptive effects of illness. This account illustrates the challenges of writing about the self, sometimes exposing oneself in unflattering detail, in order to get to the truth:

My first new body started to appear in 2004. A beer gut had accompanied me for much of my adult life, but just recently I noticed that things were getting a little out of hand. Not only was my stomach becoming hugely unsightly – though people were kind, they never commented, except for saying I was cuddly! – it was bringing problems: breathing was becoming noticeably more difficult, moving around was harder and more exhausting, energy was fast drained. But more serious were new signs that accompanied my old fatness: the feet were swelling, toes looked as is if they were going black, bending over to pull on my socks became an issue each morning. And slowly this got worse and worse. Going to bed meant finding the right angle to lie; washing and dressing started to take much longer to do; long walks had to be dropped from my repertoire of activities; shirts had to become floppy and baggy – XXL became my size; I looked out for trousers with elastic waists. Oddly, my face became more emaciated. I became less focused on things. I could not sit down comfortably for any period of time. It was when my enlarging ankles and now legs started to look blacker and blacker that I decided a doctor should be seen. Fat and obese body. Bruised and blackened body. (Plummer 2012)

Plummer goes on to tell how the hospital in Santa Barbara provided care, and ultimately discharged a 'Drained, threatened, sick body'.

From these specific, graphic details, Plummer then tacks from the personal to the social, reaching towards broader points about body, society and space. He reflects that 'with the breakdown of my body, everything in my illness world changed':

My worlds of movement, clothing, hair, drinking, eating, sleeping, washing, talking, thinking, and feeling – all moved into a different key. The people I knew took on different characteristics. Places became different. Whoever I was before, I was not now. I was a new and changing body. It was a new world of feeling. My consciousness had shifted. Here is a sense of a world so at odds with the ways in which I experienced it when I was not ill. Being seriously ill shifted the phenomenal world I lived in. (Plummer 2012)

Through this account of his own bodily experience, Plummer reflects on how 'Life and its bodies are transformed under the rule of illness'.

Arthur Bochner and Carolyn Ellis's *Evocative Autoethnography* (2016) is a textbook written as an account of a three-day workshop, complete with introductions, discussions and handouts. The authors model the method they describe and aim to teach, which by definition is designed to draw out readers' feelings, memories and insights. Some other autoethnographers draw upon a wider range of sources, triangulating their own experiences with 'external data sources' (Thompson-Lee 2017:46). Working in this way, which she identifies as analytical ethnography,

Catherine Thompson-Lee examines homophobia and heteronormativity in a rural school and community in England. She begins with her own experiences of homophobic harassment, which she later supplements with documentary sources including medical records, CBT (cognitive behavioural therapy) notes, a CBT thought diary, email and text message correspondence, and (records of attempts to access) police records. Anxiety, induced by the harassment, is manifest in worry about the safety of her cat, Lily, which prompts her to make an appointment with her doctor. Her account juxtaposes experiences of the medical appointment with the doctor's report of the same incident:

> I had a recurring thought that if Lily wandered beyond our gate onto the farm, as she often did, Mr Freeman might sweep her up by the scruff of her neck, slit her throat with the knife I imagined he carried, and toss her back over the fence to land in our garden. (Thompson-Lee 2017:66)

The doctor's notes, which Thompson-Lee quotes, reported 'exceptionally severe symptoms of anxiety' (Thompson-Lee 2017:66). From these personal experiences, triangulated with documents generated by others, Thompson-Lee works towards some broader reflections on homophobia and heteronormativity, sexuality and rurality, private and public spheres and identities.

Try this

Think of an incident from your life which you would *not* like to write about for others to read: something private and personal, perhaps something sexual or embarrassing or incriminating. Then write answers to the following questions:
1. What are all the reasons why you don't want to write about this incident?
2. How could publication affect you personally, affect others, affect your personal life, affect your professional life?
3. What other impacts could publication have?
4. Are there any potential positive outcomes?
5. What could you learn if you did write about this incident?
6. What could others learn from reading of your experience?

This exercise will give you some insight into the kinds of issues autoethnographers have to grapple with as they formulate their work.

CREATIVE WRITING IN PRACTICE

Imprisoned by metrics: an autoethnographic fiction from inside corporate academia *by Kay Inckle*[6]

Kay Inckle is a recovering academic. By her own account, she misspent much of her adulthood in higher education pursuing the naive belief that education was a vehicle for critical and creative practice which promoted social justice. Instead she found that the white, ableist patriarchy was alive and well and reproducing ever more inequality and elitism. In this piece she uses creative writing to explore the overt and insidious ways in which disability discrimination is enacted in universities and how higher education remains a hostile environment for disabled women.

It is almost daylight. The trees which twenty minutes ago were opaque black outlines on a slate grey sky are now three dimensions of multi-hued foliage. Blue tits flit between the branches and blackbirds take wing in search of the day. Woodpigeons are already scouring the lawn for errant worms and the remnants of birdseed I scattered on the ground a day or so before.

I can feel my chest tightening as daylight spreads around me. The stillness of my morning meditation which, like every day, must succumb to the workday ahead, signals its retreat in the rising tide of my anxiety. I still have my swim and breakfast before work, but most of my 2km lashed through harshly chlorinated water will be spent in mental argument with the day ahead.

Figure 2.2 Inspiration doll by Alke Gröppel-Wegener, created in response to this piece by Kay Inckle. Inspiration dolls comment on and play with genres of creative writing.

This is every morning before work, but today it is especially acute – today I have to attend an investigation meeting. The meeting is the result of multiple complaints I have made about disability discrimination.

---

[6] This contribution should be cited as follows: Inckle, K. (2021) 'Imprisoned by metrics: an autoethnographic fiction from inside corporate academia'. In Phillips, R. and Kara, H. *Creative Writing for Social Research*. Bristol: Policy Press.

Complaints which, via their own special corporate wizardry, the university have reformulated into an investigation of me. My probation period is not yet complete and I am acutely aware that what was once a straightforward failure to provide reasonable adjustments has become an assessment of my competency. It is no solace that I am not the first to find myself here, or that I won't be the last. The All-Party Parliamentary Group on Disability reported that every year between thirty-five and forty-eight thousand disabled employees are 'routinely failed on performance or health and safety grounds, and managed out of the workplace instead of being offered a reasonable adjustment' (Connolly et al 2016:7; see also Foster 2007).

I guess that I am about to be 48,001.

And I am frightened.

My fear propels my mind to the increasing number of short-column news stories quietly circulated about academics who have taken their own lives: overwhelmed by the demands, the bullying, the workloads – and all the intricacies of their punished lives which we will never now know.

Would I ...? I wonder to myself.

Would I now?

I know that insurmountable longing for the pain to end, the torture of every passing minute, and the clumsy attempts to escape forever ... foggy memories from what often seems like someone else's past.

My cat, my companion of twenty years, lets out a creaky meow and I lift her onto my lap. I gently fold my arms around her, curling my hand to stroke her soft, white under-belly. She instantly responds, purring, and her entire being vibrates with pleasure. I rest my cheek against the smooth crown of her head, breathing in her warm fur and faint cat-biscuit smell. Her now sightless eyes half close and I kiss the thick fur on the side of her neck.

No, I think to myself.

No, not now.

Even so, my anxiety takes a familiar twist into self-blame. Perhaps I shouldn't have complained? Perhaps I could have done things differently and then this would not be happening? Perhaps if I had just explained *again* why it was wrong to schedule me into teaching rooms with no wheelchair access ...? But how many times should I have to ask, beg or plead, simply to be provided with a work environment that I can do something as straightforward as get into?

Impotent rage floods through me and I can almost feel my skin blush with the force of it.

I know I cannot sustain these battles for much longer.

Things have to change or I have to get out.

I don't think that change is coming anytime soon.

And I do not think that when I leave will be at a time of my choosing.

I have been an academic for many years now, and so I have an almost numb resignation to many of the injustices of the system: watching my former PhD students leap-frog over me in the promotion hurdles; the incessant condescension: surprise that I am not a student, and then presumption that I am inexperienced and in my first academic appointment regardless of the increasing pages taken up by my CV; the obstinate, unyielding refusal to provide me with wheelchair accessible facilities; the pitying comprehension when I explain that my research focuses on mental health and disability – clearly I am not a real academic, I am a charity case let in out of good will towards the afflicted. I am cast forever as an observer while what one of my colleagues describes as 'mediocre white men', are primed for promotion and rewarded in ways that I, a disabled woman, can only dream of (see: Brewster et al 2017; Martin 2017; Brown and Leigh 2018; Hannam-Swain 2018; Inckle 2018a).

But, whatever the injustice, there is always a metric to justify it, and today the metric is going to be research.

I have been told my research is not good enough. The work I produced from a prestigious social science grant was declared a 'self-help' book and of no academic merit by a panel of 'experts' who had not even read it. My single authored work (e.g. Inckle 2014; 2015; 2018b) was only deemed to be of two star quality (that which I co-authored with ablebodied men was more merit-worthy, apparently because I need input from ablebodied males to improve my work). I had not had the courage to submit the work I have recently undertaken using creative methods, as I know it would be seen as worthless. And it is not just my current institution that does not value my research, I receive similar evaluations in grant applications where I posit creative and user-led research methods as means of promoting democratic and inclusive research among marginalised communities – people whose lives are usually appropriated and then abandoned once the researcher has met their goals. But the reviewers tell me that I, 'clearly know nothing about social research methods', and that I would need to, 'conduct psychometric testing on my research participants' if I wanted to suggest that the research could be a positive and/or empowering experience for them. At conferences I meet (white, able-bodied) male academics who submit proposals with similar methods, and theirs are 'innovative', 'impactful' and 'cutting edge'. They are rewarded with substantial grants, the accompanying prestige, and the confidence to assert that academia is certainly a meritocracy which rewards critical and creative work. Therefore, *I* must be doing something wrong, not writing clearly, not substantiating my sources, and this is much more comfortable for everyone to accept than the fact that there is routine and systematic discrimination against disabled women in academia.

I know all of this is wrong, yet, somehow, the years I have spent in higher education have forced me to accept my place at the bottom of the heap. But it is more than that. It is not simply that I have come to accept that 'the system' does not value or reward me, or even treat me as an equal. Somehow I have also come to believe that I, and my work, are not valuable, not respect-worthy nor equal to that of others: I feel a twinge of shame when people ask me what I do. I worry about presenting my research methods and findings to anyone. I feel anxiety when I go and teach. I used to love teaching, it brought something to life in me – and my students – which was exhilarating, transformative, almost spiritual. I used to be known amongst my colleagues as having 'the Kay factor', something special that I brought to my teaching, the assessments that I designed, and to my engagements with students. Now, when I go and teach my head aches and my chest tightens, I have become uncomfortable referencing my own research because I fear the students will disparage it in the same way the university does, and I am uncertain, tentative, nervous.

I used to believe that research and education could be a vehicle for social justice, that universities were places where criticality, diversity, creativity and innovation were valued. What I have found is that universities are factories where a vicious elite reproduce themselves, furnished in corporate greed and armed with 'the masters' tools' (Lorde 2017) freshly sharpened for the next assault on a minoritised group.

Perhaps I should not be surprised at the extent of the abuse I experience, perhaps I should be surprised that I have withstood it for so long (see Pring 2018a; 2018b).

Today I think my 'choice' to withstand it will end.

I take another deep breath nuzzled into my cat's soft fur, and then, with her carefully balanced on my lap, I wheel away from my resting spot and begin to gather myself for the day ahead.

Observational writing and the implied observer

Creative writing is frequently but wrongly associated with flowery language, sentimentality, loose sensuality and a surplus of adjectives. If that was right, creative writing would not be a very good way to conduct and report the findings of social research; there would be too much emphasis upon the words, too little on the social worlds the researcher is investigating. In fact, creative writing can be precise, spare, searching and observant: a research method in its own right. We call this observational writing, though others have come up with other terms such as 'writing flatly'.

We borrow the term 'flat' writing from the French experimental writer Georges Perec, who advocated this as a form of sociological and biographical 'questioning' (Phillips 2018). Perec advocated looking closely, unsentimentally and without judgement, and disciplining oneself to transcribe observation without embellishment. 'Force yourself to see more flatly', Perec (1997:51) advised, turning away from the spectacular and the eye-catching, to focus upon the things that are 'most obvious, most common, most colourless' (Perec 1997:50): the infra-ordinary (Phillips 2018). This writing is fundamentally empirical, comprising 'transcriptions of reality' (Leak 2001:26), hence the name given to it: the 'empiritext' (Armstrong 2015).

In the wake of feminist and anti-racist critique of the disembodied white male gaze (England 1994; Rose 1997), self-effacing writing may come across as uncritical, lacking reflexivity about the author's positionality. But this form of writing – in which the author removes him or herself from the picture and writes from the perspective of an implied observer – offers some particular insights into the place and the power of words in our attempts to access and understand the social and cultural world.

In *The Regional Book* (2015), David Matless brings flat description to a physically flat landscape: the Norfolk Broads. For Matless, flat writing goes beyond the obvious pun, 'cutting across styles of seeing claiming conventional, hierarchical authority' (Matless 2019:171). It 'serves as a motto for constant notice, respectful looking, the spotting of unlikely material significance in things' that are ordinary and overlooked (Matless 2019:171). The principles of writing flatly run through the composition of the book – a series of site descriptions, arranged alphabetically rather than conceptually. The description of Hoveton Great Broad follows '*An isolated broad and nature trail in the Bure valley, between Wroxham and Horning*' (Matless 2015:28, original emphasis):

> Aromatic, a broad and carr reserve gained only by water, a small Bure north bank quay. Tree and fen bar land access. Tie up and take the boardwalk, a sleeper path of half a mile, looping from entrance to exit, single file. Visits elective, no stray humans. Public authority trails nature, national reserve maintained. The warden has a hut.

Signs warn not to stray, muddy danger lurking. Experience sensibly channelled. Hides give on the broad, free of navigation, birds undisturbed. Mud accumulates shallows. Chained binoculars see terns, platform nesting. Coot graze. Kingfisher darts.

Petrol engines made this grow. Hay lost horse demand, and cutting ended. Signs mark succession, and intervention, deflecting for sedge. Numbered posts match guiding text, for moss and fern, peat solid and thin, turf ponds and the greater broad. Bird life passes by, or perches. Branches frame a sunlit tawny.

Boat noise fades into wood, traffic forgotten. River water nose drops, carr scent rising. The fruits of damp, sweet gale of fen. Currant, wild. Reserve confinements, aromatic. (Matless 2015:28)

This flat description of a flat place seems not to impose order. It tends towards the form of a series or list, organised into thematic paragraphs, accommodating the ordinary and ordinarily unremarked.

Matless's description of Hoveton underlines some of the choices a writer must make when attempting to transcribe a place and a social setting. His word choices mirror the setting itself; small semantic differences can indicate subtle variations in the things they describe. But, when we describe things, we necessarily make choices about which words to use, and which categories. However spare and self-effacing, plain and factual our descriptions might seem, they are a product of the semantic and taxonomic choices we have necessarily made. As such, flat writing can be searching – empirically observant and theoretically insightful (Becker 2001).

Try this

If you can be in a public place to do this exercise, so much the better; if not, look out of the nearest window. Write a description of what is in front of you. Do not use the first person pronoun 'I'. Do involve all five major senses – sound, smell, sight, touch, taste – if you are able. If you wish, include some of the other senses, such as balance, and sensations of temperature and vibration. Focus your writing entirely on the environment and what you perceive there, and not at all on yourself.

Stories and storying

Imagine, in one global day, the pages of prose turned, plays performed, films screened, the unending stream of television comedy and drama, twenty-four-hour print and broadcast news, bedtime tales told to children, barroom bragging, back-fence Internet gossip, humankind's insatiable appetite for stories. Story is not only our most prolific art form but rivals all activities – work, play, eating, exercise – for our waking hours. We tell and take in stories as much as we sleep – and even then we dream. Why? Why is so much of our life spent inside stories? Because, as critic Kenneth Burke tells us, stories are equipment for living. (McKee 1999:11)

The far-reaching significance of stories within human lives, captured here by Robert McKee, speaks to social research in at least three different ways. First, stories are social practices, involving writing and other media, which may be subjects of research in their own right. Second, stories can be a means of gathering data: by getting people to tell stories and by paying attention to the stories they are already telling. Third, stories offer a means of exploring, distilling and sharing research findings.

Stories are attracting a lot of attention in the social sciences and humanities, and in other fields including the natural sciences and engineering. Researchers and teachers are increasingly recognising the power and possibilities of stories, with heavily subscribed academic conferences, schemes through which researchers are coached in the art and craft of storytelling, and a proliferation of publications on the subject.

For all these reasons, social researchers who are interested in creative writing also tend to be interested in stories. Creative writers sometimes tell stories. Stories are often (but not always) written; some are scripted before they are spoken or performed. Written and other stories work with and against a number of different shapes or ways of writing – including those explored throughout this book – and reach across fiction and non-fiction. The stories people tell about their lives and relationships – from anecdotes about dating to accounts of bereavement – work within genres and assume conventional forms, even when they appear most personal (Bochner et al 1997). Poems, songs, and plays can also be stories, though this is not always the case. So, though they overlap with other strands of creative writing, stories have a distinctive place of their own, one which demands the direct attention provided here.

'Every research project is made up of stories' (Sword 2012:88). But what is a story? This term is being used increasingly loosely and liberally, as are variants including storytelling and storying, so it helps to begin with the foundational, simple definition that: 'In the everyday sense' story refers to 'any narrative or tale recounting a series of events' (Baldick 2015:342). Literary critics complicate this definition by distinguishing story from narrative, and both of these from plot. Here are some points of departure. Story has been defined as 'the sequence of imagined events that we reconstruct from the actual arrangement of a narrative (or dramatic) plot' and encompasses the 'full sequence of events as we assume them to have occurred in their likely order, duration, and frequency' (Baldick 2015:342). Storytelling is a broader term. It involves ordering experiences and events; evoking mystery and awe; and finding order and meaning in the world

(Atkinson 1998). Storying is broader still. It reaches beyond the narration of events to the exploration of ideas and images, which may be fragmentary rather than coherent. This inclusivity is generative, extending from the stories already in circulation to those that have yet to be found or created (Sandelowski 1991).

These definitions are helpful, but circular and tangled, as they define the terms in relation to each other. Since it is important to be as clear as possible at this point, we have attempted some definitions of our own, which distinguish between narrative, story and plot. Narrative and story are often used synonymously but they are not the same. 'Narrative' is a description of a series of events, usually in chronological order (Richardson 1997:27). Hence a 'narrator' is someone who relates a narrative. A story is designed differently from a narrative. It is likely to have a beginning, middle and end, often has one or more climactic moments, and usually has some kind of message to convey. The 'plot' refers to the way a story is designed. This may not be in chronological order; flashbacks and time-jumps are commonly used in fiction. If designed well, a plot will enable the story to hold its readers' attention through the use of tension-creating devices such as delay and partial reveals. In a really good plot, everything in the story prompts something else, such that everything (after the first thing) is a consequence of some previous element of the story.

Another way to put this is:

- narrative = what happened
- story = why it happened, and to whom
- plot = how it happened

At a very simple level, and with thanks to Forster (1974 [1927]):60), here's a narrative: the queen died, then the king died. With a little causation, this could become a story: the queen died, then the king died of grief. With a well-designed plot this could become an entire novel or full-length film. This might start with some description or footage of the newly bereaved king, showing his shock and bewilderment, rage and denial. There might be flashbacks to moments in the king and queen's relationship, to help the reader or viewer understand more fully the nature and extent of his loss. There might also be scenes from the time of bereavement, to show his decline and eventual death from grief. In a novel or film there might be more characters and subsidiary storylines (who is next in line for the throne?) These might come with an overarching message, perhaps that everyone is ultimately alone, or that love is more than life, or that love is ephemeral and not to be trusted – this story, like all stories, could be told in many ways.

Conventional academic writers would have you believe academic journal articles are made entirely of narrative, but in fact – at least in the social sciences, arts and humanities – they often have significant elements of story. This is often described, confusingly, as a 'narrative arc', that is the path the author creates to take the story from its beginning through its middle to its end, a path that readers can follow and which will assist their comprehension. Of course, story is used extensively in creative writing, and social researchers who use creative writing make good use of story, as shown by many of the examples and contributions in this book. Researchers also, sometimes, use narrative, and occasionally plot.

Though it helps to define 'story' and related terms in the abstract, they are better understood in contexts of use. Stories as objects and means of social research are also examined, in more detail, in a growing number of dedicated books and articles on the subject (for example, Lewis 2011; Phillips and Bunda 2018; Parfitt 2019).

Collecting and transcribing stories

Stories, in written and other forms, are fundamental to social life. They run through the things we say to and about each other: the tales we tell, the fantasies we relate, the happenings we narrate, the identities we project, the ways in which we account for and present ourselves to others. Stories circulate among children (Theobald 2016) or co-workers (Gabriel and Connell 2010), between patients and carers (Sandelowski 1991), students and instructors (Parfitt 2019), neighbours and community members (Sandercock 2003; Cowie 2017). We use stories to say who we are, who we think we might be, and who we want to be. We tell stories to therapists, doctors, teachers, friends, family members, priests and imams, and perhaps most fundamentally to ourselves (see, for example, Jennings and McLean 2013). And, of course, we hear, watch, read and otherwise consume stories.

For all these reasons, there is a lot of scope for social research involving stories. Researchers can collect stories that have already been written down and transcribe those from other forms such as the spoken word. These stories interest researchers because 'stories economically communicate experience, ideas and emotions and help make sense of potentially perplexing situations' (Gabriel and Connell 2010:507). Though some stories do this better than others – Yiannis Gabriel and Con Connell (2010:507) highlight those that are 'told well, in the right context and at the right time' – all stories reveal something, even if only that the writer or teller is muddled and still searching for what it is they want to see or say. Indeed, the least fluent stories can be the most illuminating, exploring experiences that may not yet be clear to the writer or speaker. Here, stories have particular potential, since they can get at subjects indirectly, for example through fictional and allusive figures and narratives. Through sometimes circuitous routes, storying can circumvent conventions and restrictions about what can be said: where, when and by who (Plummer 1995).

One way of collecting and transcribing stories is elicitation: asking people to tell their stories (Atkinson 1998). This is most practical where it involves stories that people are ready to tell. Ken Plummer (1995), exploring the sex lives of non-heterosexual men and women in the 1980s, found many people ready to open up to him. Their readiness to speak may have reflected the time, a moment in the history of sexuality in which queer people were increasingly ready to come out, and conscious of the significance of doing so. Their fluency and loquacity also reflected Plummer's skill as a researcher, and the safe space that he, as a gay man, had offered them. For some, coming out was a liberating moment of what Finola Farrant (2014:461) calls 'unconcealment'. For others, it meant discharging a responsibility, to self and community. Their fluency was also made possible by the language that was readily available to those who wanted to speak. This included scripted coming-out narratives that gay men and lesbians increasingly performed, and encouraged and pressured others to perform. Be yourself, young people have been told, but be yourself in the same way as everyone else! Tell the story of 'your (real lesbian) self' through a formulaic story of coming out (Crawley and Broad 2004:39). Sexual relationships are not only described *through* stories; they are experienced and conducted *as* stories (Bochner et al 1997). This is true not only of particular relationships, but also of relationship histories: the series of desires, encounters and relationships that make up a sexual life. More generally, we use the life stories we tell to find order in our lives (Polkinghorne 1988), to gain perspective, affirm the life choices we have made, connect with others, establish belonging within a group, and more (Atkinson 1998).

Some other stories are more difficult to elicit, some other subjects more difficult to put into words. This may be the case where people are not ready to tell their story, do not feel safe or do not know how to do so, perhaps because they lack the language that would make this easy. This might be said of earlier generations of gay men and lesbians, who were not only pressured to conceal their sexuality, but also had less exposure to language in which to articulate their sexual desires, identities and relationships (Morgan 2000).

In addition to the stories that researchers directly elicit, there are many in circulation, which it is possible to collect, whether by transcribing spoken words or by gathering and interpreting stories that have been written down. There is a long history of transcribing the stories of oral culture. Well-known examples of this practice include the transcription of folk tales, which formed the basis for great anthologies including *Grimm's Fairy Tales* and the *Arabian Nights* (see Warner 2012). These literary transcriptions have counterparts in contemporary social research, where researchers have overheard and found spoken words in settings such as barbers' shops and sports grounds. In each of these examples, transcription is active and productive, not simply writing down stories but retelling them in written form. Tracey Bunda, an Australian Aboriginal woman who works in Aboriginal and Torres Strait Islander higher education, tells stories about her family which speak, as her research collaborator Louise Phillips puts it, 'of separation from family from a young age and ongoing daily lived encounters of racism' (Phillips and Bunda 2018:xii). Bunda tells how she has passed down the storytelling traditions of her family, learned from her mother, translating these from oral to textual form:

> There are many within my large family who are storytellers, finessed performers who can reduce a listener to tears from laughing and crying in equal measure. I continue to hold the love of stories close to me and contemplate that perhaps a contribution I have is the capacity to write stories and give back through this ability. (Phillips and Bunda 2018:2)

The following extract is from 'Taken', which Bunda presents as 'the story of my mother' (Phillips and Bunda 2018:54); it is included in *Research Through, With And As Storying* (2018), which is the result of collaborative work and conversations with Louise Phillips:

> A small ramshackle house of rusting corrugated tin, slapped-together old timber boards for walls and a dirt floor could be found down the bush track. It is away from the town that bustles with its own importance and only becomes known, is seen, when the lives inside the shack have percussion with the important things of that town where white people live. The bush track, lined with white gums and scrubby bush that have taken shape from too many battles with the wind, travels parallel to the sea. Pale-blue skies, slow-moving puffed-up clouds and a taste of salt in the air paints a picture complete.
>
> The shack ordinarily holds a messy tangle of children, lean of body and light of feet. Some of that messy tangle is outside, playing imaginary games that will keep them occupied for hours and days and weeks. Inside, on the iron-framed bed strangled tight with a grey blanket, GOVERNMENT stamped in red, sit the three.
>
> The youngest is aware that this is not another ordinary day. (Phillips and Bunda 2018:52–3)

The tension grows later on, when an official vehicle pulls up outside the shack and '[a] white man opens the car door' and approaches, 'a piece of paper in hand'. He gathers three of the children, leading them to the back seat of the car, which takes them to 'the Salvation Army-managed Aboriginal mission of Purga' (all quotations: Phillips and Bunda 2018:54):

> On arrival, the three who had endured a strange and terrorising kidnapping were separated again. The oldest boy was placed in the boys' dormitory, whilst the two girls were placed in another dormitory. The youngest of the three had arrived in Purga. It was her birthday. She was 7. (Phillips and Bunda 2018:54)

This story intersects with the autoethnographic writing introduced earlier in this chapter, with the writing and telling of stories by researchers.

Another form of storying research involves stories that have already been written down. Here, where 'all' that remains is for the researcher to collect and interpret them, the work of the social researcher intersects with literary and cultural criticism. We have defined the scope of this book (in Chapter 1) to avoid straying too far into subjects and fields that we could not do justice to. Our focus, we explained, is on creative writing rather than literary criticism. That said, stories (and other forms of creative writing) that are already in circulation, in written and other forms, are too rich a source to pass over completely at this point.

One example of stories being used in social research is by organisational researchers Mike Zundel, Robin Holt and Joep Cornelissen, who used stories from a TV series to inform their analysis of institutions as dynamic systems. *The Wire*, which ran on HBO from 2002–08, is centred around the trade in illegal drugs in the US city of Baltimore. 'The stories implicate agents (traders, police, politicians, addicts), institutions (commercial markets, courts, standards, language, laws), and objects and symbols (clothing, electronic surveillance) within narratives of organisational creation and dissolution, performative success and failure, and personal accomplishment, frustration, and tragedy' (Zundel et al 2013:103). These stories were written by two men, David Simon and Ed Burns, who had worked in Baltimore as journalist and detective respectively. '*The Wire* is self-consciously fiction, yet it remains intimate with the everyday, unresolved atmosphere in which those living and working in Baltimore breathe (or cease to)' (Zundel et al 2013:106). To produce this fiction, the writers conducted a great deal of research, spending over two years in the field with people from the criminal justice system, people directly affected by drugs, and politicians. Zundel et al (2013:106) aver that 'the meaning generated by social investigation is not exhausted simply because it is not conveyed in a propositional language of science'. For Zundel et al, the fictional *Wire* provides richer data about institutions as dynamic systems than the conventional, non-fictional accounts gathered by organisation researchers. This data allows the researcher to examine events as they happen and to understand them, at least to some extent, experientially for themselves rather than vicariously through someone else's re-telling of experience (Zundel et al 2013:106–7).

Having found such already written stories, we need to decide what to do with them: how to interpret them. These challenges are similar to those of interpreting stories that we have elicited and/or transcribed. Like many other things people say and write, but more so, stories demand interpretation; their truths tend not to be literal. Plummer (1995:1) explains that: 'Whatever else a story is, it is not simply the lived life. It speaks all around the life.' Not simply the representation of a life, the story may be an orientation device, which 'provides routes into a life, lays down maps to follow' (Plummer 1995:1). Through stories, we 'play with possibilities' (Cameron 2012:585). It follows that we should not read stories too literally.

Each story offers a 'view from "somewhere"' (Diversi 1998:133), which is expressed through perspective or point of view. By writing stories from particular points of view, rather than as all-seeing or omniscient narrators, social researchers are able to complicate and extend their now-established understanding that all knowledge is positional. The recognition of positionality, belying the universal knowledge claims of white western men (Rose 1997), launched the feminist first-person writing explored earlier in this book. Stories, in which writers explore particular points of views and voices, take this project further.

The idea of point of view is closely related to another: voice. It is often said that writing works best when it has a coherent and recognisable voice. But what does this mean? This term has two distinct meanings in creative writing. Most literally, characters in a story have their own particular voices. Marcelo Diversi explained that his goal, in telling stories about street children, was to 'give voice to street kids' (Diversi 1998:132). Voice also refers to the tone and style of the writer, who may or may not be present as a first–person narrator. This understanding of voice originates in the teaching and criticism of fiction, but it is also applicable to non–fiction writing (Neale 2009:181; Morgan 2011:128). Each of the contributions to this book has its own voice, which is different from the voice of the main text, and from each other.

Try this

There is a writing exercise for voice, which involves telling a story from a particular perspective and in an appropriate voice. This is fun to do with one or more friends or colleagues if you can. Helen developed this from a patois/dialect exercise she found in 2006 on Stet, the blog of the linguist, editor and writer Ria Bacon. Imagine this happened to you:

You were travelling in a city by bus. A man got on, dressed as a clown, and kissed three passengers on the cheek on his way to a seat. A little girl sitting opposite him started to cry, and climbed onto her mother's lap for a hug. The man didn't react. Two stops later, he got off the bus, and you saw him dance along the street, kissing random strangers.

Now decide which character you would like to be:
- police officer
- beauty therapist
- excited ten-year-old
- actor
- taxi driver
- retired army colonel
- rap artist
- dairy farmer
- human rights campaigner
- government minister

Rewrite the story as if you were that character recounting the experience to your best friend. Give yourself a maximum of 10 minutes. If you are working with a friend or in a group, it can be fun to write characters on strips of paper, fold them up, mix them around and then pick one (and a second, if you really can't face the first one). Don't tell anyone which character you picked. Write the pieces, then read them out in turn and have the others try to guess each character.

CREATIVE WRITING IN PRACTICE

Worlds within worlds: Mohammed the watchman *by Hayden Lorimer and Ruth Olden*[7]

Hayden Lorimer is a writer, broadcaster and Professor of Cultural Geography. He led a research project exploring ruined heritage sites through experimental methods, including creative writing. **Ruth Olden** is a cultural geographer, landscape architect and landscape writer based in Glasgow. She is interested in the bonds that tie people and place. Here, Hayden and Ruth experiment with ways of seeing a ruin, focusing upon the experiences of a security guard called Mohammed. Their account is interspersed with slivers of commentary on their methods: the ways in which they write and observe, and their responsibilities towards Mohammed and the ruined site itself.

i. Stories are Journeys

You can put a fence around something, but you can't contain its stories.

To begin with this seemed like the most important lesson we would learn. It helped us make sense of Mohammed's story. He's someone all too easily portrayed as a victim of history. But someone who we would rather characterise on different terms: as a survivor of geography.

But there's a burden of responsibility that comes from telling a story such as his. (Which is to say nothing of the good fortune we have in being able to tell it at all.) To write of Mohammed, we know we need to do right by him. To respect the blank spaces, because the lines of a life, and the paths it takes, are not clear cut. And on reflection this is surely the

Figure 2.3: Inspiration doll by Alke Gröppel-Wegener, created in response to this piece by Hayden Lorimer and Ruth Olden. Inspiration dolls comment on and play with genres of creative writing.

---

[7] This contribution should be cited as follows: Lorimer, H. and Olden, R. (2021) 'Worlds within worlds: Mohammed the watchman'. In Phillips, R. and Kara, H. *Creative Writing for Social Research*. Bristol: Policy Press.

lesson that will linger longest. Taking proper care to craft an ethic of storytelling ought to be something that takes its measure from his discipline, determination and dedication.

ii. The Unruliest of Ruins

It was researching the social life of a ruin that brought us to this sort of reckoning.

Ruins are the kind of place that create certain habits of mind. In matter of fact, being a ruin-botherer can make you feel like there are forces at play that won't be subject to your control. Or anyone else's for that matter. After all, a ruin is a place where entropy feels like the only law which is being enforced, pushing what-once-was towards what-no-longer-quite-is.

And ruins are where weird stuff tends to happen too. When no one is keeping watch, where everything is out of sight of adults, there is licence to do pretty much as you like. Smash shit up! Tear it down! Set it alight! Take too much! Take it all off! Turn it up! Stare wildly!

But complete abandon, year upon year, can take its toll.

Try to picture our ruin if you can. Up close, it has spalling surfaces and mildewing corners, the clutter of former worlds underfoot, and wall streaks left by gleeful all-night sprees. Step further back – *carefully* though – better to take in the scene. There are holes that gape, between curving blocks and tilting slabs. Awful spaces yawn where staircases and windows once slotted in. This isn't the heritage version of tumbledown. Real ruination is what happens when the pageantry of faded glory slackens, then sloughs away for good.

Our ruin has a certain notoriety. A great concrete carcass. It looks, as one student of architecture quipped, like the place where Modernism crawled up a hill to die.

iii. Shadowlands

It's an insider's joke, and it would have been lost on Mohammed during his first day on the job. Architectural appreciation was not part of the security man's brief. The place just looked grim. A shadowland, deserted, hidden deep in the woods.

He took the nightshift, which was all there was on offer. Six through to six. Part of a ramped-up security regime, newly imposed to keep the trespassers out.

> "Young folk being a danger to themselves."

That was how his manager put it. There were less polite descriptions too.

The firm's contract was with an arts company, which was in the process of taking the property off the hands of its long-time owner, the Catholic church, which itself was desperate to get shot of the place, which was a turn of events that would please the public body charged with ensuring that historic buildings listed for their architectural importance in the life of the nation do not go neglected. Wrangles among stakeholders over the ruin's future had been going on for decades. Occasionally, real estate speculators circled the site, excited enough by a unique opportunity to dream fanciful schemes of residential development only to admit defeat when the complexities of the site became fully apparent.

For the church, an arts company represented the option of last resort.

'A moon-shot effort', was how the press reported things, seeing as there was no single source of cash to cover the costs involved in converting a dilapidated former seminary, abandoned for more than thirty years, but still admired for its daring design, into a major cultural asset.

"Stabilise *that* thing?"

The sceptics reckoned these new guardians were tilting at windmills.

iv. Who Goes There?

For Mohammed, none of this mattered a jot. What did were the tools of the trade: ID, keys, torch, work-boots, and rainwear (standard-issue hi-vis). And, above all else, an electrical heater to keep the security cabin warm. The mobile generator to the rear of the cabin doubled as his bike-stand. For long stretches, its puttering and rough cough was the only other presence discernible on site. There's nothing companionable about the silence when you're on nights, and all alone. Phone reception is patchy up there. The depths of winter swallowed everything.

Mohammed worked at keeping himself occupied, getting attuned to the seminary's nightlife. For a start, there was a beat to learn. The site's perimeter steel fencing marked the limit of his patrol. As the front line of defence, palisade steel fencing comes industry-approved. Each railing has a trident-top; spikes splayed for preventive effect. Going over the top is not advisable. But the most determined of "ruinistas" come equipped to find a way through.

He checked for breaks in the fence-line, and squeeze-throughs where the spars had been bent out of shape. And he got his ear in, learning how to listen hard, for the ways that sound travels through the ruin's spaces, and the tricks its acoustics can play. For any encounter, there was a code of conduct to internalise, and physically embody. Strong, clear commands, issued with authority, but without aggression. Would-be intruders, he learned, came in all shapes and sizes. Some went in for politeness and pleading. Others feigned defeat, only to redouble their efforts at some out of the way corner. A few banshees, the local lords of misrule, came to the ruin to get fuelled or wired, and were ready to threaten violence or vengeance.

v. Driven to Extremes

To say he'd seen this all before is true enough. But familiarity brought little relief. It felt like its own kind of traumatic return. Back to Khartoum's streets, to criminality and police work, to civil war and accusations of wrong-doing. None of this had been kids' play. Nor was leaving behind everything that he held dear. Or the trials of a sea crossing, or journeying overland through Europe, or the decision to stow-away in a desperate bid to reach the UK. There was his family to think of, still living in Sudan, and efforts to present a case to the authorities, that in the interests of safety, they be allowed to join him. Fences and walls, barriers and borders, securitisation and fortification, containment and detainment: these days it's a global business.

With spring's passing, and the arrival of summer, the job got harder. Would-be intruders came in numbers, determined to keep up customary rights of access to an informal adventure playground. Fresh greenery offered them a thick canopy of cover. They toyed and teased, using decoys and dummy runners. Scare tactics too. He felt under siege. At points all control was lost. Retreating to the cabin, he called for backup.

His manager was not best pleased, making the situation plain: if an accident happened on Mohammed's watch then it would be him to blame. Duty of care, liability too.

"The whole effin lot of it. On *your* watch."

Precariousness of employment is a powerful means to exert pressure, and to disown legal responsibility. What is core to a supplier's contract can be reconfigured as an outsourceable service.

Members of the local constabulary were little better. Airing their own suspicions about what, or who, actually counted as an alien presence. The wrong colour, from the wrong country, with the wrong language. One of them, not us.

vi. Metalwork

We all know how it feels to fret so much that you grow sick with the worry.

As the days lengthened and nights shortened, fortifying the ruin demanded 360° attentiveness. Mohammed posted himself at vantage points most suited for keeping watch, monitoring the approach routes from on high. Doing running repairs along the fence-line became a practical kind of response. Friends helped. Sourcing all sorts of stuff useful for patching up, battening down, covering over and holding together.

Whatever they could lay their hands on really. Bike locks. Padlocks. Plumbing clasps. Steel hasps. Heavy-duty mesh. Metal sheeting. Mohammed carried a tool-bag, ever ready.

Today, the keen-eyed ruin-goer will find tell-tale tangles along the fence-line. The legacy of one-man's handiwork, suturing wounds and tending to soft spots.

vii. A Mixed Bag

His letter of notice came in the post. Word was that the arts company had decided on a new approach. If the gate-crashers couldn't be deterred by a security presence then installing an anti-intruder alarm system might do the trick. Getting laid-off brought relief, of a sort. Abandonment is no condition for someone in need of solidarity and support. Up there he could only ever feel half-connected, somehow at odds with himself. Like the ruin had become a blueprint for his emptiness. He'd only been employed to defend the place. Not as its champion. And never its martyr. Redundancy meant parking some of the fears that nagged, easing one knot of anxiety in his gut.

There are certain lines of work that, in one way or another, we all come to depend on. And yet we know next to nothing about them. Faceless jobs, numberless shifts, the toil undertaken by "unpeople". The nightwatchman is one among them. Old clichés prevail: about it being an easy gig, recruiting retired cops, ageing bouncers, angry blokes, misfits and cast-offs.

But the truth about security work is different. Or rather, it's full of social difference.

viii. Word Travels

Some years ago, the geographer Doreen Massey wrote about what she called 'geographies of responsibility'. It is a resonant term. What did she mean by it? Massey stressed the importance of recalling how 'we are responsible to areas beyond the bounds of place not because of what we have done, but because of what we are' (2004:16). Grounding the concept mattered to Massey. And she recognised the imperative of personifying it too.

Mohammed's nights standing watch over an empty ruin, alone in the dark, is one such geography of responsibility. It brings Sudan into closer correspondence with Scotland, and makes our conditions of interdependence a little more apparent. In narratives the likes of his, the outlines of a larger life can be charted, and the politics of connectivity charted.

The experience of exile among Sudanese refugees has been reported in a series of portraits by the 'Voice of Witness' project (Walzer 2008), and in the form of a semi-fictionalised autobiography written by novelist-activist Dave Eggers, in collaboration with Valentino Achak Deng, one among a generation of Sudanese 'lost boys' (Eggers 2007). The portraits show how the legacies of displacement can be lifelong, and exhibited or expressed in a sense of unease. As a new life is slowly pieced together, who you are remains something self-contained. You are a recessed presence, prone to withdrawal, cautious of drawing attention to yourself. You are compelled to occupy the shadows because your status remains so precarious.

The lesson is clear enough. To venture into the intimacy of another life requires storytellers to consider how an ethic emerges from being economical with words and resourceful with language. The creativity of the exercise can be as much about taking away, and paring back, as it is about filling in.

ix. Onwards

The last we heard from Mohammed he was picking up different bits of work back in the city, security stuff at construction sites and jobs on store refits. No happy, or unhappy, ever after. That's not how it goes.

And the ruin? As yet, it remains a ruin.

Writing about ideas: essays and lists

There are imaginative and analytical capacities and components in all creative writing (Harper 2019:12). That said, the previous sections have focused on the imaginative – on images and imagination, description and notation – and now it is time to examine the analytical more directly. To this end, we turn to creative writing about ideas, in the form of essays and lists.

Essays

In the social sciences, the term essay is widely misunderstood and underestimated. Instructors and study skills manuals teach and often force students to write what they call essays when they are really looking for miniature theses. These consist of structured arguments in which core statements are unpacked through paragraphs that proceed in a straight line, elaborating and evidencing opening claims, and working towards conclusions, which bring few surprises when they finally arrive.

The essay, in contrast, is a freer, more creative form of writing, a 'tentative, unsystematic exploration', a 'toying with ideas' (Forsdick and Stafford 2006:8–9; Phillips 2018). The essayist eschews the certainties, predictability and linearity of formal academic writing. The essay is characterised less by signposts than unexpected changes of direction. Max Bense (1947, quoted by Adorno 1984:164) argued that: 'He writes essayistically who writes while experimenting, who turns his object this way and that, attacks it from different angles, and in his mind's eye collects what he sees, and puts into words what the object allows to be seen under the conditions established in the course of writing.'

Writing in this way, we may be able to explore subjects from different angles, and in different ways, typically beginning with a personal experience or observation, and reaching out to broader reflections. These are hallmarks of research, which is – or should be – exploratory and open-minded. Since essayists reach from personal to shared experiences, many are also social observers and researchers.

The essay has a long and living history, one which reaches back to Michel de Montaigne (1533–92) but also looks forward, thanks to contemporary writers who are continually exploring the possibilities of this form of writing and reinventing the essay and the essayistic. Contemporary essayists include the humourist David Sedaris, the sociologist and writer Tressie McMillan Cottom, and public intellectual and broadcaster Rebecca Solnit, as well as younger writers such as (the late) Marina Keegan, Charlie Fox and Jon Day.

Since the essay is a meandering form, exploring its objects from different directions, it crosses over with writing about walking and other forms of locomotion in which the writer/narrator criss-crosses a place, coming at it from different angles. Jon Day's *Cyclogeography* describes the *Journeys of a London Bicycle Courier*, as its subtitle explains. Its title is a pun on psychogeography, which involves walking against the grain of the modern city. From the seat of a bike – with all that can be seen, felt and heard from that vantage point – this book turns the city this way and that, and works towards some broader reflections. There are many twists and turns in the chapter on 'Circulation': beginning with a quotation from Thomas Pynchon; quickly moving on to some observations about the cyclist's sore bottom and some novel ways of protecting it; to specifics of getting dressed for cycling on a particular day:

> It's Friday morning and I'm getting ready for the day's work. I put on a woollen cycling jersey and pull on my shoes, still slightly damp from the previous day's rain. Outside, a woman throws batches of sodden bread from her balcony. Pigeons wheel in to feed. I drink a pint of milk and turn on the radio attached to the bag strap that runs like a bandoleer across my chest. I don't talk into it yet – this time is still my own but its gentle burble of static and talk breaks the silence. (Day 2015:20)

From these immediacies, the text cuts back to some historical context and out to some wider reflections. Day retells the story 'that track bikes were first used on the city streets by Jamaican couriers in New York' (Day 2015:21), alongside the more personal history of his own bike. He writes about the mechanics of cycling, where 'the first pedal strokes of the day' generate the energy needed to overcome 'the inertia of my wheels and the friction of rubber on tarmac' (Day 2015:22–3). And there are broader ideas about the ways in which bodies flow through cities, and how cyclists feel the streets through their wheels, experiencing and revealing otherwise invisible geographies. These thoughts are interesting, but they do not come across as the culmination of this work, and there are no real conclusions. This is not a thesis … it does things a thesis cannot.

There is no simple formula for writing essays, though some manuals and manifestos for creative writing may help (see, for example, Cioffi 2005). To those who would like to try this form of creative writing, we suggest that you start by reading essayists, paying attention to how they write, and learning by example. And so, rather than ending with a seemingly simple tip or instruction, we end with a brief reading of two modern essayists: Marina Keegan and Rebecca Solnit, followed with some practical suggestions.

Marina Keegan draws out broader points. In an essay written for Yale University's student newspaper, she reaches into her own experiences, reflecting on a quality of connection with fellow students, which she felt was 'not quite love' and 'not quite community' (Keegan 2014:1). Keegan's personal point of departure – admitting to anxiety that she would soon be leaving her student life behind – is rendered all the more poignant by the fact, known to her readers, that she died in a car crash shortly before the piece was first published (Keegan 2012). The 'opposite of loneliness' is what she was 'grateful and thankful to have found at Yale' and 'scared of losing' (Keegan 2014:1). Trying to put her finger on this feeling – in the tradition of the essay, the form of writing that explores a subject from different angles, rather than driving home a point – she writes of a 'feeling that there are people, an abundance of people, who are in this together' (Keegan 2014:1).

In Solnit's essays, we find 'the coincidence of language, philosophical reflection and bodily sensation' (Forsdick and Stafford 2006:46), which marks the essay as a literary form, and a form of enquiry. 'Open door', the first chapter in Solnit's *A Field Guide to Getting Lost* (2006), is in itself a masterclass in the essay as form and method. This piece begins with memories of Passover, getting 'drunk on Elijah's wine' (Solnit 2006:3) and the tradition of leaving open the 'door to night', thus to symbolically 'leave the door open for the unknown' (Solnit 2006:3). From these personal memories and religious and philosophical reflections, Solnit moves on to reflect on the nature of curiosity, differentiates between getting lost and losing oneself, takes the reader to the Rockies and introduces 'a lost eleven-year-old, a deaf boy who was losing his eyesight as part of a degenerative disease' (Solnit 2006:9), the subject of a search-and-rescue mission which ended well. Periodically, throughout this engaging and challenging essay, thoughts coalesce in quotable sentences. But we have resisted this 'highlighter pen' approach to reading Solnit. Instead, we suggest that every sentence counts, and that to learn the art of essay writing, it is important to read Solnit and other essayists as slowly and fully as possible. Then, steeped in the essay as a literary form, one may start to write essays of one's own, and ultimately to decide what particular kind of essayist one wishes to become.

Try this

We end with a practical tip for exploring the essay form. Read an essay by a writer who is new to you, such as Rebecca Solnit (2006), Peter Jackson (2013), Marina Keegan (2014), or Tressie McMillan Cottom (2019). When you have finished reading, write down your responses to the essay. How did it make you feel? Why do you think it made you feel that way? What did you like about the essay? What did you dislike? If you were going to write an essay, on a subject of your choice, what would that subject be?

Lists and listing

We now turn to another form of writing about ideas: one that explores taxonomies (the categories we put things and ideas into) and language (the words we use to label things and ideas).

Lists are all around us: shopping lists, to-do lists, reading lists and bucket lists; bullet points and numbered points in articles and reports; course lists; performance listings; the list goes on!

These can seem like the lowest form of writing: apparently artless, lacking even in punctuation. 'Are you sure we can get away with bullet points?' a co-author once asked Richard, explaining that this would not do in her own discipline. To answer this (not unreasonable) question, we should ask another: why might it be acceptable or, more than this, intellectually meaningful to use bullet points, or any other kind of list, in one's research? Let's answer this by way of another list, before going on to some examples:

- As anyone who has ever drafted an index will know, lists force the writer to identify important names, ideas and things, and to put them into some kind of order, alphabetical or otherwise, which may or may not include categories and sub-categories (Magné 2004). In other words, lists are exercises in or explorations of taxonomy. As such, lists also reveal tensions within taxonomies: 'strange, extraordinary, inopportune' things that don't fit a class or category can disrupt the entire system and force a rethink (Lakoff 1987; Maciel 2006:47).
- Lists are efficient and digestible, and therefore appeal to communicators, particularly when they are writing for concise-format media. These include newspapers and online platforms such as The Conversation, the influential platform for the dissemination of academic research. The list-form article, making three to five points, possibly in some media-friendly mnemonic order, has become sufficiently common to merit a neologism: the listicle. The modest, accessible listicle promises concision and clarity. A famous list is worth quoting because it speaks so directly to this book. It is by George Orwell, from his essay 'Politics and the English Language' (written in 1946, available online) and it proposes rules for writing, at least one of which warns against words like listicle!

  i. Never use a metaphor, simile, or other figure of speech which you are used to seeing in print.
  ii. Never use a long word where a short one will do.
  iii. If it is possible to cut a word out, always cut it out.
  iv. Never use the passive where you can use the active.
  v. Never use a foreign phrase, a scientific word, or a jargon word if you can think of an everyday English equivalent.
  vi. Break any of these rules sooner than say anything outright barbarous.

- Some lists have an aesthetic, a literary and visual appeal. Many (not all) lists are vertical, running down the page, each beginning with a capital letter. The arrangement of the list on the page, the typeface of a printed list, or the quality of handwriting and implements used – pencil, pen, and the presence or absence of colour – can transform lists into visual art. Like poems, and artworks that demand a closer look, lists can set the pace, slowing down the act of reading, instilling a rhythm of their own. There can also be an aesthetic – more than a logic – to the order in which the elements of a list appear. This aesthetic can revolve around a number of possibilities: how the words sound when read in sequence; how they look on the page; whether they hint at a story, open a window, or gesture towards an idea, all of which may spark the reader's curiosity.

Jonathan Meades' memoir of his childhood and adolescence, *An Encyclopaedia of Myself* (2014), includes a 'period product inventory' of the items for sale in his nearest shop:

> Weston's Wagon Wheels; Nestlé's segmental chocolate bars with green mint filling and green wrappers, Fry's segmental chocolate bars with white mint filling and navy wrappers; Fry's Turkish Delight; Crosse and Blackwell Russian Salad; Trex; Robinson's Lemon Barley Water; Kia-Ora (which meant good health – it was everyone's single word of Māori); Walls' disgusting pork sausages; Millers' even more disgusting pork pies … bottled sauces – A.1., HP, OK, Daddies, Heinz Salad Cream and ketchup … Rowntree's Fruit Gums (which caused mouth ulcers) and Fruit Pastilles (which didn't) … . (Meades 2014:19–20)

Meades' *Encyclopaedia* presents a version of a life, situated within a time, place and cultural context. This list speaks not only of the author, but also of time and place, the culture and society in which he lived. Its attention to the details of provincial life in postwar England – the food people ate, the clothes they wore – builds up a picture of what urban sociologist Darrel Martin calls 'the everyday and its materialities' (Martin 2019:191; see also Becker 2001).

Meades' list also illuminates the taxonomies of material culture. Word choices matter: the common and proper nouns; the sequence in which they appear and the connections implied, the distinctions drawn; the things left out, the linguistic inconsistences; the fluctuating ways in which things and events are recorded (Sheringham 2000; Maciel 2006). This list gets us thinking about words and the way we use them to explore our experiences and realities.

Though we may think of lists as vertical, unpunctuated sequences or words, lists take other forms including prose. Such lists confound some fundamental conventions of academic writing: make a point, evidence it, evaluate the evidence, and restate the point. Prose lists, in contrast, pile up material without always spelling out why, or explaining what the material is intended to evidence. Here is an example from Iain Sinclair (2008), in a piece about (and against) the London 2012 Olympic project:

> In the mornings, there is a clinging, overripe smell that some people say drifts in from the countryside, a folk memory of what these clipped green acres used, so recently, to be. Mulch of market gardens. Animal droppings in hot mounds. The distant rumble of construction convoys.
>
> The heron dance of elegant cloud-scraping cranes. Flocks of cyclists clustering together for safety, dipping and swerving like swallows. Hard

hats and yellow tabards monkeying over the scaffolding of shrouded towers, the steel ribs of emerging stadia. (Sinclair 2008)

Sinclair's writing can sometimes come across as a rant: … and another thing! But his lists have other effects: establishing a rhythm; accumulating words and paragraphs, establishing momentum; developing a kind of anti-aesthetic, which evokes layers of ugliness, excess and absurdity; presenting a busy collage of late capitalism.

We also find lists in the arts. Some of these are by writers and poets whose work interests some social researchers; others are by researchers working with poetry and visual art. In the work of earth artist Richard Long, these impulses converge. *A Straight Northward Walk Across Dartmoor, 1979–2010* takes the form of a vertical list of places encountered on two walks, undertaken at different points in time. This work brings together artistry and enquiry. It reflects the broader significance and potential of the seemingly humble list: as a means of exploring broad questions about the environment, economy, politics and society (Phillips 2012).

Try this

You have won a competition to be in the first human research team to land on the planet Hashkath and study the Aandrisks and their complex society (Chambers 2015). The air on Hashkath is breathable for humans. The Aandrisks are reptilian, reproducing through eggs. Individuals cycle through three genders: male-aligned, female-aligned and neutral. Aandrisks have three families: their egg family (biological relations, to whom they are rarely close), hatch family (who they live with as children) and feather family (the family they choose as adults). The adults in hatch families are usually elders; in Aandrisk society, young adults are deemed unqualified and unready to raise children. Hatch and feather families are usually polygamous. Write a list of your initial questions.

And, for another exercise in listing, try this: make a list of items on your desk or in your workspace. Now, play with the list so that it changes shape. First, try a number of different ways of ordering the items on the list. These may be alphabetical, or according to some other principle, such as the shapes of the words or the sounds they make when read aloud in succession. Second, rewrite your list, such that you use a different word to label each of the items. For example, rather than pencil, you might say writing implement or pointed object. Now play with this list, exploring different ways of ordering it, as before. Compare your different lists. What do they tell you?

Doing it yourself: following through

Having introduced a number of ways of writing, and made suggestions for how researchers new to creative writing can get started in each of them, we are now ready to follow through by developing the writing you may have started. We recognise that you may only want to do this for some of the creative writing you begin. In other cases you may feel that the initial exercise has been enough, and that you have hopefully learned something from it, if only that you do not wish to continue! That said, where you have started some writing you would like to improve, here are some suggestions.

Drafting and editing

Sustained writing typically needs to go through multiple drafts: usually at least three. One way to think of this is that you write the first draft to tell yourself a story, and in the second draft you edit to make that story comprehensible for other people. The third draft is for polishing the text: making sure your sentences and paragraphs are well crafted, your story flows, your word choices are optimal, and your punctuation is effective.

Before you start writing – or, at the latest, before you start writing the second draft – ask yourself who you are writing for. Your boss? The readers of a specific publication? Your future self? Your peers? Work out who makes up your intended readership and think about their characteristics, then make your writing appeal to them and/or meet their needs.

We advise you always to read your work out loud when it's almost done. Reading aloud can seem unnatural, onerous, embarrassing, or pointless. However, this reading can help you identify errors and clunky sentences that you wouldn't spot on the page. Also, it helps you to create a consistent voice for your piece of writing. Helen reads all her work out loud as she finalises her texts, including full-length books. Richard does too, though he distinguishes between writing for silent reading and writing scripts to be read in presentations and other performances. He tailors his writing to these different media, but in each case he finds it helpful to read aloud, sometimes to an empty room, sometimes within a workshop. We advise others to do something similar: listen to your work.

Reading others' work is not a passive occupation. Readers create meaning as they read, from the place where the writer's words meet the reader's past experience and current emotions (Elbow 1998:314–15; Kara 2017:106). This in turn creates a new experience for the reader, often evoking new emotions in the process (Elbow 1998:315–16; Kara 2017:106). As a writer, you cannot have total control over this, because you don't know what a reader will bring to your work. Your job is to express what you want to say as effectively as you can. Then you have to let the reader do the rest. Thus, while it is helpful to listen to your work being read aloud, whether by yourself or someone else, you cannot know quite how it will sound to others.

Seeking and receiving feedback

Seeking and responding to feedback are important parts of the writing process. Sometimes feedback is useful at first draft stage. This tends to be the case for writers who are either very experienced (because they have learned how to make use of feedback at an early stage) and those who are novices (because they need help to find their way). More often feedback is useful at second draft stage. Here you have already worked hard to make your writing effective for others, and it's time to test the results of your efforts.

You can ask for different types of feedback, such as criterion-based feedback or reader impact feedback (Elbow 1998:240) or expert feedback (Goodson 2017:91). Criterion-based feedback focuses on the quality of the writing. There are many questions you could ask here, such as about levels of detail, organisation of ideas, and effectiveness of language (Elbow 1998:252–4). Reader impact feedback focuses, as the phrase suggests, on the impact the writing has on its reader. What does it make them think and feel? For Goodson, discussing academic writing, expert feedback should be from an expert in the field and should focus on accuracy of content and quality of argument (2017:91). However, in the context of writing creatively for social research, expert feedback could equally be from an experienced poet, novelist, playwright or other writer.

When you are seeking feedback, take time to think through what you want to know, and pose some specific questions. This makes your feedback reader's task easier. You may also want to include a final catch-all question such as, 'Is there anything else you want to tell me about this piece of writing?'. That can enable someone to give feedback on areas you might not have considered.

Although feedback is useful, it can be hard to take (Elbow 1998:237). Try to get feedback in writing. Read it through and give yourself time to absorb the emotional impact. This can be anything from delight to rage, bewilderment, pleasure, or irritation – and often involves a combination of emotions. Let yourself feel whatever you need to feel, and do whatever you need to do to acknowledge your emotions. Talk to a friend, eat chocolate, jump up and down – whatever works for you.

When your emotions have settled, go back to your feedback and treat it as data. Read it carefully and extract the key elements. Feedback can be confusing (Thomson and Kamler 2016:83) so seek clarification if necessary. Ideally that would be from the person who gave you the feedback; failing that, get a second opinion from a trusted colleague or friend.

Feedback tends to fall into one of three categories:

- No Chance – where you are not going to do what the feedback suggests, perhaps because the person has misunderstood an aspect of your work;
- No But Yes – where the feedback makes you realise change is needed, though not in the way the giver intended;

- No Brainer – where the feedback is spot on and you can see it makes sense to do what the person says.

It can be helpful to create a table from your feedback, with three columns headed Key Element, Category, and What/Why. In the first column, write one key element of your feedback in each row of the table. In the second column, categorise that feedback as a No Chance, No But Yes, or No Brainer. In the third column, write down what you will do as a result of the feedback and why. Then your What/Why column can be used to create an action plan for implementing your feedback. Dealing with feedback systematically in this way helps you to make the most from the input you have received.

Writing together

Writing is often thought of as a solitary activity but, as we shall see in Chapter 3, some people enjoy or benefit from writing in the presence of others. There are a huge number of ways this can be done, from two friends meeting in person or online to write together, to luxury group retreats led by bestselling writers on tropical islands lapped by turquoise seas.

Rowena Murray asserts that any writing which is not completely private is at least relational and often a social activity. Writers are in relationship with their readers at the very least, and often with colleagues, managers, reviewers, supervisors, editors and so on (Murray 2014:6). Any writer can benefit from the opportunity to discuss their writing aspirations, problems and successes with others. It doesn't matter whether you're talking to a writer who is more or less experienced than you, working in the same or a different genre, a peer or a mentor; discussion is almost always helpful.

Some groups and organisations host 'shut up and write' groups, which can be very helpful when you need to churn out a first draft. Writing workshops are usually tutored and can last for anything from a couple of hours to a couple of weeks. And retreats are increasingly popular. These can be solo retreats where you book some accommodation, or borrow a friend's house while they're away, to concentrate solely on writing for a few days or weeks. Or they can be organised retreats. These may be tutored retreats where you spend most of your time writing and have a few taught group sessions and one-to-ones with a tutor. Or they can simply be catered retreats, such as those run by the Arvon Foundation in the UK, where you have your own room to write in a big house with other writers doing the same.

So if you find being alone off-putting, and that is getting in the way of your writing, there are other options. Find another writer, or a group, or start a group. Or go on a retreat – search online to find retreats all around the world catering for writers at all levels. Or get creative and create your own retreat!

Another way of writing together is to collaborate as joint authors. This is more common with some ways of creative writing. Scriptwriting is sometimes seen as more amenable to collaboration than, say, poetry, though it is not difficult to find examples of collaborative poetry (for example, Eshun and Madge 2012). Writing with others can be a joy, though it can also bring challenges (Sword 2017:130). These days, people don't have to be co-located to write collaboratively. Documents can be shared and meetings held online to facilitate international and global writing collaborations, as long as everyone has internet access. For creative writing, it can be more fun and sometimes more productive if you can work together in the same room, but it's not essential and may at times be counterproductive. The key to success in collaborative work is to decide how each person will contribute, then to stick to what you say you're going to do.

One particularly innovative approach to collaborative writing was taken by Charlotte Wegener, an ethnographer based in Denmark. She worked with a fictional character, enlisting Phineas from A.S. Byatt's novel *The Biographer's Tale* (2001) as her co-writer for analytic work. Having no real people with whom to collaborate, 'I ended up inviting into my writing process a bewildered and naive fictional character' (Wegener 2014:352). She found that creating dialogue between herself and Phineas, largely – though not exclusively – using his own words from the novel for his speeches, 'inspired me to interact with my data in new ways and make decisions about which categories and narratives to craft' (Wegener 2014:358). Here is an example of the dialogue (Wegener 2014:358 – page numbers in the excerpt are from *The Biographer's Tale*):

Phineas: "I seemed to understand that the imaginary narrative had sprung out of the scholarly one, and that the compulsion to invent was in some way related to my own sense that in constructing this narrative I have had to insert facts about myself, and not only dry facts, but my feelings, and now my interpretations." (pp. 236–237)

Charlotte: Yes, these lies made you reflect upon your assumptions of reality and how to write about reality.

Phineas: "I have somehow been made to write my own story, to write in different ways." (p. 237)

Charlotte: Your writing is fragmentary just like your story consists of fragmentary information about fragmentary lives. Your data is a range of odd artifacts—unfinished manuscripts, marbles and index cards—not fitting into categories and not really making you or me more informed. One narrative, however, runs through the fragments, and that is the story of writing as a life-extending human activity.

Phineas: "Reading and writing extends—not infinitely, but violently, but giddily—the variations we can perceive on the truth we thus discover." (p. 237)

For Wegener (2014:358): 'Fictional genres and cowriting with fictional characters as research tools generate, if not unquestionable "facts," then at least some truths about the field under study.' Wegener's idea is one which other researchers could take forward, using characters from novels, films, plays, animations, fairy tales – there are many choices here.

CREATIVE WRITING IN PRACTICE

From a beat and a melody come a lyric and a truth: Honey's story *by Kitrina Douglas and David Carless*[8]

Kitrina Douglas and **David Carless** have been researching, writing and performing together since their doctoral research. In this collaborative autoethnographic piece they use creative writing to show how songwriting can be used to help social researchers uncover subconscious knowledge. The piece includes a song they wrote during fieldwork on a project exploring the physical activity experiences and lives of women over 55 living in rural Cornwall, UK, commissioned by the Women's Sport and Fitness Foundation.

In this contribution, we explore some of the creative processes of lyrical and musical inquiry as social research. We use autoethnography as a way to illuminate our experiences of using the body and a musical instrument as a basis for uncovering truths we didn't know we knew.

> At its most basic we are only discussing a learned skill, but do we not agree that sometimes the most basic skills can create things far beyond our expectations? We are talking about tools and carpentry, about words and style ... but as we move along, you'd do well to remember that we are also talking about magic. (Stephen King 2000:155)

Figure 2.4: Inspiration doll by Alke Gröppel-Wegener, created in response to this piece by Kitrina Douglas and David Carless. Inspiration dolls comment on and play with genres of creative writing.

Honey's Story

'Honey used to creep into my bedroom,' David said, halfway through a conversation about dogs and field notes. 'I remember one night I woke up and couldn't feel my

---

[8] This contribution should be cited as follows: Douglas, K. and Carless, D. (2021) 'From a beat and a melody come a lyric and a truth: Honey's story'. In Phillips, R. and Kara, H. *Creative Writing for Social Research*. Bristol: Policy Press.

legs. I couldn't move them. I was terrified! Then I realised it was her – she'd climbed onto my bed and fallen asleep lying on my legs!'

'She sounds a lovely dog,' Kitrina said laughing. 'I wish we had been allowed a dog.'

'She was a rescue dog,' David said carrying on, 'and a real gannet, it was so funny, she'd eat anything she could get. She'd even try to peel chewing gum off the pavement with her teeth if you'd let her! We used to let her lick the empty peanut butter jars, I laughed so much watching her, she'd totally clean out every last bit with her tongue.'

David finished his story and they finished chatting about themes. Then, after the phone call, David returned to their thematic analysis, looking again at the words spoken by Nell and how her story fitted with the themes or challenged what they thought they showed. Then he looked through all the extracts that related to one of their themes and chose a couple of extracts as illustrations. Then he went on to write a little more about what they'd learned. But when he read back what he'd written he wasn't pleased. In fact, it was somehow devoid of the life he'd experienced while he was talking with the women – in their homes, the coffee shops, standing in a queue at the post office. *Where was the energy? The humour? The spirit of resistance?* he asked himself. And where was *the feeling?* He'd lost it. He thought back to the phone conversation a few moments earlier and the spirit of what he felt when he'd talked about his dog, Honey, and how she would clean the peanut butter pot and how it made him *feel* – laughter, connection, love, joy. In a similar way, when he looked at what he'd written about the women and their lives, friendships, dogs, activity, he'd somehow lost something he'd known and felt when talking to the women in Cornwall.

Blaming this failure on tiredness, he stopped work for the day, had dinner, watched a movie, and then aimlessly picked up his guitar. He'd retuned it the day before and now all he had to do was bar a fret with one finger and a harmonious chord would ring. He fingerpicked the strings, then let his hands skip down the neck to pick higher notes. It brought a feeling of lightness and connection. He suddenly saw, in his head, Honey bounding towards him at full speed and unable to stop, bowling him over. His body remembered the feeling of her softness, her bulk, her muscles in tension. His hand swept down to the other end of the guitar neck where he plucked other chords, and other scenes emerged from his body, fragments.

He thought back to Nell again and her talking about her 'well-meaning' friends who wanted her to get married again after she'd lost her husband, not wanting her to live out in the country alone, nor paint her ceiling, nor, in fact, do anything outside the narrow 'norm' expected of an 83-year-old. He suddenly had the urge to write so, putting the guitar down, he scribbled a few lines, driven by emotional fragments still in his head, the music still ringing, forming a stream of awareness, bubbling, dancing over rocks, a different telling about her life than the one he wrote earlier. He was aware too that they both shared this sense of people wanting to get them 'married off' – her because she'd lost her husband and him because parents like their kids to 'settle down' and 'start a family'. As Nell had said: *'First they try to get you remarried,'* she'd told them. *'When they realise you don't want that they start on ...'* David stopped. What had she said? He looked at his notes: *'Poor old soul up there on her own! But I like being on my own, I don't want company for company's sake!'* He turned the page of his notebook and selected words and phrases for an emerging poem:

First they try to get you remarried
When they realise you don't want that
they start on 'Poor old soul up there on her own'
But I like being on my own
There's always a dog
Dogs always turn up when you need them

David smiled, lay back and closed his eyes again, allowing his arm to loll off the sofa. His hand relaxed.

Honey's nose nuzzled into the open hand. It was damp, rubbery and had a slightly rough texture. Next it was her tongue, with millions of soft micro bumps, warm, licking his hand, finding the gaps between his fingers, tracing their edges. It tickled, made him laugh. He stroked her head, soft, warm, and she put her head in his lap. Did they both feel secure? Was this love? Was it unconditional acceptance? Why was this moment so peaceful? So uneventful? Was it more than company? David looked down at Honey and, as he did, her eyebrows lifted and she turned her eyes towards his. Was it trust he saw in her eyes? What was she not telling him in those big dark windows? She licked her mouth and yawned revealing a dark pink flash of colour and white sharp teeth. Then she swallowed and put her head down again in the warm spot she'd created on his lap.

David woke from his dream, aware suddenly of how many of the women had talked about *not being touched anymore*, because when you are old, they said, no one wants to touch you, caress, hold you. Feeling heavy and saddened by this thought, yet remembering the feeling of Honey touching him, he picked up his guitar again. What else had the women said?

The shape of the instrument and the smell of the wood created a secure foothold which allowed an otherwise hidden world to be opened up to him – but at a subconscious level. Placing his fingers on the frets he experimented with different chord shapes and began finger picking some progressions. To an onlooker, it might have seemed like aimless, repetitive meanderings. To those who understand the songwriting process it might have looked like he'd gone fishing. Fishing for a new song. Still cloaked in the feel of Honey's body pressed against him, his fingers danced across the strings and he smiled, remembering Fran and Betty talk about the touch they received when they went dancing. He heard their voices, imagined them swirling across the dance floor, invited to dance, their skirts and dresses flowing, in the arms of a man or woman who would hold those ageing bodies close. And then, in a few magic moments, from the stirrings of their stories, tiptoed the song *Our Dancing Feet*.[9]

Take me dancing
Cause I've spent some time alone

Now I'm ready
To feel a warm touch on my arm
Let's go dancing
Take me to that place
Where there's music, movement
a smile upon my face

I'm dancing
Waltzing and I'm flying
and I'm looking
into another dancer's eyes
I'm dancing
A child as life begins
and I'm starring
in 'Gone with the Wind'

My reflection says I'm older
My heart and mind have never changed
I'm still a dancer and a mover
and this dance never fades

Now the dance is over
lead me to my seat
You might linger a little longer
here with me
Maybe tomorrow
we'll meet out on the street
and we will laugh as we talk about
Our dancing feat

Epilogue

The song *Our Dancing Feat* and poem *My Murderous Face* (the beginning of which also appears here) were written during fieldwork on a project exploring the physical activity experiences and lives of women (over the age of 55) living in a rural area (Cornwall) in the UK. The project was commissioned by the Women's Sport and Fitness Foundation. We created a performance ethnography from our field work (for additional information see Carless and Douglas 2010) which has been performed live for participants and local groups in Cornwall, in lectures, invited seminars and conferences, as well as across the UK, in the USA, Europe and New Zealand. The performance is available on CD. A selection of poems (https://youtu.be/AcJCjtTHaLw) and songs (https://youtu.be/R4EGRN_blw8) from the project are also available on YouTube.

3

Doing research, generating data, working with participants

Introduction

Social researchers are using creative writing in all aspects of their work: from gathering, exploring and analysing data to presenting and disseminating findings. They are doing so in many different forms, including diary entries, letters, stories, field notes, lists, poems, comics, written dialogue, play scripts, screenplays and more. They are doing this through the creative writing they do themselves, which we explored in Chapter 2, and by working with participants, which we move on to examine here in Chapter 3.

This book takes a broad view of social research for creative writing, drawing on a wide range of examples from the literature, and taking inspiration from an array of social researchers. That said, this is a field in which the authors of this book are active, and so we also draw upon examples from our own work. Here, Richard's research is particularly relevant. Some of this research is collaborative, conducted with fellow researchers who deserve a proper introduction at this stage, since they will reappear in the course of this chapter and later in the book. These researchers include: Afshan D'souza-Lodhi, a writer who identifies as a queer Muslim woman, who facilitated workshops in a project led jointly by Richard and Claire Chambers. Claire teaches postcolonial literature at the University of York, and specialises in Asian and Muslim women's writing. Nafhesa Ali, the researcher who worked with Claire and Richard to convene workshops in which young British Pakistani Muslims explored and learned creative writing, also contributes a piece of her own to this chapter, exploring research involving creative writing with participants.

Rationale

Creative writing is a participatory social research method when it involves people – framed as participants rather than mere informants or subjects – who get engaged in creative writing and, in doing so, provide insights into social experiences and issues. Their 'writing' – as verb: the process, facilitated and observed by the researcher; and as noun: the products of writing – forms the data for this research. This potentially covers a range of forms: from script and screenwriting to fiction, poetry, blogging, journal and diary writing, among others.

Participants can be involved in creative writing in different ways and to different extents. We can think of participatory creative writing for social research as a spectrum. At one end, participants play important but limited parts: doing some writing, perhaps; taking part in discussions about the writing process; providing the writer with material, such as in the form of an interview; reading and responding to drafts and performances; and so on. At the other end of this spectrum, participants are much more deeply and thoroughly involved, shaping and owning the project and the outputs (see, for example, Campbell et al 2017). The latter can be a form of action research. In this chapter, we explore work at both ends of this spectrum, and in between.

Participatory creative writing has a number of advantages. These include generating data that may be difficult or impossible through other means:

- Fostering exploration of personal or sensitive topics. Creative writing more generally provides windows on some otherwise hard-to-reach subjects and experiences. These include issues that some people see as personal or sensitive, making them difficult to broach through more conventional research methods such as face-to-face interviews and focus groups.
- Through the privacy afforded by writing, creating a safe space for exploring and articulating issues about which participants experience uncertainty and vulnerability (Djohari et al 2018).
- Exploring experiences that participants may not be aware of. Sometimes reaching beneath the conscious to the subconscious and the latent, sometimes reaching banal blind spots: things so ordinary and seemingly unimportant that we overlook them; the 'infra-ordinary' (Perec 1997; Phillips 2018). Through creative writing, we are saying, researchers and participants may come to understand things that were hitherto invisible or unknown (Richardson 1997:87).

Other advantages of participatory creative writing include benefits for participants:

- Enabling participants to develop transferable skills in creative writing as an art or craft and as a form of communication.
- Offering a vehicle for exploring rather than reporting experiences. E.M. Forster (1974 [1927]) asked, 'How do I know what I think until I see what I say?' More questions follow, such as: How can I know what I am experiencing if I don't put it into words? Writers are often advised to write 'what you know' (Neale 2006c:44), but this is only the beginning. In a handbook of creative writing, Derek Neale teaches that 'writing about what you know is a route to a different understanding of your own experience, and therefore also a route to finding out what you don't know' (Neale 2006c:55). So, he concludes, writing reaches towards 'what you come to know' (Neale 2006a:56). Jeanette Winterson (2005:134) puts this another way: 'The stories themselves make the meaning'. This is the fundamentally creative aspect of creative writing: the making of meanings, development of understandings, rather than simply the representation of the already known (Harper 2019:12).

- Enabling us to explore possibilities. Sociologist Ken Plummer (1995:1) reflects that, '[w]hatever else a story is, it is not simply the lived life. It speaks all around the life: it provides routes into a life, lays down maps to follow, suggests links between a life and a culture'.
- Being transformative – in good ways – for those involved in participatory writing. Finding and sharing stories can be cathartic (Parr and Stevenson 2013). These activities can 'unconceal' truths that were previously bottled up (Farrant 2014:461), revealing experiences that would otherwise remain hidden (Iser 1997:4).

Participants in creative writing projects stand to benefit collectively as well as individually because these projects typically involve working together, usually in workshops.

- As discussed in Chapter 1, some forms of creativity benefit from interaction with others, and take place relationally rather than individually. Interactions with other participants and workshop leaders can therefore be generative, enabling individuals to work creatively and to explore phenomena in ways that would not be possible alone.
- Working together, participants learn, practise and develop skills, gaining competence and confidence. Collective storytelling can be transformative (Richardson 1997:32–3).
- Some people enjoy connecting with others, and value the social dimension of writing together, as an end in itself.
- Participation in a group also provides a context in which creative work may be recognised. For example, participation may provide opportunities for sharing work, beginning with reading to the group, and sometimes leading to performances to wider audiences. Also, it may sometimes provide opportunities for publication.

We are not saying participatory creative writing is always a good idea. Like other methods, it has its time and place, but it also has risks and limits:

- The 'findings' of creative writing should not be taken too literally. Mitch Rose argues that stories should not be mistaken for 'empirics'; and that we should remember the 'distance between words and the world' (Rose 2016:135). That said, with sensitive interpretation, data from research involving creative writing stand to complement more conventional counterparts that can be taken more literally, such as interview data.
- Where sensitive and private matters are likely to be raised, participatory research runs the risk of compromising the privacy of individuals. It is possible to assert 'Chatham House rules' – that 'what happens in the workshop stays in the workshop' – but not to enforce them.

- While it can be liberating to 'unconceal' truths that were previously bottled up (Farrant 2014:461), this can also be scary and dangerous.
- Where creative writing reaches experiences beneath the surface, to the subconscious and the yet-to-be-articulated, participants may face realisations they are not prepared or ready for, and they may do so in public. Things may come up and come out with unexpected consequences.
- Particularly where participatory creative writing involves collaboration on a single output, such as the script for a play or film, group dynamics can take over, such that certain voices are amplified while others are silenced. This is partly a matter of personality as individuals may dominate. The parts people play in groups are shaped by factors such as gender, age, sexuality and marital status.
- Writing, even when it is ostensibly creative, is not necessarily free or radical. We write – and otherwise tell stories – within the means available to us, and the most readily available means include dominant discourses, genres, familiar expressions, and clichés (Amis 2001). This leads Leonie Sandercock (2003:12) to 'question the truth of our own and others' stories' by remaining 'attentive to how power shapes which stories get told, get heard, carry weight', with the recurrence of 'certain plots and character types'. Richardson (1997:42) comments that, 'How we are expected to write affects what we can write about'; this applies equally to an academic article for a specific journal and to an established poetic form such as a sonnet. Thus, while creative writing can be searching and illuminating, even subversive, it can also be conventional, and hegemonic (Brickell and Garrett 2015).

Some pitfalls of participatory creative writing revolve around the setting in which this work is typically conducted – the workshop – and the group dynamics therein.

- Working with other people is not always easy or effective. It involves constraints and compromises. There is no reason to assume that each participant has an equal say over the final product or performs equally in the collaborative process. Minority voices may be marginalised when they do not fit the story being told. Dissenting views are sometimes watered down, giving way to a consensual but potentially insipid story. Collaboration also subjects participants to collective decisions about working methods, which may constrain them.
- Participation in creative writing workshops can be challenging and uncomfortable, particularly for some people, such as those who have difficulties with writing, literacy, or being in groups. Workshops tend to involve reading aloud – sometimes required, sometimes invited, but difficult for participants to entirely avoid – and commenting on each other's work. This can be nerve-wracking.
- Some forms of participatory creative writing can be risky, exposing personal secrets that the writer may not intend to share, and may not even have been aware of, prior to writing.

Finally, there are downsides to creativity itself, which extend to creative writing:

- Creative writing is off-putting to some people, and this may not only be a matter of personality, but also class, gender and cultural difference. Some groups are more comfortable than others with the idea of creativity, and with writing, and with creative writing. It is important for researchers to remember that creative writing is not for all, when reflecting on the difficulty they may experience when recruiting participants, and to consider the questions of who is *not* present in a project; who has *not* been attracted.
- Creativity, as we explained in Chapter 1, is not intrinsically good, enjoyable, inclusive or productive (Hawkins 2015:249; Mould 2018). Some researchers have reported that participants can struggle with creative activities such as writing and drawing, finding them difficult and unpleasant (for example, Richardson 2015; Mannay 2016). For example, Kerri Kearney and Adrienne Hyle (2004:377) found that drawing 'could not be described as a positive factor in getting respondents to participate in the research; if anything the knowledge that they would be asked to draw may have deterred them from participation'. Those who have taught creative methods to students, or set assignments that involve creative work, will have noticed a range of reactions: some students welcome the chance to be creative, whereas others panic at the thought. Learning from this, we need to be careful not to pressure people to be creative, allowing them to opt in and out of creative activities, and we need to think about how we label these activities; whether as creative, or in some other way: perhaps just as writing.

Ethics

The attractions and risks associated with participatory creative writing revolve around ethical issues, relating to how researchers may observe workshops, what commitments they make to participants, and how confidentiality and anonymity are preserved. These issues in turn raise others, about who the writing belongs to and what is done with the material.

Many researchers are drawn to participatory research for ethical reasons, since this approach often comes with commitment to the wellbeing and interests of participants and their communities (Manzo and Brightbill 2007). This 'ethics of engagement' (Pickering and Kara 2017:299) is amplified when participants are offered a range of means and media – going beyond conventional social scientific methods to include creative practices and forms – to explore and represent their own experiences (Mattingly 2001). Still, no method is intrinsically ethical, nor can it 'guarantee liberatory or ethical research' (DeLyser and Sui 2014:300). This means that participatory creative writing requires as much ethical reflexivity and vigilance as any other method.

Research ethics begin with doing no harm or, more realistically, with understanding what harm could potentially be done and then seeking to minimise the risk that it will be. (This is a minimal ethical ambition. Many social researchers are more proactively ethical, both in relation to participants, and more widely.) These ethical considerations involve trying to ensure that research takes place within as safe a space as possible. We have to assess risks on a case-by-case basis, always considering: whether participants may be exposed in some way that puts them in danger; whether the research might raise matters with which participants are not equipped to cope; whether any of the participants have support needs; whether their privacy and confidentiality might be compromised through the research (Kara 2018).

A common way of minimising risk is to anonymise data – including diaries of writing workshops, interviews with participants, and published outputs – and to ensure that no recognisable visual or voice recordings are shared or published. This conforms to the default social science approach to the attribution of findings: anonymise unless there is a good reason and clear agreement not to (Ní Laoire 2007). In practice, anonymity 'cannot be considered completely protective of the participant' (Richardson 2015:619); and it is not possible to ensure that the research takes place within an absolutely safe and confidential space (Hunter 2008). Still, anonymity provides a degree of protection and, so long as the limits of this are explained and understood, it may give some participants the confidence to explore issues that they might have otherwise avoided.

We should acknowledge, though, that the paternalistic imposition of anonymity by researchers on participants who want to be named can also cause harm. This is particularly relevant when creative writing is being used in research, as it is common for authors to have their names associated with their written work. Indeed, this is regarded as the author's right in the laws of many countries. There is a wide range of reasons why research participants may want their names to be used. The best approach here is to offer participants the options of anonymity or of being named, and let them decide (Kara 2018:99–100). Participants are often better equipped to make their own decisions than researchers or research ethics committees (Gerver 2013:135).

While some risks of participatory creative writing are obvious – the danger that one participant will gossip about another, for example – others are more subtle. Writing is not for everyone, and this is not just a matter of personality; it may also stray into class, gender and other forms of difference. Creative writing may benefit from forms of literacy – and cultural capital – that some people have more of than others. Divya Tolia-Kelly (2007:132) has observed that researchers 'wanting to engage with the experiences of those marginalised within society' have sometimes turned to non-verbal research methods, such as drawing and autophotography. Rather than asking street children in Kampala to write or speak about their experiences, Lorraine Young and Hazel Barrett (2001) gave them disposable cameras and asked them to take pictures of places reflecting their daily lives. The ethical risk of imposing creative *writing* where it is not appropriate is that potential participants will feel uncomfortable, exposed, even stupid; the practical risk is simply that they will not participate, and that there will be no findings. Indeed some people cannot participate, for example if they have dyslexia or a brain injury that adversely affects their ability to write. But, as we go on to show, there are ways around this which include devising projects with a variety of roles such that, for example, some participants may do the writing while others contribute in other ways.

Some researchers try to do more than simply avoid harm and discomfort in the course of their research. Action researchers, whom we have introduced briefly and return to later, are particularly proactive in this respect. They typically seek to ensure that their work benefits participants and their communities, and they seek to share rather than own the research process. Action researchers tend to work with individuals and communities who are 'excluded' and 'oppressed' in some way (Kindon et al 2007:9) such as people with disabilities (McFarlane and Hansen 2007), migrants (Pratt 2012) and ethnic and racial minorities (Hume-Cook et al 2007). Conceived as 'research "with" rather than "on" people' (Heron and Reason 2005:144), participatory action research is designed to 'challenge hierarchies between researcher and researched' (DeLyser and Sui 2014:299), involving participants and their communities when deciding what to research, how, where, when and why.

That said, action researchers are not alone in their pursuit of proactive ethics that seek to go beyond the avoidance of harm and try to benefit participants. Nina Woodrow combined this ethos with creative methods in her collaborative research with refugees in Australia, which involved the co-creation of stories. Woodrow described her ethical project as 'a form of socially engaged activism' (Woodrow 2016:2). Indigenous researchers worldwide regard mutual benefit as a prerequisite for research (Kara 2018:26–7).

To develop these claims about the ethics of creative writing in participatory social research, we end this section with a more sustained illustration of ethically driven research: a project called 'Graphic Lives'. Sarah McNicol worked with a group of British-Bangladeshi women to research their life stories and the histories of their communities. They began with a variety of preparatory activities including museum visits, reading graphic novels, and learning some computer skills. McNicol (2019:242) says: '… the aim was not to make them expert comics creators, but to give the women sufficient skills and understanding of comics to enable them to tell their stories'. Then the women used the 'Book Creator' app to tell their stories in their own ways through digital comics, using their own and others' photographs, drawings they made, and text in any language (see Figure 3.1) (McNicol 2019:241). The Graphic Lives project began with a series of ethical principles: in addition to the skills training and creative outlets already mentioned, the researchers decided to accept and respect participants' stories as they chose to tell them, and to apportion authorship to participants who wished to be named (Harley and Langdon 2018:195–6). As McNicol (2019:244) explained, Graphic Lives did 'not seek or attempt to represent a verifiable truth' and it 'acknowledged and accepted the presence of fictional elements of autobiography', embracing the blurred 'boundaries between fiction and non-fiction … as a strength'.

Figure 3.1: Panel from 'Graphic Lives' project by Saddika.

I have been through many struggles, but I don't complain because the things I have been through make me stronger.

Source: McNicol 2019:243

Getting started: participatory creative writing for social research

Participatory creative writing as a research method brings a number of challenges:

- Who is a participant?
- How to invite or recruit participants?
- How to get started? How to warm up? How to build confidence?
- What role(s) to play? Is anyone in charge?
- When should people work as individuals and when as a group? How can people work effectively together?
- What is the best way to review and revise drafts? How can people give and receive feedback constructively?

- What 'data' can the researcher collect?
- What are the roles of process and product?

Manuals and handbooks on creative writing, which we draw upon, answer some of these questions more exhaustively and authoritatively than we can do here (for example, Anderson 2006; Neale 2009; Beck 2012). Those books include suggestions for how to facilitate creative writing, usually through workshops, and how to get these groups started and keep them going. Here we will focus on the applications of each of these methods to social research, and address the challenges that researchers are likely to face when working with creative writing. These challenges – like the field of creative writing itself – are largely practical. Contrasting creative writing with reading and literary criticism, Graeme Harper reminds us that 'creative writing cannot exist without actually doing something' (Harper 2013:133).

Doing something, in the context of creative writing pedagogy and practice, often involves workshops. We tend to imagine creative writers as individuals, working in glorious isolation, occasionally appearing to sign books and conduct readings, but otherwise remaining aloof, alone with their pens, typewriters and laptops. And yet, for better or worse, many people who teach, learn and practise creative writing today do so in workshops (or other group settings). Working in groups, participants typically write, read and comment on each other's work, usually in the presence of a facilitator, who will set tasks and explain ground rules including mutual respect and constructive criticism. Workshop techniques – involving reading to the group and commenting on each other's work – work best with the number of people who can fit around a table and get to know each other. The participatory workshop method raises two preliminary questions: what is a participant, and how can participants be recruited?

What is a participant?

Participants are individuals and groups who get involved in participatory projects, in this case participatory creative writing. Involvement in participatory creative writing for social research does not necessarily mean everybody writing. Some participants write; others may provide writers with content, contribute to conversations around the writing, get involved in editing and revisions, bring the participants together, and so on. In this chapter, we are particularly interested in participatory creative writing that involves everyone in the writing itself, but we also want to acknowledge some other ways of doing this research. One example of the latter comes from Vancouver, where Geraldine Pratt conducted interviews with women who had left their homes and families in the Philippines in search of employment as domestic workers (Pratt 2012; Pratt and Johnston 2017). A professional writer used the interviews as the basis for a script which the women read and co-edited. In this way, they contributed to the writing process without actually writing. Doreen Mattingly (2001) worked in much the same way in the making of a play about residents of City Heights, an impoverished, diverse neighbourhood in San Diego. Local teenagers gave interviews, providing content and ideas, which the researchers handed over to a professional writer and director. This was a participatory creative writing project, but not everyone put pen to paper, or hand to keyboard. Some ceded 'narrative authority' to the researchers and writers (Mattingly 2001:451). Much the same could be said of subsequent work in a similar vein, including Michael Richardson's (2015) participatory theatre project in which participants provided content and were invited to correct and comment on drafts, but were not involved in actual drafting (see also Denzin 2003).

But, while participants in creative writing workshops need not necessarily write, many do. For them, and arguably for participatory creative writing as a research method, hands–on writing is where a project comes alive. So we shall have a lot to say about actual writing by participants in the following pages.

How to invite or recruit participants

There are advantages in conducting research with individuals and communities in which the researcher has already established relationships. Heather Castleden, Vanessa Sloan Morgan and Christopher Lamb (2012:160), framing their participatory creative research with Indigenous peoples in Canada, put it this way: 'I spent the first year drinking tea.' Similarly, Ruth Raynor (2017) joined a women's group and attended for over two years before initiating a drama workshop with them. Too much familiarity can be counterproductive. There are also disadvantages of knowing a group well; it can be easier for participants to open up to a stranger; an outsider can retain a professional mystique, which inspires trust in some people. Also the vast majority of potential participants are able to weigh up the likely risks and benefits of taking part in research, whether or not the researcher is known to them (Dresser 2015:312; Pickering 2018:423). Still, when it comes to setting up and running a participatory creative writing workshop-based project, the advantages of knowing and being known tend to outweigh those of anonymity. Consequently, many of the following tips for researchers seeking to do this are effectively shortcuts for those who do not have the time to spend the 'first year drinking tea' and for those who are struggling to connect with potential participants.

Tip 1: Setting up

Impersonal approaches – appealing to potential participants through traditional and contemporary channels such as leaflets and social media posts – sometimes work, but the odds are stacked against them. People find it hard to walk through the doors of creative writing workshops, tending to need reassurance and confidence.

In some of our own research, we have learned the hard way not to trust shortcuts to setting up participatory research; and to take the time needed to build trust and relationships before getting started, particularly when participants will be invited to take risks in their writing. Working with Richard, Afshan (introduced earlier) wanted to recruit non-heterosexual Muslims to creative writing workshops she would lead on sexuality and faith. Afshan posted invites online. Her social media appeal was well received, with many likes and shares, so Afshan had cause to be confident that at least 15 participants would be there. In the event, only two people came. One was a personal friend who had been directly invited. The other, neither LGBT nor Muslim, was a filmmaker, wanting to observe gay Muslims for a script he was working on. The workshop was cancelled. Afshan later reflected that, when she was younger, she would have been equally reluctant to walk into a room of LGBT Muslims whom she didn't know, but who might know her, or know people who knew her. A more direct and personal approach was needed. And we would have to be more patient.

Tip 2: Offer, don't ask

However you approach participants, it is a good idea to offer them something they want, rather than asking a favour. To do this, you will have to understand something about the people you are hoping to attract: what they might be looking for or open to, and what they might like to get out of creative writing. It is important to use the right words. To think of just one example, some young men may be resistant to poetry but drawn to (writing for) spoken word, even if the content is much the same. And some people may be keen to learn certain technical and creative skills: how to make films, for example, or to write for stage or screen (Parr 2007), or simply how to write (Guidi 2003). For some, skills are transferable and open-ended, but for others they are part of a bigger plan. Farah Ali, who worked in creative partnership with Richa Nagar (Nagar and Ali 2003:361), explained her interest in collaborating: 'Do you know what my fight is about, Richa? I'm fighting to speak my way so that no family member, no community, no organisation, no researcher, no media person gets to distort my story to sensationalize my life!' Of course, not all potential participants are as articulate or as strategic as Farah Ali, though most have some idea of what they are looking for and open to.

Tip 3: Be upfront

Before the first workshop has begun, explain the ground rules and outline what will happen if people attend. You can do this through a variety of ways and settings: in a taster session, in leaflets, participant information sheets, preliminary emails, a phone conversation, or in several of these ways. Be clear about the ground rules, including arrangements for confidentiality and anonymity. Explain to potential participants how their privacy will be respected, and how they will be asked to respect the privacy of others. If the creative writing activities will explore a particular theme, explain this at the outset. This way, there will be no surprises on the day, and there will be fewer no–shows, since attendance will be less daunting. Those who attend will do so knowingly.

Tip 4: Work with trusted individuals

If you don't have contacts within the community you are researching, try to work with someone who does. Making a similar point, social scientists often speak of 'gatekeepers'. We are not keen on this terminology. The gatekeeper is defined from the perspective of the instrumental and unilateral social scientist, who wants something this figure can provide: access. And the gatekeeper's position revolves around his or her control over access to a community or group; there can be something self-serving about this. Rather than gatekeepers, we prefer to speak of pivotal figures, whose authority is more organic than instrumental. This point came home to Richard and Nafhesa when they were trying to start some creative writing workshops at a school in Yorkshire. They needed the support of a senior member of staff and so had to convince him that the workshops would be a good idea. The administrator agreed, explaining that he was keen to support 'anything that would get the students reading and writing more'. He suggested suitable times for these activities to take place, provided a room, and helped with the design and distribution of leaflets and posters. However, when the workshops began, very few young people showed up, and almost none returned. Richard and Nafhesa began to suspect why this was happening: the teenagers may have been ambivalent towards creative writing, but something else was putting them off. Was it that the administrator kept popping into the workshops and looking through the glass wall? Was it that he could be heard commenting on the participants, including a female student he said he was surprised to see? Was it that he was an authority figure, whose role as a gatekeeper was determined by the school rather than the young people? Was it that the set–up felt too much like another lesson? In any event, we eventually gave up. This wasn't working. Contrast this with Nafhesa Ali's collaboration with a community leader in Rochdale. Nafhesa was trying to recruit young Muslim men to join a creative writing workshop. She worked with Asaf (not his real name), who is well known and liked in the community there. A number of men came forward. They wanted to help Asaf and trusted his judgement. They had come to the group 'for him' as much as for themselves.

Tip 5: Work with existing groups where possible

It can be hard to get people through the doors of creative writing groups, even when they are free and welcoming. This is particularly the case when research projects are targeting particular groups of people, as they typically do, such as members of a given age group or social class. Many people find it hard to walk through the door of a workshop to join a group they do not already know, particularly when the workshop brings challenges and risks of its own: though appealing to some, words like creative and writing are intimidating to others.

Another approach, which is less scary to some participants, is for the researcher to seek to work with groups that already exist. This means supporting and engaging with such groups, in keeping with their interests and priorities, which may be as loose as spending time together or as firm as learning together and perhaps even reflecting on specific issues.

In her piece later in this chapter on running and documenting creative writing workshops, Nafhesa refers to groups and sessions she convened in Glasgow. Rather than recruiting participants directly, she sought out groups that already existed but lacked resources and leadership. Nafhesa approached the Glasgow Women's Library, which put her in touch with women's reading and writing groups. With some research funding to hand, Nafhesa was able to provide books for the reading group and facilitators for some writing – fiction, blogging and playwriting – sessions. She was able to tilt those sessions towards the themes of the research project, which Nafhesa was conducting with Richard and Claire. But, as the project developed, nobody could remember who had recruited whom. The researchers started out thinking they were in charge, but learned that they were not, and that it was good not to be (on another workshop, within this project, see: Phillips et al 2020).

There are practical reasons for working with groups that have formed: since the trusting and meaningful relationships which underpin successful workshops already exist, much of the difficult work is already done. There are also ethical reasons for seeking out and working with pre-existing groups; doing so is consistent with the spirit of participatory action research. In its purest form, action research is responsive, existing to support groups which have preformed and taken the initiative to make contact with the researcher. This is why Richa Nagar has:

> actively identified specific groups and individuals who are interested in building collaborative relationships with me, and reflected with them on the conditions, goals and processes that could give a concrete form and language to our evolving dialogues and collaborative agendas. My efforts have emanated from the belief that discussions surrounding the politics of representation – and of reflexivity, positionality and identity – have reached an impasse. (Nagar and Ali 2003:358)

Of course, not everyone is sufficiently well connected or organised to know they can reach out to a professor, not least one with Nagar's standing, so the purely responsive mode is not as inclusive as it might first appear; and some researchers may find themselves waiting a long time before anyone approaches them. It can therefore be more practical to look for existing groups and try to work with them, or perhaps seek to join their group as a participant observer before proposing any collaborative research.

CREATIVE WRITING IN PRACTICE

Working with what's there *by Andrew McMillan and Sarah McNicol*[1]

Andrew McMillan is a multi-award-winning poet and Senior Lecturer in Creative Writing in the Manchester Writing School at Manchester Metropolitan University. **Sarah McNicol** is a Research Associate in the Faculty of Education at Manchester Metropolitan University. Having convened some workshops, Andrew and Sarah found that facilitators need to adapt to the group they are working with rather than expecting the group to adapt to their plans.

Running community creative writing workshops, we have learned to identify and work with existing ways of writing and knowing, rather than imposing preconceived ways of doing things. Facilitators need to be adaptable to the group they are working with, not the other way around.

Here, we take a broader-than-usual notion of creative writing, starting with the dictionary definition of 'making marks, letters, words or other symbols on a surface'. This broad understanding of writing – involving more than words on the page – stands to make processes and workshops more open and democratic. Even so, in the literature we read to inform our work, we are used to seeing frequent reports of a 'skills gap' and lack of confidence reportedly acting as a deterrent to participation. We feel this concern is overreported. We approach this problem from another angle: allowing a community's existing ways of writing and knowing to come through.

Figure 3.2: Inspiration doll by Alke Gröppel-Wegener, created in response to this piece by Andrew McMillan and Sarah McNicol. Inspiration dolls comment on and play with genres of creative writing.

Researchers who speak of a skills gap tend to approach participatory creative writing as a means of building skills and confidence where these are lacking. They begin with

[1] This contribution should be cited as follows: McMillan, A. and McNicol, S. (2021) 'Working with what's there'. In Phillips, R. and Kara, H. *Creative Writing for Social Research*. Bristol: Policy Press.

the assumption that participants do not write, or are scared of it: a deficit model (for example, Mannay 2016; Kearney and Hyle 2004).

While it is true that most people in the less-privileged communities we often work with do not see themselves as 'writers' or 'artists' and frequently have little or no formal experience of 'creative writing', we have found that many are open to writing (and drawing), when these terms are defined broadly.

During a project looking at the legacies and 'hauntings' of social traumas in post-industrial areas, members of the project team visited a community centre in Sunderland which sat in the middle of a social housing estate, very close to the site of the Nissan car factory. When we arrived, we found only two 'participants' – local women – had answered the advertisement, alongside a local community organiser. People had been asked to bring along an artefact or photograph that sparked an important memory for them.

The initial plan had been to do some writing based around this. However, it soon became clear that the participants were more comfortable talking than putting their words onto paper, and so the session evolved into one where the 'writing' the participants were doing would be oral rather than written. We decided to try and physically map the history that the women were discussing. Rather than asking them to write a poem, or sketch out their memory, we simply laid out lots of blank pieces of card on a table. The card in the middle would be where we were now, the community hall. We then asked the women to map out the rest of the area as it had been when they grew up – writing on each card the name (as they had known it, the dialect or slang name perhaps) of each landmark, pub or street, and we arranged them on the table to create a map of memory. With new cards we then overlaid what the area was like now, and then overlaid again with hopes for what it might be in the future. We were using writing and drawing to explore urban futures, come up with dreams and plans for the local area. All this came about because of a willingness to abandon our ideas of what 'writing' or 'drawing' might mean for participants, and because of a willingness to mould the session around the interests and needs of those taking part, rather than the strict requirements of the researchers.

On other occasions, we have worked with groups with health-related conditions that might initially appear a barrier to using creative writing as a method. Working with people living with dementia, a condition which can affect both language and motor skills, we collaborated with a cartoonist. The group were initially resistant to the idea of working with comics, but they overcame their reservations, using this medium to explore experiences of dementia. We encouraged them to work in pairs and small groups, as a way of removing pressure on individuals. We also provided structure to make the task manageable, using pre-drawn characters with speech bubbles for participants to complete. Their ideas, which fed into a final comic, include a 'dementia journey', which contrasts with a bus map that always displays the same routes.

In another residency, poetry was written by people with severe cognitive and physical disabilities, some of whom could only communicate with their eyes, in movements which only their specific carer was able to decode. Again, this did not preclude writing taking place; it just meant opening up and democratising the idea of what writing could be. Almost complete lines of poetry were written up, with the ends of lines being left for participants to make their own choices. Sensory items such as different textiles and textures, or shower gels with different smells were then shared with the group so that they could make their own decisions about how each line should end and about the direction the poem should take, with each new line begun in response to the choice which participants had made for the previous line. In this way, a group poem was written and the participants had a real sense of ownership over what was created.

Another widely reported barrier to the use of creative writing as a method with some groups is a lack of literacy skills, in English or more generally. We worked with a group of women who migrated to the UK from Bangladesh as adults and therefore have fairly limited English skills, especially in written language. Through the project, they produced individual comic books about their life stories using images and text in English, and in some cases in Bangla too. Whilst some of the women typed their comics themselves, others preferred to have help typing in English from one of the facilitators or another participant. Women who had very limited knowledge of English wrote their stories in Bangla, then the group helped to translate them together. Perhaps the greatest success of this project was in stimulating a change in the way some of the women thought about themselves: as one commented, 'I feel like I'm a writer now!'.

Our experiences with a number of diverse groups suggest that it is likely that the circumstances under which participants are asked to write or draw can affect their willingness to do so. For example, in their research with training school staff, Kearney and Hyle (2004) asked individual participants to draw whilst the researcher moved away, but remained in the interview room. It is perhaps not surprising that this may have been a deterrent for participants as they suggest; in that situation, most of us would surely feel the same. Perhaps unsurprisingly, if the atmosphere is more relaxed, requests to write or draw may find a much more willing response.

Tips for workshop facilitators: adapting to groups

1. To help create trust, facilitators may make themselves vulnerable in some way: by demonstrating their own naive drawing skills; drawing with their non-dominant hand; or speaking about their own personal connection to the issue at stake. Similarly, it can be valuable to demonstrate where participants have considerably greater skills than the facilitator, for example reading or writing in a different language.

2. Get a sense of what the group are interested in, and equally anything they are likely to find difficult or off-putting, before starting work with them. Alter

prompts and resources to ensure they are a) appropriate for participants' level of English, and b) culturally relevant – or open to interpretation across multiple cultural backgrounds.

3. Giving participants a range of options is another way to ensure that an activity is accessible for all, especially when working with a group you are less familiar with. Having the option to use multiple languages or senses, appointing someone as a scribe, or working as a group can make creative writing activities more accessible.

4. Be prepared to step outside your own comfort zone. Be open to new research skills and methods, and to the sometimes unexpected needs of participant groups. Allow participants – their expertise and their notions of what 'writing' might involve – to lead. Skills are not something to be 'given' from experts to participants, but something to be negotiated and jointly explored with, and indeed learned from, participant groups.

Workshops and groups

How to draw participants together into a cohesive group

Where workshops begin organically, with groups that have formed themselves, participants may be ready to start creative writing. Where individuals are relatively new to each other, though, it can be helpful to spend some time loosening up and warming up. Cohesive groups are happier, more productive and more sustainable. When people feel part of something, they are more likely to attend subsequent sessions, and tend to be more freely creative and engaged.

It can help to start with some icebreaker games, which serve a number of purposes:

- establishing a relaxed atmosphere
- helping people to learn each other's names
- building trust
- building concentration
- energising the group

Examples of icebreakers, appropriate to creative writing workshops because they get people talking to each other and thinking about creativity and writing, include asking each person to:

- Think of something they have done for the first time this year and something else they would like to do. Tell others.
- Say three things about themselves, all of which are strangely plausible, but only one of which is true. The group will try to guess which is which: the bluff and the truth.
- Tell others about their favourite book or film: what and why?

One way of helping groups to gel is to put individuals in touch with each other, to the extent that they are comfortable to share their details, and without infringing anyone's privacy. Forming a social media group, for example, can be helpful in bringing individuals together and providing them with space to encourage each other, and to feel part of a group. The anonymised WhatsApp exchange in Figure 3.3 illustrates how a group cohered through social media. Through these exchanges, individuals learned names, reminded and encouraged each other to attend future meetings, found space in which to arrange meetings outside the main workshops, shared ideas and work, and ultimately formed friendships.

Though workshop participants can and do make friends and form cohesive groups – as Nafhesa goes on to illustrate in her piece on 'Muslim women laughing in the library' – it is important to remember that group members do not play equal or identical parts. Those who use and advocate participatory research methods stress the importance of attending to the power relations and what Richa Nagar

Figure 3.3: Connecting through WhatsApp. Nafhesa Ali used social media platform WhatsApp to draw together a group of young Muslim women who had joined a workshop at the Glasgow Women's Library.

[11/03/2018, 12:15:55] Marwa GWL: 🐚🐚
[11/03/2018, 12:16:04] 🌀🌀🌀: Assalamu alaikum beautiful ladies!

Hope you're all well and spoiling your Mums (or being spoilt if you're a Mum 😊)!!!

Just wanted to say thank you for coming yesterday and welcome to the GWL creative writing whatsapp group 😊🎞️
[11/03/2018, 12:17:02] Noura GWL: 👐💗 hello lovely ladies!!!
[11/03/2018, 12:19:14] 🌀🌀🌀: Hi Marwa and Noura 😀

Everyone: Please do join the Storying Relationships Facebook group and find me, Nafhesa Ali (researcher), Ruby (library facilitator) and Nina (Author) on FB! And let's get those creative juices flowing 😊
[11/03/2018, 12:19:51] Nina: Hello all!! It was lovely meeting you all yestetday. Hope you all enjoyed the workshop as much as i did
[11/03/2018, 12:20:21] Marwa GWL: Yeah I really enjoyed it!
[11/03/2018, 12:20:29] Nina: 👍
[11/03/2018, 12:22:55] Asma GWL: It was really nice meeting everyone. Excited to start writing and taking part in this project! :) ✒️ Asma
[11/03/2018, 12:23:21] 🌀🌀🌀: Hi Nina and Asma 😊

All: please do use this space for GWL writing stuff, speaking to each other about your writing, challenges, joys, tears 😢 etc. 😊 you can also use this space to support each other with relevant things, but please do not use it for random promotions.

Enjoy Xxx
[11/03/2018, 12:23:51] Fatima GWL: Hey everyone, it is Fatima
[11/03/2018, 12:24:24] Heena GWL: Hey! Im not on social media so won't be able to join groups. It was lovely meeting you all yesterday. Looking forward to the next few weeks. Heena xx
[11/03/2018, 12:24:46] Fatima GWL: I am off Facebook as well
[11/03/2018, 12:25:30] 🌀🌀🌀: Hi Fatima.
Hi Heena.
That's fine, this is our alternative, more personal space for contact 👍

has called the 'multiple and difficult borders' between themselves and participants (Nagar and Ali 2003:360; Pratt 2009:17; see also Parr and Stevenson 2013). The dynamics between participants matter too. These dynamics revolve around power and personality. There is no reason to assume that women will have as much agency as men within a mixed group, though sometimes they do. Nor should we assume that young people will be free to speak in the presence of elders. Meanwhile, inequalities exist within groups, which are never homogeneous, but are shaped by intersections of gender, race, class, sexuality and other forms of difference and power, as well as by personalities and personal relationships. For all these reasons, participants are unlikely to speak as one, on behalf of 'consensual' or 'harmonious' communities (Mohan 2001:160). One of the advantages of creative writing workshops, in which people typically work together but produce individual outputs, is that there is no expectation of consensus or of finding a single voice. That said, it is also important to remain alive to the dynamics, and sometimes the tensions, within the workshop process.

Playful workshops

Creative writing with participants can take various forms: from working through the conventional writing exercises and building skills in the manner recommended and taught in creative writing classes and manuals (for example, Anderson 2006), to other methods that involve writing, but take other approaches. These include working with comics, which involve both words and images. We've already seen examples of these other forms in Andrew McMillan and Sarah McNicol's piece, 'Working with what's there'. Kate Wall, a specialist in visual research methods, worked with colleagues to develop 'pupil view templates' for use in their educational research (Wall et al 2005). The researchers were investigating school pupils' views of interactive whiteboards. Their 'pupil view template' was a hand-drawn scene of a classroom, with a teacher at an interactive whiteboard, and three pupils of indeterminate gender, two of whom each had a speech bubble and a thought cloud (Figure 3.4). All the characters' faces were blank, as was the whiteboard. Pupil participants were encouraged to draw and write whatever they liked to represent their views of using an interactive whiteboard in the classroom. This method enabled the researchers to gather rich data about pupils' perceptions and feelings about interactive whiteboards, and to draw conclusions about the impact of interactive whiteboards on pupils' educational development.

Andrew McMillan and Sarah McNicol have found adopting a 'playful' approach to be one of the most effective ways of engaging with community groups. At first, this might sound a frivolous suggestion, but this is an important aspect of planning a workshop, especially one that may address difficult topics. Used appropriately, they argue, a playful approach allows challenging topics to be discussed in thought-provoking ways, while retaining an optimistic, relaxed and hopefully enjoyable atmosphere. This can take time. Quite reasonably, participants can be reluctant to accept the word of the facilitator that a workshop is in fact a 'safe space' and will need time to establish this for themselves (see 'Working with what's there'). Previous experiences of writing or drawing (and being judged on these) are also likely to impact on participants' attitudes. One problem may be the fact that many people associate activities such as these with being at school, so adults who have unpleasant memories of school may be reluctant to participate. Adopting a more playful attitude and avoiding types of activities people remember from school are likely to help here. It is also important to remember that a single approach will not work for all groups or individuals. Approaches need to be tailored and adapted to particular groups and group members.

Figure 3.4: Visual prompt, known as a 'pupil view template', used by Kate Wall and colleagues, who invited participants to write dialogue in speech bubbles and thought clouds.

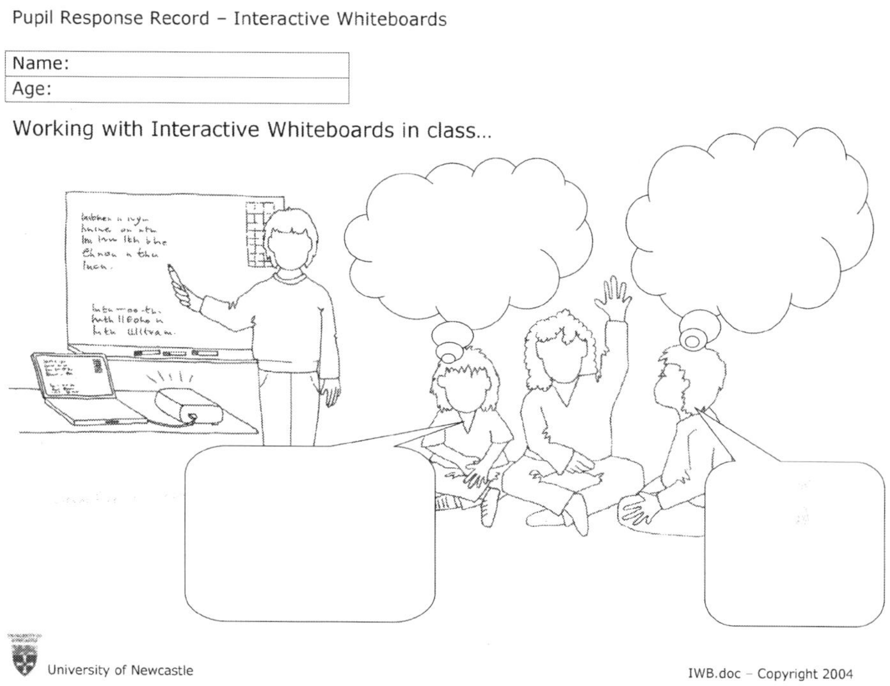

Pupil Response Record – Interactive Whiteboards

| Name: |
| Age: |

Working with Interactive Whiteboards in class...

University of Newcastle   IWB.doc – Copyright 2004

Getting started, warming up

Having found a group or brought one together, you might attempt to run the workshop yourself, or you might work with someone who is more experienced in doing and teaching creative writing. The facilitator is likely to begin with some tried-and-tested techniques which are fundamental to creative writing practice. These are explained in more detail in creative writing handbooks and manuals (of which there are many: see our recommendations in Chapter 1); however, an overview of some of these techniques is appropriate here, with suggestions for how these techniques apply to social research specifically. Three of the most important methods are clustering, freewriting and (what we shall call) character conversations.

Clustering typically begins with group discussion, followed by free association exercises, which group members attempt individually and then collectively, with the help of the facilitator. This practice, named and explained by Gabriele Lusser Rico in *Writing the Natural Way* (1983), generates a flow of connected images and ideas, bypassing the analytical brain functions that otherwise constrain and filter writing and thought (Anderson 2006:24). In a group setting, clustering may begin with a prompt – typically a word or image – that may spark free association and lead to conversation. In this way, individual participants may create lists or diagrams: webs of words, expressed visually through chains of connection. An example, in Figure 3.5, shows a cluster on the theme of 'green', generated by a participant in the first of a series of creative writing workshops. Participants can also do this exercise together, speaking the words that come to them, while the facilitator writes these on a board, forming a collective list or cluster. In this way, free association and clustering may unblock the writer's mind – and writers' collective minds – getting their pens flowing, and generating points of departure for more sustained writing, in which the analytical mind may be more helpful.

Prompts for clustering may be words with multiple meanings like 'water' or 'green', or topical phenomena such as 'climate change' or 'neighbours'. Though it can be helpful to start with the former, which can help to warm up participants and get words flowing, researchers with specific ideas about what they want from this activity tend to move towards words or phrases that speak to their particular aims and interests. In some cases, it may be necessary to work a little harder to get the group going, perhaps by introducing a more pointed and sustained image or text. Thus, for example, rather than simply prompting a group of young Muslims with a word like love or dating, researcher Claire Chambers handed out copies of a short, engaging article: 'Islamic Tinder' by Triska Hamid (2017). She gave everyone a few minutes to read the piece, and then led a short discussion of the themes it raised. This sparked an open-ended conversation, which began with a form of free association, and led some of those present to tell stories about their

Figure 3.5: Word cluster on the theme of 'green', generated by an individual participant in a creative writing workshop (anonymised).

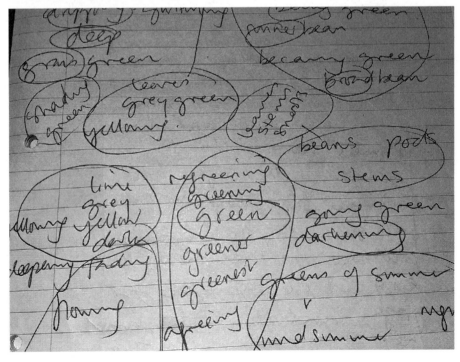

lives, their friends, and other real and fictional characters (Chambers et al 2019). This exercise ultimately led the participants to write their own story about what they called 'halal dating' (Phillips et al 2020).

A second exercise, which is commonly practised in creative writing workshops, is known as freewriting – a term coined by Peter Elbow (1998). This involves writing freely and quickly without censoring or editing, in response to some kind of prompt, with just a few minutes to write, and little or no time to think. The prompt may be entirely new or it may have been generated in a clustering exercise. When freewriting, 'we permit ourselves to associate freely, that is to write down the first words that occur to us, then whatever that makes us think of, following the train of thought wherever it goes' (Anderson 2006:23). For academic researchers, accustomed to analytical writing and slow, careful, precise expression, this can feel unnatural, even scary. For participants with less academic training, this can be a little easier. In any case, creative writing instructor Linda Anderson (2006) promises that freewriting can be rewarding and productive:

> It can feel uncomfortable, especially at first. You may feel that what you are writing is silly or unseemly or banal. You may feel a strong urge to stop or control it. But don't. You will often be surprised, even delighted, by the liveliness and power of the ideas and words that emerge. (Anderson 2006:23)

In freewriting, we can lose a little of the control we normally have over what we say and how we say it. This can be revealing and risky too, signalling possibilities and dangers, which researchers need to take into account when using this form of creative writing. If, as creative writing instructors claim, this 'fast, unpremeditated' writing accesses our 'deepest ideas, feelings and memories' (Anderson 2006:23), exploring themes we routinely censor because we see them as private and personal, and others we conceal even from ourselves, freewriting may be illuminating. It may access experiences that other research methods cannot. But there is a danger in revealing things that people normally keep hidden, and may even not be aware of themselves. This danger is doubled when it takes place in full view of a workshop, when an individual reads out their work, presenting an unedited version of him or herself for others to see. This raises ethical issues about whether and how to use freewriting in social research workshops. At the very least, it suggests, participants should not be forced to read what they have written out to the group; these and other traditions of the workshop should be reconsidered.

Another common creative writing workshop method – which we call the character conversation – involves inventing characters, giving them names, back stories, worries, jobs, relationships, physical characteristics, personal histories. These conversations may be kickstarted with a prompt of some kind. Participants may invent and exchange names upon which to build characters, or they may invent their own. They may start with an image, such as a photograph in a newspaper, or a portrait on a postcard, and work from that. Sometimes, members of a workshop are asked to do these things individually before discussing them with the group. Alternatively, a group may have a brainstorming session, developing characters collectively. In social research, these characters may be used to address specific issues. For example, in a project on relationships, the researcher may invite participants to invent a character's sexual history (or lack thereof) and describe someone he or she desires, sexually and romantically. In a project on migration, the researcher may invite participants to introduce and flesh out a fictional migrant. Through these characters and scenarios, it may be possible to broach subjects that would be more difficult to address directly and autobiographically by speaking personally. The space of the workshop or stage enhances this possibility, providing distance from everyday life and normal conversation, which can free up the imagination, once again loosening the tongue or the pen. As Ibrahim, a participant in a theatre project put it, 'it was easier to talk about certain things on stage than directly with our parents' (Gembus 2018:437). Once characters have been invented, whether individually or collectively, they may form prompts or building blocks from which workshop participants begin to tell stories or sketch scenarios.

For a more sustained example of collaborative, workshop-based creative writing, we now turn to some research led by Ruth Raynor, whose work is also featured elsewhere in this book. Ruth used drama workshops to explore women's experiences of government austerity in northern England. Her workshops were led by a facilitator, who began by asking small groups of participants to make an advertisement selling 'what is good about being a woman'. One group combined voice-over with mimed actions, and mentioned: 'having boobs', 'getting dinner bought for you by your boyfriend or husband', 'being daddies [sic] little girl' and 'having Ann Summers parties'. This exercise led the women to discuss the play they wanted to write: its theme, style and genre. 'Ideas became more and more extravagant. Plot lines including things like murder and incest were passed around and Gabbie and [Ruth] worked hard to keep things focused on the experiences that are most relevant to the lives of these women.' They steered the group to write a play in which women would recognise themselves, while maintaining some dramatic tension: 'we needed conflict in the script for it to work dramatically for an audience' (Raynor 2016:113; see also Raynor 2017).

Another medium, which has been found to help participants express themselves more freely than they tend to do through conventional research methods such as interviews or focus groups, is poetry. Poetry has been used both in the training of medical professionals (McCulliss 2013:99) and also to explore the experiences of trainees in this field. Student mental health nurses in the US were asked to write poems 'about their clinical experience or about the experience of mental illness from the client's perspective' (Kidd and Tusaie 2004:404). The researchers then analysed the poems to improve their understanding of the lived experiences of student mental health nurses. Similarly, in the UK, first-year nursing students were asked to write poems about compassion. These were analysed to learn 'how student nurses experience and understand compassion' (Jack and Tetley 2016:1).

How to write, review and revise together: workshopping

The writers' workshop – a method developed at the University of Iowa in the 1930s (Wandor 2012) – has become 'the world's most common venue for creative writing education' (Harper 2019:4). This method has filtered down from postgraduate writing programmes to undergraduate, amateur and therapy groups and, as we have seen, to social research. In addition to the methods which we have already introduced (and which include clustering, freewriting and character development), workshops are important settings for reading, revising and rewriting: taking work forward.

It is customary for participants to read their work to the group for discussion and comment, or to share their work in written form (Haslam 2006b:379). Feedback typically includes a mixture of encouragement and critique. Workshop convenors typically explain ground rules, explaining how participants should and should not comment on each other's work. Feedback involves a mixture of 'saying nice things first, pointing out what you "like", is "good"'before venturing some criticism, 'pointing out what is "wrong" or what does not "work"' (Wandor 2012:54). This format is adapted to different settings. Therapeutic and recreational workshops tend to be encouraging, whereas formal creative writing programmes are more challenging and rigorous, for obvious reasons (Morley and Worpole 1982; Wandor 2012).

Social researchers need to decide where to position themselves and their projects on this spectrum, and this may be something to negotiate with participants. Some may be content to enjoy writing in a social setting; they may want to pick up a few tips but not be challenged too directly. Others may be more ambitious, perhaps because they are serious about writing well or because they want to push their engagement with the substantive themes introduced through the writing workshops. And, while social researchers need to find a suitable balance between encouragement and criticism within the creative writing groups they convene, they also need to decide on some more fundamental questions. These include whether workshops are right for their research, and – if so – how these workshops should be convened. There are also questions about whether and how participants in creative writing projects should work together. Through these questions, social researchers may speak to some more generic problems, which creative writing experts have raised, in relation to the dominance of the workshop methodology. We return to this in the next section.

Scope

The workshop techniques introduced in this chapter – beginning with clustering and freewriting – are the building blocks for many different forms of creative writing. We have had to be selective, given the sheer number of different forms and genres in which creative writers work. Some of these different forms, each with their own conventions and techniques, were introduced in Chapter 2, though again we were selective, given the many different ways in which it is possible to write creatively and the impossibility of doing justice to all. Practical introductions to specific forms of creative writing are provided in handbooks and manuals of creative writing, written by specialists in their respective fields, which can be read and used alongside this book (we recommend some of these in Chapter 1). Therefore, we present this as an illustrative introduction to the ways in which creative writing pedagogy and practice may be applied to social research and adapted to social research projects.

CREATIVE WRITING IN PRACTICE

Reflexive storytelling: 'Muslim women laughing in the library' *by Nafhesa Ali*[2]

Nafhesa Ali is a sociologist based in the Department of Geography at the University of Sheffield. This piece is centred on extracts taken from Nafhesa's reflexive diary during a research project titled 'Storying sexual relationships', with young British Pakistani Muslims. Nafhesa draws upon her diary as a basis for exploring the (in)visibility of the researcher and their insider-outsiderness through the relationships between people and stories, highlighted in this tale of multiple identities.

The Setting: Positioning the 'I'

On a side street in East Glasgow stands a red brick library.[3] It contrasts with the mesh fence opposite, which is adorned with striking images and poetry about women and their life stories. As I walk across the street and under the red gothic arch of the library's entrance, my eyes adjust to the darkness. This is the Glasgow Women's Library – hidden away from the bustling city street – where the hum of the city is left behind. Blue and white mosaic tiles are bright against beautifully carved stone statues. Dark, heavy wooden doors lead me into a sanctuary created for women's literature and the celebration of women's writing.

Figure 3.6: Inspiration doll by Alke Gröppel-Wegener, created in response to this piece by Nafhesa Ali. Inspiration dolls comment on and play with genres of creative writing.

Inside, I see endless rows of shelves with books written by female authors. High-backed chairs covered with throws and cushions, inviting visitors to find a book,

[2] This contribution should be cited as follows: Ali, N. (2021) 'Reflexive storytelling: "Muslim women laughing in the library"'. In Phillips, R. and Kara, H. *Creative Writing for Social Research*. Bristol: Policy Press.

[3] This piece draws upon the research diary I kept when I was convening a series of creative writing workshops with Muslim women in Scotland. The project explored sexual relationship practices through fiction, non-fiction, blogging and playwriting.

sit and read. I hear muffled voices and the sound of the kettle, whistling in the kitchen. The building offers privacy, through veils created by the bookshelves. In the back corner, away from visitors, a long wooden table awaits. Twelve chairs neatly tucked under the table, each with a pre-loved cushion. This is an ideal place for creative writing, and it is where I shall host our writing workshops.

The Characters: Positioning the 'We'

We host a Welcome Event for Muslim women's writing in the main hall. It is a large public room with impressive Victorian glass windows that reluctantly allow light in through the thick lead-lined panes, which are set above mahogany panelled walls. Some of the women arrive in pairs; others alone. Some recognise each other; others wait nervously for the talks to begin.

The playwright and author share their experiences. They tell of their passion for writing as Muslim women. The group listen attentively. Words of writing, theatre and screenplay spill out onto the audience and stir interest through the room like confetti on a newly married couple.

The women ask questions: "Why did you start writing?", "How difficult was it to publish?", "How does it feel to be a Muslim woman playwright/author?" The hows and whys fill the room. A tangible atmosphere builds, emboldening the women to attend the creative writing workshops and revitalising their ambitions to write.

Next, we show *Halal Dating*, a short animated film, created by participants in a previous workshop in Yorkshire. An image pops up on screen with the word 'halal' being squeezed out from a towel. The voices in the short film share their thoughts of what is and is not acceptable in personal relationships. It is a new theme on dating for them. Something which challenges the understanding that dating is not allowed. The women listen intently. The film stops and they turn to face me. I hold my breath in anticipation, searching their faces, anxious about their reaction to the potentially controversial themes of relationships, intimacy and dating. A smile breaks out among the audience and the women begin to clap. They like it. We have made a connection. An English Pakistani Muslim researcher *doing* research in Scotland. Steaming hot chai, paper plates, pakoras and rocky road tiffin are served, and a calm fills the room.

Setting the Scene: Positioning 'Them'

During the writing workshops, it is clear the women enjoy each other's company. I see it in their faces, when they arrive. They are bonding as aspiring writers; amateur or expert. They come in smiling and eager to learn. It is wonderful to see friendships

Figure 3.7: Workshop welcome event, 2018. Photograph by and reproduced with permission of Nafhesa Ali.

extend. Comfortable in each other's company, the women challenge and support each other in equal measure.

As the workshop series proceeds, I take more of a back seat. I am visible at the table with the women, listening closely as they read out their stories. I follow the discussions and laugh at the plays being read in funny accents and voices, but mostly I am silent. They don't need me to facilitate or interact anymore, they have taken ownership of their group. I enjoy the safe space, which has been created for them. My pencil moves quietly, trying to capture as much as I can. I choose not to tap away on my laptop, which sits silently in my bag. Right now, I am the unobtrusive researcher.

Some women type on tablets or top-of-the-range laptops in Ted Baker cases. Others scribble with pens or pencils or in notebooks brought for the workshop. They write hard and fast, putting their multi-cultural world to rights. They are Scottish, Pakistani and Muslim. Their multi-dimensional words fill the pages. Joy, fear and sadness. Entwined

Figure 3.8: Muslim women's fiction writing workshop. Photograph by and reproduced with permission of Nafhesa Ali.

in relationships and expectations that are lived out across duplicate lives wrapped up in culture, religion and Scottishness – all striving for a single identity. The reverence that enfolds during the writing is beautiful to see. Heads bowed. Elbows on tables. A silent fervour that realises the need to carve out their own stories. The writing ends and heads come up, sighing aloud, released through their writing and creativity.

During one session a woman, wearing a hijab and full abaya, reads a text out loud, her Scottish accent imitating a Yorkshire lad, swearing and asking a girl on a date to Nando's. Laughter echoes around the library, between the bookshelves and carpeted floor. Sitting together around the table, the women are laughing and talking about sex and relationships. Everything is open for discussion: from virginity and the first bleed, to anal sex. The women speak of their fears: about introductions, loveless marriages and women's rights. They explore these themes through the medium of creative writing and the safe space of our writing workshops.

"It's so lovely to see a group of Muslim women laughing in the library", the non-Muslim library assistant says to me as I walk back to the table with pots of tea. The image of the passive, oppressed Muslim woman has been unsettled, here within the library. I nod and smile in agreement.

Working with individuals

The creative writing workshop is paradoxical in the sense that it invites individuals – however private or introverted they may be – to practise their solitary craft not only in the company of others, but also in socially challenging settings that favour extroverted and gregarious individuals. For some people, reading out is hard, and reading out and otherwise sharing potentially revealing preliminary work for the scrutiny and criticism of others is terrifying; for others, it is great fun and welcome attention (Holland et al 2003; Haslam 2006b).

Thinking primarily of the workshops that take place in formal creative writing programmes, Michelene Wandor (2012:57) argues that creative writing pedagogy 'needs to be reconceived, freed from the straight-jacket of the workshop, which involves teachers abandoning the hard-cop, soft-cop routine, and developing other approaches'. She argues for a rethink, moving towards whatever form of creative writing teaching – or research – 'allows students to begin to see how they already use language, how they think and imagine, and see possibilities for ways in which they might use language imaginatively in the future' (Wandor 2012:58). In other settings – where creative writing is a means to other ends including pleasure, therapy and research – we may either rework or replace the workshop in other ways.

Where social researchers work with creative writing, there is sometimes a case for abandoning the group format, which works better for some people than others, and for abandoning the methods that put pressure on individuals to write and read aloud, which they may not want to do, or may not feel they are able to do. To this end, Rowan Jaines' contribution – 'Starting to write about the Fens' – shows how, in place of workshops, it may sometimes be better to work one-on-one, talking and writing with individual participants in order to draw out words, initially through speech, and later in written form. This may be particularly important where individuals have specific needs: for those who may not be natural, accomplished or experienced writers; and for those with dyslexia, literacy or language issues, or other reading and writing difficulties.

Another way to produce a piece of collaboratively written work for research is by rethinking the parts played by different group members, and not pressuring everyone to do the same things. This can help researchers to reshape the creative writing workshop approach by tailoring it to the needs and talents of its various members. In other words, this means recognising that it is possible for an individual to participate in a creative writing workshop without necessarily writing or doing other things like reading out and taking criticism.

Varying roles for participants and facilitators

Some participants may provide content, perhaps by giving interviews or telling their stories to researchers, while others may get involved in wider conversations around the writing project, or help with editing and revising drafts. For example, in

Michael Richardson's collaborative theatre project, which explored intersections of Irish heritage and masculinity in North East England, participants gave interviews, corrected transcripts, and commented on drafts of a play, which they had not directly written. Their involvement illustrates how, in participatory creative writing, there are different ways to participate. Researchers have come to this conclusion from a number of different angles: from collaborative film projects (Parr 2007) to participatory storytelling for urban planning (Cowie 2017) and management (Gabriel and Connell 2010). Yiannis Gabriel, who has advanced creative research methods in management studies, argues that researchers should help each participant to 'find his/her own voice' and feel that the outcome is 'jointly created and jointly owned'; this is more important than involving each person in every part of the process (Gabriel and Connell 2010:507).

Writing is not necessarily an individual act; groups may write. Participants in the Mustaqbal youth theatre project, which set out to explore the experiences of descendants of Arabic and Somali migrants in North West London, were involved in a rather different way. For them, collaborative writing meant developing a script, beginning with brief ideas of what each scene should involve, then improvising to develop scenes, which were transcribed by a member of the team (Gembus 2018:434). This is more deeply collaborative than the individual writing that takes place in conventional workshops, in which participants are alone-but-together, writing individually but relying on workshop facilitators, other workshop members and audiences for direction and encouragement, within creative work that 'is simultaneously individual *and social*' (Reuter 2015:vii, original emphasis). As Harper (2019:xvii) puts it: 'Creative writing is both an individual practice, based in the self (you, me, other creative writers), and a holistic one, reflective of cultural, societal and historical influences upon us and upon those around us.'

The shared – collective, relational – experience of creative writing is illustrated through research that involved telling, listening and writing. Researchers from the University of Northern British Columbia wanted to explore the potential for using spoken and written stories as a means of improving healthcare in rural communities. One activity, implemented at a workshop involving 25 Indigenous and non-Indigenous people, involved working in pairs. Sarah de Leeuw explains that:

> Each member of a pair was asked to tell the other a story about an important event or aspect of their life while the second person listened and recorded that story without interruptions. After each hearing a story, all participants were asked to write, in their own words, a retelling of the story they were just told by their partner and then to reflect on what it felt like to tell their story to another person and to have it transcribed. (de Leeuw et al 2017:160)

While different participants may play different parts, these parts may be fluid, changing over time as individuals explore possibilities, find talents they didn't know they had, get excited by some things and bored of others, and generally decide how and what they want to contribute. Convening a collaborative art project, Kye Askins and Rachel Pain watched how 'interaction among the young people increased *and changed*' over time (Askins and Pain 2011:814, original emphasis). They found that, in the course of working together, participants explored experiences and views they held in common, and others in which they differed. The project – bringing people together and introducing stimulating objects and materials to work with – provoked and embraced unplanned and unpredictable interactions and actions' (Askins and Pain 2011:815). Similarly with creative writing: we never know what will happen; this is the point, the reason for doing research; to find out something we didn't know before.

If the contributions and roles of participants are ideally worked out in the course of research, the same is true of researchers and facilitators. Ken Plummer (1995:21) disentangles the parts played by researchers: variously coaxing, coaching and coercing people to tell their stories. This observation raises questions about the parts played by convenors in shaping creative writing. Should it be self-effacing, simply helping participants to get their words out, in the most authentic way possible? Or is there more to finding a voice? Does this involve learning a craft, accepting input and direction from an editor, and seeking to write better rather than simply more authentically? Katherine Brickell and Bradley Garrett argue that it can sometimes be right for the researcher to 'handle, and potentially even intentionally shape, stories that matter' (Brickell and Garrett 2015:947). Annette Markham takes this further, arguing that 'the researcher must take seriously the role of cultural interpreter, and gain interpretive authority through rigorous and constant practice of their craft' (2012:347). We agree, and would ourselves argue that the 'craft' of research includes the craft of writing. Many of those who attend creative writing workshops, including workshops convened within the course of research projects, do so because they want to improve their writing, which means learning the craft and accepting editorial input. Others come to creative writing in the hope of finding a voice, which means accepting help from workshop facilitators.

Social researchers work with participants to explore their experiences and perspectives in their own words. This raises questions about whether researchers should help participants to edit and refine their writing. Social scientists would not reword interview transcripts, so should we treat creative writing scripts with equal respect? The answer is yes, and no. Yes: the process of finding words – and sometimes struggling to do so – is illuminating, and social researchers would do well to pay attention to scribbles and drafts in their original form. But no: first drafts are not sacred. Creative writing is largely a matter of revising and rewriting, editing and polishing, and finished pieces also matter. It would be naive to imagine that people write most authentically when they do so without any understanding of the craft of writing. More likely, when we do this, we unwittingly work within genres and conventions we have internalised but not examined. Better, then, to respect the wishes of participants who are seeking a greater command of the writing process: by providing feedback and editorial input, to help them to find their voices as writers, thus to 'write better'.

Getting involved in editing and polishing other people's work can feel strange to social scientists trained in listening to participants rather than talking over them. But, as we point out repeatedly in this book, many people are involved in creative writing, even where only one is named as the author. Typically, editors suggest ways of improving pieces of work, and facilitators and instructors suggest ways of improving and developing writing skills. In social research, this can feel uneasy (Josselson 2011). Shouldn't participants be left to speak for themselves? Whose text is it? Whose voice?

Editing an anthology of writing by emerging young Muslim women writers, some of whom had participated in workshops convened as part of a research project investigating sexual relationships, Claire Chambers suggested edits and worked with contributors to improve their writing. In this project, Claire was working with Nafhesa and Richard. This research departed from orthodox social research methods in which a speaker's words are elicited, but not edited, and are quoted unvarnished. Claire worked with the ongoing involvement of participants who sought her comments and suggestions. Feedback can be difficult both to give and to receive, and requires tact and trust. When we get it right, and avoid bruising or being bruised, feedback is crucial to creative writing, to finding a voice, to writing 'what we know' and 'what we come to know' (Anderson 2006). Showing the new writers how to reduce repetition, tighten their prose and choose more effective turns of phrase, Claire helped them improve their writing and get published – all of which they said they wanted, and welcomed. Doing so, she supported their attempts to find their voices as writers, to explore their experiences and desires through newly gained writing skills, and ultimately to appear in print alongside established writers (Figure 3.9).

Figure 3.9: Anthology of writing by British Muslim women. Around half of the stories in this book were written in creative writing workshops that formed part of a participatory research project led by the editors of this anthology, published by HopeRoad in 2020.

CREATIVE WRITING IN PRACTICE

Starting to write about the Fens *by Rowan Jaines*[4]

Rowan Jaines is a doctoral researcher in the Department of Geography at the University of Sheffield. Her PhD project focuses on rural landscape in the Fens of the East of England. Here, she explores the Fens with the people who live their everyday lives there. She explains how she helped people to start writing about that place.

Beginning is difficult. Seeing and telling equally so.

I work in Fenland, a district in the North of Cambridgeshire that makes up half of what was once the Isle of Ely. Fenland is a confusing place to study because often people use the term Fenland to describe the whole district of what was once (but is no longer) a fen, or rather a collection of fens. This area spreads across parts of Norfolk, Cambridgeshire and Lincolnshire. People don't often talk about the little area that houses Wisbech, Chatteris, March and Whittlesey. They talk about the area as a whole but more often than not they prefer to talk of Wicken Fen (the reconstructed Fenland to the south) or Cambridge city itself.

Figure 3.10: Inspiration doll by Alke Gröppel-Wegener, created in response to this piece by Rowan Jaines. Inspiration dolls comment on and play with genres of creative writing.

Perhaps the area makes it difficult to construct a sense of space. The huge drained flatness lacks the undulations, the sense of up and down and near and far that provides the eye with something to rest on.

Fenland District sits right at the centre of the drained fen and often feels liquid in its drained state: edgeless, seeping off in all directions and bleeding with the light into the overarching skies. People often talk of time rather than place if they do speak of

---

4   This contribution should be cited as follows: Jaines, R. (2021) 'Starting to write about the Fens'. In Phillips, R. and Kara, H. *Creative Writing for Social Research*. Bristol: Policy Press.

the area. They imagine their gaze travelling back to the swampy morass the region once was. Writers talk of spectres in the wider fens, time looping in this landscape.

The place has neither hills nor mountains to climb and so there is no vista from which to look over the area. The economy is based on food production rather than desk based services. Indeed the fertile underlying land in myriad ways prevents the presence of tower blocks. No manmade hills, no corporate cliffs. Without the possibility to look from atop, a perspective is hard to gain and the everyday rises up to eye level.

As part of my research I came to sit, one by one, with ten local people. Together, we tried to find a way to talk about the everyday in Fenland and attempted to put something of the place into words. I met the contributors through my daily meanderings around the area – walking with the dog, conversations in shops, pubs and museums, asking people I already knew in the area, through making phone calls to ask if I may visit. We met in pubs, in people's homes, work offices, in libraries and at the little cottage where I stayed. A method emerged through the relationships. We fashioned it together through noticing the most ordinary aspects of day-to-day encounters – through meeting and talking and figuring our way together. This piece is about that method, which shifted with the relational dynamics but held fast in its aim. It is also about noticing and about the surprise of noticing oneself noticing.

Figure 3.11: Fen field at dusk, November 2016. Photograph by and reproduced with permission of Rowan Jaines.

Writing Together

We sit together and we begin. Really we begin before we begin, noticing the repetition of certain words – the music of our voices, cadences, rhythms, sighs and what is not said. We do not discuss any of this. But it happens nevertheless. Next time you meet a new person, take a second and listen as the song of your speech strains to harmonise. Sometimes it doesn't happen and no music gets made. This is fine. Indeed it makes room for something other than music.

We start to talk places. Stories of journeys to places, and the journeys of places away from what they were and into something new. I am told that a place – once played in – can run through the fingers like sand in an hourglass. As time moves on the memory erodes. Quietly, it is acknowledged that places are places in time. We talk about the weather and notice the quality of the day's light and the temperature on our skins. The weather takes us again to other times and places.

I ask that places and times are narrowed down. Or I might say "choose three", noticing a skewer of anxiety enter the room, a feeling of a school test. Replies come staccato: "my mind has gone blank" or "none of them are very interesting".

Crash, an interlude.

Figure 3.12: Not quite sunset in Fenland, Northern Cambridgeshire, October 2016. Photograph by and reproduced with permission of Rowan Jaines.

Disruption, rupture. A fear slips in and forms a crack. Perhaps a shaft of light so that we can see a little more clearly.

We move back, stepping much more slowly and the conversation slips around into the details previously thought too obvious to be of interest. Place begins to form in the mind's eye but we steer back around again to the beginning. We discuss the place on a specific day at a specific hour. A young woman describes:

> *Wearing lots of layers so it feels heavy but I'm still cold.*
> *Not quite sunset, beautiful orange hue across the sky.*

I scribble quickly, noting down the turns of phrase unless we decide a Dictaphone is more comfortable or practical. Either way my job is to listen, to transcribe and to ask questions so that across from me the mind's eye is forced – as the French experimental writer Georges Perec put it – "to see more flatly" (Perec 1997:51). Sometimes we do a better job together than other times. Sometimes the place keeps drifting out of focus and constellating as places do – with other places, times and ideas. At these points we keep going back. I ask questions like: "Tell me about the day? Is it morning or night? What is the light like? What can you smell? Hear? Tell me what you can see around you ..."

Sometimes I am very irritating. Seeing flatly does seem like a very interesting thing to do. I might be asked, "what is this project about again?"

Another rupture, another turn around and we find ourselves back at the start together.

But then suddenly we look up, time has jumped and we've been somewhere else. Perhaps we have carved out a slice of the place as an artefact, or rather they have. I passed the tools whilst they worked.

After

I transcribe the notes and pass them across to the speaker to edit. Sometimes time means I email it to them later, sometimes we sit together until the end. The speaker keeps the piece for a week before I file it, I email to say thank you and to check if they want to change anything else. The contributors move things around, check facts and names which maybe I've misheard, take out colloquialisms replacing them with standard English. They do this more at the start of the piece, perhaps enjoying the rhythm of their own phrasing as the piece goes on. Or indeed because perhaps seeing flatly remains quite dull.

I find myself driving down the roads and walking down the streets described to me. I recognise all the features and begin to get an uncanny feeling of having been somewhere same but different. The landscape becomes fantastic – oversaturated and strange. The light is so dissimilar, the days themselves are held in different seasons, the feelings are so totally removed from the scenes described and yet they are so clearly the same places. I wonder how the describers feel in the places they described.

A participant emails me:

On the way back I thought about what it is that I had written and how everything seemed to me, it was a strange experience for me, it is hard to describe how something feels and seems to you because we all perceive the world in different ways, and it isn't something I have done before so it was difficult at first but it got easier. It was an enjoyable experience for me, it felt as though I had to look at the world in a different way, because we see the world, but how much of it do we truly take in, how much of it stays the same in our memory? While driving to my house we went down the road that I had described in my story, I looked at every part of it, there was details I got spot on but others not so much. It made me come to a realisation that we may see something every single day of the week but we have to ask ourselves; do we truly take in all of the world as what it is ...? It has made me want to take in more of the world and to see it for what it truly is and to appreciate the world more. I now go down my road everyday like I always have but I see so much more of it. I see all of the things I missed out.

Figure 3.13: Fen road, November 2016. Photograph by and reproduced with permission of Rowan Jaines.

By constructing pieces where we tried to put things 'flatly' we saw the lack of feature in the landscape differently and undid it. Another contributor spoke about a time he had gone up onto the roof of the Corn Exchange. Afterwards he said:

Then it was back to earth with a bump so to speak. I went out on the bike after that, that weekend and basically sort of like looked at ground level at what I'd seen on the roof and it looked completely different. It looked bigger, from up there everything looked smaller but when you got down to it everything was a lot bigger.

Perhaps getting started in this way provides a space where things that have blurred into insignificance can move into a new focus, a site where the ordinary becomes strange and the opportunity arises to see the edges within the expanse. Indeed, this way of getting started made space for the familiar to emerge in all its strangeness. The project allowed for the landscape to be remade as eerie to myself – already a stranger in this place. More importantly perhaps, it made the concept of a fieldwork *method* stand out as a familiar kind of weird. A method is to some extent a gaze that sees only what it is already looking at and thus, to some extent, what one already perceives. This is perhaps an unhelpful point on which to end. There is of course no answer, no neat ribbon to tie up at the end. But it is good to notice, to be surprised and forced to advance tentatively to the next step, not knowing what it will require.

Figure 3.14: Fly tipping and morning sky, November 2016. Photograph by and reproduced with permission of Rowan Jaines.

Data and findings: process and product

Some creative writers are more interested in process, others in product, and the same is true of researchers who use creative writing in their work. Donald M. Murray, the Pulitzer Prize-winning author credited with differentiating process and product, advocated attention to the former (Murray 1972). Those who regard creative writing as a practice-led discipline tend to agree. For Harper (2019:xi), 'the "doing" of creative writing has always been paramount', and that means 'studying the practice rather than the outcomes/texts of creative writing'. Some social researchers come to similar conclusions, even though they tend to see process rather differently: less a matter of technique and wordcraft, more a matter of creative and participatory practice and what it can reveal about those who are doing it, and what it can do for them.

Similarly, participatory action researchers tend to stress process over product because, as they see it, the way in which research is done leaves a lasting trace: on those involved and on their wider communities. Participatory research includes but reaches well beyond participatory creative writing, and the products of such research are equally broad, including a range of impacts and artefacts, of which texts are just one possible example. Dydia DeLyser and Daniel Sui argue that 'research processes are as important as research outcomes' because those processes have the potential to 'challenge hierarchies between researcher and researched' and 'equitably engage community research partners' (DeLyser and Sui 2014:299; see also Kindon et al 2007; Askins and Pain 2011; Castleden et al 2012). Process is important to many participants, whose motives for involvement include gaining skills, connecting with others and enjoying themselves, rather than simply helping the researcher out (Parr 2007). The process of writing is just one part of this broader participatory process, in which involvement with a group is as important as the details of what group members do. In participatory action research, these motives help shape the project; hence the importance attached to process. Some other researchers, working with similar methods, stress process for a different reason, which revolves more around the insights that can be gained from observing creative practices, rather than focusing upon their tangible outcomes, in this case written work.

Notwithstanding the emphasis that many creative writers and social researchers place upon process, the products of creative writing are also important of course, both in creative writing practice and in its applications to social research. The products of creative writing have a number of different things to offer social researchers. First, well-crafted written work stands to provide eloquent answers to research questions, and to speak to research interests from original angles. Second, the production of quality outputs can benefit participants who see their involvement in this research as a means of developing creative skills, producing work they are proud of, and exploring the possibility of working as a professional writer or artist. Researchers may or may not be interested in making artists of participants, but if they see their work as a form of action research, they may be keen to accommodate participants in this way. There are, in any case, advantages of being associated with high-quality outputs, since these can attract attention to the research project that spawned them. Third, high-quality outputs can provide material for the dissemination of findings and the cultivation of pathways to impact. These outputs may take the form of accessible and high-quality work: books and articles that people may want to read; plays and films they may watch; and, in each case, circulating material with the potential to affect readers and audiences, and in this way to make an impact (Lorimer and Parr 2014:543).

Every researcher has to work out the balance between process and product which is right for them and their participants. Here are some contrasting examples of how the balance has been struck. First, Richard (researcher) and Stacy Bias (facilitator) discussed the priorities for a film which a group of participants would script and make (Phillips et al 2020). Stacy was originally concerned that the process would not produce a film with the professionalism or 'virality' of her previous work, *Flying While Fat*, which attracted millions of views online (see 'Your stories are moving' in Chapter 4). She felt that a polished outcome would be possible if she were commissioned to work through and animate some of the interview transcripts generated by the project team the previous year. But that would not be participatory film, and it would require Stacy to depict young Muslims (she herself is not a member of this group). Richard and Stacy agreed that the priority should be on the participatory process and that the film should be about and by Muslims, facilitated but not made by Stacy. This meant managing expectations about the output's quality and its potential to make a direct and immediate impact online.

Other researchers come to other conclusions about the balance between process and product. Working with refugees in Australia, Nina Woodrow (2016) did not simply stand back and let participants speak. She actively 'co-created' stories because, as she explained, stories 'can evoke empathy and effect powerful changes' (Woodrow 2016:2). Given the prevailing hostility towards refugees in Australia at the time she conducted this research, Woodrow saw that by working with refugees she could help them tell their stories in a way that could make a difference. As Geraldine Pratt and Caleb Johnston put it, well scripted stories can 'induce empathy' (Pratt and Johnston 2017:280), affecting employers, policy makers and members of the public. But, even when decisions are made about the relative importance of process and product, tension between priorities can linger. Kye Askins and Rachel Pain sensed 'considerable tension between the perceived need for a professional product' and their own 'goals in knowledge coproduction' (Askins and Pain 2011:812), and this tension resurfaced when they allowed an artist to smarten up and change art works, upsetting some participants, who felt their own work had been compromised.

Though some researchers prioritise process and others product, most recognise the importance of both, and therefore the importance of being able to collect and interpret data relating to each of them. In fact the boundary between process and product is always blurred in creative writing, where anything from the very first phase of the process may become part of the final product. Most social researchers are better equipped to work with the processes than the products of creative writing. This is because we tend to be trained and experienced in interviews and focus groups, participant observation and participatory research, all of which come in handy in observing, documenting and interpreting the doing of creative writing. Still, as Graham Mort (2013:219) observes, 'creative writing process can never map easily onto other social scientific or scientific models'. And if this is true of process, it is doubly so of product. Though some creative writing texts are readily understandable by anyone with a reasonable grasp of literacy and language, others are less literal, and revolve around metaphors and allusions that may be more difficult to read. Interpretation of these more complex texts requires skills that are more akin to literary criticism and perhaps to psychoanalysis than conventional social science.

But these skills are not unrelated to those honed in the interpretation of complex interview and focus group data, where the interesting findings lurk beneath the surface and in the ways in which things are said and the silences that remain, rather than what is directly said. And, of course, it is possible to learn to work on a more literary critical level and, failing that, to collaborate with those in other disciplines, whose research training and experience may complement those of the social scientist.

Observing and documenting the creative writing process

The creative writing process can be observed and documented in a number of ways, beginning with diaries and journals:

- Research diaries: in which researchers and workshop facilitators maintain diaries of their observations, experiences and reflections of the research process. These diaries are wide-ranging, beginning at the planning stage and continuing through fieldwork, including any workshops that are undertaken, and subsequent analysis of findings. Though the importance of the self-reflexive diary is established in ethnographic research, its importance is worth reiterating in this discussion of product and process, since the diary is closely attuned to collecting data about the research process. That said, it might become a product in its own right.
- Audio diaries: Rachel Pain's audio diary of participatory arts workshops, recorded while research was taking place, covered events and observations during workshops and reflections outside, as well as preparatory work and meetings and phone calls with the artist, their collaborator and facilitator. Pain also recorded her recall of and reactions to events around the workshops, including conversations outside the venue with former participants who continued to hang around (Askins and Pain 2011). Other researchers use video diaries and social media to record and share research experiences as they unfold (Carrigan 2020).

Where more than one member of a team keeps a research diary – which is a good idea – it may be possible to compare and contrast different perspectives on and experiences of the same events. Compare, for example, diaries of a single workshop, kept by Afshan (the facilitator) and Nafhesa (the researcher) within a research project led by Richard (Phillips et al 2021). Afshan recorded in her diary that she had introduced 'free writing exercises of a minute long, a way to get [the participants] warmed up'. She asked them to write for a minute about 'various different topics' such as 'time, home, love, death' and 'relationship'. 'We then talked about how it was writing for a minute and I mentioned exercises similar to this that can be done every morning as a way of getting your brain trained to write on demand.' In contrast with Afshan's factual record, Nafhesa records the way in which she experienced the activity, and the ways in which she felt the participants were feeling. Nafhesa found it 'intense' and wondered if it could be less formal. 'As I am watching the group I can see their un–comfort once they start and them wanting to leave.'

Diaries of the research process are mentioned in many accounts of participatory research, but often in passing, and briefly, since diaries tend to be taken for granted. Researchers who pay more direct attention to the diary include Dan Mahoney, who collected, transcribed and distilled gay men's stories about their lives. He kept a self-reflexive research diary which he began in the preliminary stages of his project. Mahoney explains that the journal covered 'what I was seeing, feeling, and hearing at the time, and my analytical understandings of these issues'. The journal found a dual focus: methodological and substantive. 'How the fieldwork relationships were forged had a profound effect on how the stories got told' (Mahoney 2007:579). Direct attention to the 'self-reflexive fieldwork journal' in Mahoney's account of his research brings this often taken-for-granted, textual research method into view. Mahoney explains:

> This reflexivity through journaling … taught me: (a) how to value and be transparent about the tools and sensibilities I brought to the research context; (b) how to articulate my emotions, empathy, and feelings toward my study collaborators; and (c) how this emotional context was an important analytical tool for the promotion and success of the research project. (Mahoney 2007:580)

But the diary is not the only means of recording the experiences of participatory creative writing. Other means include:

• Traces of the process of creative writing including 'the notes, the scribbles, the emails, and so on, that are produced during creative writing' (Harper 2013:150).
• Informal conversations, interviews and focus groups with participants and facilitators, conducted in a range of settings: before, during and after creative writing workshops. Through these conversations, it is possible to explore experiences of writing, and to look beyond the most tangible, superficial

traces of writing workshops: the words left on a page or on a flip chart. Some people tense up when recording devices are switched on – even with their permission – and interview schedules are produced. This can break the spell of creative workshops and close people down. So it can be helpful to conduct these conversations and interviews as informally as possible. Rather than asking people to step aside and 'be interviewed', it can be a good idea to join them in quiet moments of their own making: during cigarette and food breaks, for example, and while hanging around outside a venue. For other people, who may be more comfortable with structured conversations, more conventional interviews may be appropriate (Gembus 2018:433).

- Photographs and films: recording research activities – including creative writing workshops and performances – while they happen. Drawing and sketching are also options for those who have the necessary abilities. This can be more appropriate in some settings and with some participants than others. It is essential to seek informed consent.

- Tracking readers and audience reception to creative writing: observing group discussion of drafts read aloud in workshops, and using feedback from these discussions in revising and refining work; tracking reactions to readings and performances of finished work; organising and documenting 'talk back' sessions following these events (Pratt and Johnston 2017); and tracing circulation, for example though download and viewing figures for material posted online. Where audiences are involved in meaning-making through reading, listening and watching, audience research may be seen as a form of participatory research in its own right (Cowie 2017), even though such audiences are accorded a limited role, which happens after the story has been researched, written and relayed.

Before any of these data can be collected, it is important to ensure that participants understand how they are being observed, and to seek their permission to work in this way, with every opportunity for them to say no. Not every participant will be comfortable with every form of observation, or with the circulation or reproduction of certain records, and it may be appropriate to go ahead with some forms of observation but not others. To name the most obvious example, photography and film recording may inhibit some people, even if they have granted permission for those recordings to take place, so it may be appropriate for the researcher to stand back and adopt a less intrusive, less voyeuristic stance.

Product: outputs and impacts

Whereas there is always a process in creative writing, there is not always an obvious output. There may be a half-finished poem, crumpled and left behind, or a few words written on a phone, perhaps then deleted. Still, some trace of the writing process usually exists, even if this proves preliminary, scrappy and ephemeral. As Harper explains, 'not all creative writing produces a final work' – which is 'only one component of … the practice of creative writing, the doing of it'. He concludes that the final work, if it ever materialises, is 'both a very significant thing and the least significant thing' (Harper 2019:xvi).

Somerset Maugham tells the story of a man who died before finishing a book, declaring his life – and the years he had devoted to reading for and planning the book – a success. He found fulfilment in reading, sketching out chapters and making notes, and living with a goal in sight; and he 'never knew the bitterness of an end achieved' (Maugham 1951:174). But Maugham, who saw many ends achieved, could afford this dry humour. For most writers, it is important to finish, and for social researchers who work with creative writing it is important to understand their finished work. Doing so requires skills somewhat outside the comfort zone of many social scientists and next we give you some pointers.

First, don't take creative writing too literally or read it too directly (Rose 2016). Writers draw upon unreliable memories and selective perceptions; they speculate about how others see and experience things; they enjoy writerly licence; and in addition to all these inadvertent distortions, they deliberately distort and invent. Creative writing revolves around 'fantasy, fabulation, distortion and invention … to create the illusory fabrication of space/time that is a work of art' (Mort 2013:218–19). Creative writers are not newspaper reporters or witnesses in court; their accounts do not have to be 'entirely true' to experiences or memories (Neale 2006c:55). That said, while creative writers may not be aiming for factual accuracy, they do typically seek to explore some kind of truth (Tracy 2010). We return to this subject in Chapter 4, where we explore a form of convergence between social researchers and creative writers.

A second point follows: creative writing is illustrative rather than representative. A short story or play by a refugee does not represent the experiences of all refugees any more than any other qualitative data about that refugee would do. Nor does it necessarily represent the experience of its writer. Michael Richardson, reflecting on the play he had been involved in, storying the lives of Irish heritage men, struggled with this issue. 'The local press, the theatre company, even the ethical framework of the University wanted the story to be representative as it is seen as "safer" and more significant' (Richardson 2015:628). Richardson (2015:628) preferred to 'see the play as symbolic', not necessarily depicting specific circumstances, but exploring wider themes including masculinity, Irishness and religion, and doing so freely, indirectly.

Pointers about what creative writing is not, and how it should not be read, lead to others which are more positive. Graham Mort (2013:218) may be a little too modest, for himself and his craft, when he writes that 'the creative writer is unlikely to be able to create new knowledge in the way that a scientist can – based upon new and observable phenomena – which partly explains our residual discomfort with the research culture of the academy'. But he then reflects on what creative writing *can* do, and argues the more positive case that it can reveal 'psychological, political, social and cultural' realities 'every bit as much as the social scientific analysis' offered by researchers in the social sciences (Mort 2013:219).

This is the point: though unreliable on some levels, creative writing is truthful on others, and our challenge is to decipher this 'different kind of truth' (Neale 2006a:56). Patricia Leavy (2015:58) puts this in another way, arguing that fiction-based research 'is about truthfulness more than "truth". Fiction can come closer to truth than mere "facts" may'. We develop this point in Chapter 4, where we explore how fiction and other forms of creative writing can 'ring true'.

CREATIVE WRITING IN PRACTICE

On storytelling and social research *by Kristina Diprose*[5]

Kristina Diprose is a social researcher and a writer. In this piece she reflects on the separation and intersection of these interests, and how stories can surface at unexpected moments.

... the stories I want to tell you will light up part of my life, and leave the rest in darkness. You don't need to know everything. There is no everything. The stories themselves make the meaning. Jeanette Winterson (2005:134), *Lighthousekeeping*

It's 2011 and I'm a PhD researcher on a team building weekend with a group of young climate change campaigners who are meeting for the first time. This is the first of many such weekends planned for us over the next few months. I am part-participant and part-observer, scribbling fieldnotes in the downtime between introductions and lively chatter. I'm trying to find my feet as an ethnographer, unsure of where to draw the line between my personal interest in climate activism and my research interest in how NGO youth

Figure 3.15: Inspiration doll by Alke Gröppel-Wegener, created in response to this piece by Kristina Diprose. Inspiration dolls comment on and play with genres of creative writing.

participation schemes such as this shape the next generation of activists. I want to blend into the background, but this proves impossible as we begin a training session on 'Public Narrative'. The session facilitator introduces this as a movement-building technique from community organising in the United States, specifically Barack Obama's first election campaign. She explains that each of us will leave this training having crafted a *story of self*, *story of us* and *story of now*. The idea is that we will use these public narratives in blogs, speeches and conversations to inspire climate action, sharing something of our personal struggles, doubts and triumphs over adversity to

---

[5] This contribution should be cited as follows: Diprose, K. (2021) 'On storytelling and social research'. In Phillips, R. and Kara, H. *Creative Writing for Social Research*. Bristol: Policy Press.

show others that change is possible. To illustrate how this works, she shows us emotive YouTube clips of US activists sharing their stories to huge audiences whooping, crying and enthusiastically applauding. A palpably awkward silence follows as fifteen British strangers groan inwardly and wait for someone else to go first.

It's 2016 and I'm working as a postdoctoral researcher. I've just finished a focus group with some older women who know each other through volunteering at a local park. The tape recorder has been switched off and we are nattering as we leave the community centre, when the conversation takes an unexpected turn. Amidst much laughter, Mary (not her real name) is complaining of her family's well-meaning but bothersome efforts to make her an online dating profile. In a matter-of-fact tone, she remarks: '*I've told them I don't want anyone but my Bill. We were happily married for over forty years. He let me go as far out to sea as I wanted, but he always came for me if I was drowning.*' This catches me off-guard. I murmur goodbye blinking back hot tears and scribble these words in my notebook on the train home. Mary's faith in the bond she shared with her late husband stirs a multitude of emotions. I usually use this train journey to write field notes and answer emails. Instead, by the time I arrive home I have the first draft of a poem with a stolen title: *Lighthouse Keeper*.

Whenever a stranger asks 'What do you do?', I am torn. Knowing this simple, polite enquiry merits an equally simple answer, I tend – as most of us do – to talk about my job. *I'm a researcher*, I say, donning the mantle of someone scholarly who methodically gathers data and analyses evidence for a living. Sometimes, for no reason other than a glimmer of intuition, I lead with my other passion. *I'm a writer*. It's a relief to say it out loud, this admission of a second life as a fantasist and embellisher of the truth.

When Richard and Helen invited me to attend their *Creative Writing in Social Research* workshop, I was initially unsure of its relevance to me. I've always maintained a careful distinction between my writing and my research, or so I believed. In recent interdisciplinary research projects – *INTERSECTION* (Diprose et al 2019) and *Storying Sexual Relationships* (Chambers et al 2019) – I had collaborated with writers and explored insights generated through creative writing workshops with research participants, but I had treated this writing as data to be analysed, another method in my toolbox alongside interviews, questionnaires and field observations. The workshop promised something more: an opportunity to reflect on the relationship between social research and the stories people tell about themselves and others. It prompted me to look again at the various ways in which stories surface in the course of research.

I was struck by the way that contributors such as Katie Collins and Andrew McMillan described creative writing as a mode of enquiry, furnishing characters with inner worlds as a way of understanding what it is to be human. This reminded me of why I love to read and write – because stories help us to make sense of the world, or at least some part of it, sparking tiny fires of recognition and empathy between strangers. Likewise, I became a researcher because I am interested in the stories people tell to navigate their lives. As I listened, my thoughts drifted to one of my favourite books, Jeanette Winterson's *Lighthousekeeping*. An orphan named Silver describes herself as 'part precious metal part pirate' (Winterson 2005:3). She is apprenticed to a lighthouse keeper, Pew, who teaches her that stories are the maps we live by. The events of the novel bridge plausible fact, history lesson and fantasy, the remote lighthouse serving as a metaphor for the meeting of solid and moveable worlds.

In the workshop's opening keynote, Mary Evans observed that the truth of a story is a question of judgement. We all want to tell a good story, which means that very few people tell 'the truth', so how do we judge what people are telling us? How is it true? How do we analyse something that is not untrue, but true in the sense of a fantasy, something that a person wants us to know about their experience? Drawing on her own childhood in her first novel *Oranges Are Not the Only Fruit*, the narrator Jeanette observes that 'People like to separate storytelling which is not fact from history which is fact' (Winterson 1985:93). Revisiting this theme in *Lighthousekeeping*, Winterson argues: 'In the fossil record of our existence, there is no trace of love. You cannot find it held in the earth's crust waiting to be discovered. The long bones of our ancestors show nothing of their hearts' (Winterson 2005:170). In other words, the storied truth – the language we find to show others who we are – is a vital part of any quest for knowledge. Reisman (2011:11) suggests that by juxtaposing reality and fantasy, Winterson 'complicates the "truth" of each setting, disrupts the binary imperative, and reveals the space where change can occur'.

When I was trained in public narrative as a novice PhD researcher, the point of the exercise was that the stories we craft to make sense of our lives can be powerful, urging us and others to act. Except, at that moment, it didn't work – at least, not for me. I hadn't come prepared to share a *story of self* with a room full of people I hardly knew. I felt exposed and vulnerable, and I had no idea how to wrestle my journey as a young climate change activist into a cohesive narrative. I panicked and probably made something up. Now, looking back, I wonder how often I have put others in similar situations when interviewing them for a research project. *Tell me a story. Explain yourself. Know why you did that. Make sense.* Storytelling can be liberating, but it can also be uncomfortable and manipulative where it seeks to impose structure and meaning on someone else's experience.

An especially helpful reflection that I took from the *Creative Writing and Social Research* workshop is that it's okay for stories to be messy and unfinished. Brendan Stone gave a provocation on the kaleidoscopic nature of identity and how people's inner worlds rarely consist of a unified self. This elicited a discussion of how we can research and write in ways that allow fragments to breathe, rather than insisting on completeness. I thought again about *Lighthousekeeping*, the characters' multiple, improbable stories of self and Winterson's insistence that 'there are lit-up moments, and the rest is dark' (Winterson 2005:134).

I interviewed more than 150 people during the course of my postdoctoral research project and it is Mary's words – *he let me go as far out to sea as I wanted* – that I recall most vividly. In crafting a hastily scribbled draft of *Lighthouse Keeper* into a published poem (Diprose 2017), I took many liberties with the scant facts of her marriage as I tried to honour a story that struck me as worth re-telling. On the same research project, which was not in the least focused on relationships, but rather climate change and what we owe to future generations, another group of older people said that if we were going to talk about sustainability, we should talk about 'how we can sustain ourselves'. I think, fundamentally, that's what stories do, and that's why they matter – not as artefacts to be deciphered and mined for truth and order, but as guiding lights to live by.

4

Exploring and articulating findings

Introduction

The separation between different 'stages of the research process' is quite artificial. Of course, it is useful for purposes of teaching, learning, discussion, and so on. But really all research involves exploring and articulating phenomena.

As we have already seen in this book, creative writing offers opportunities for fruitful exploration and articulation work with participants, enhanced observational research, generating and developing ideas, and many more. This final part looks at how social researchers can use creative writing as we explore our data and articulate our findings. Whereas Chapter 3 drew upon Richard's research, Chapter 4 is informed more by Helen's work on writing as a research method. We examine a number of ways or shapes of writing that are particularly applicable to analysis, followed by some others that are associated more closely with dissemination, before bringing these together through the cross-cutting theme of storying.

Data analysis

The idea of using creative writing in data analysis may at first seem quite contradictory to good-practice maxims of working systematically and with great attention to detail. However, we argue that these approaches complement each other and add richness to analytic work. It is possible to demonstrate rigour in the use of creative writing for analysis by practising transparency: describing the process of sense-making from raw data to findings; giving examples of dialogue and interactions (perhaps from composite accounts); and making visible your own role in that process (Markham 2012). Forms of creative writing that have already shown potential for the analysis of social research data include fiction, poetry, and play or screenplay writing.

Fiction in data analysis

Fiction has great power 'to disturb and disrupt the familiar and commonplace, to question and interrogate that which seems to have already been answered conclusively, and to redirect the conversation regarding important social issues' (Barone and Eisner 2012:101). This raises questions about truth claims. Fiction offers what we might call 'authentic' truth, that is, the truth of experience, as opposed to 'literal' truth, that is, the truth of evidence-based or empirical work

(Pickering and Kara 2017:299). We say of a story that it 'rings true' (or doesn't). This metaphor, of a sound or a cracked bell, is a sensory metaphor of experience. Through stories we experience, vicariously, the experiences of others.

Several commentators (for example, Barone and Eisner 2012, Leavy 2015) draw on the work of the 20th-century literary theorist Wolfgang Iser as inspiration for ways in which fiction can be used in analytic work. Iser identified three stages in producing fiction: selection, combination and self-disclosure. Selection refers to the choice of elements to include in the work. American arts-based research specialists Tom Barone and Elliot Eisner suggest that for research purposes we think of these as empirical elements (2012:104). Combination is the process of bringing those elements together (Leavy 2019:195). And self-disclosure refers to the ways in which a text reveals or conceals its fictional nature (Barone and Eisner 2012:108).

One fairly common use of fiction in qualitative analysis is the creation of a composite piece (Saldaña and Omasta 2018:194). This can take a range of forms, such as a description of a person, or a monologue, or a story of experience. The aim is to protect the anonymity of individual participants while creating a piece that 'rings true'. This is often done by patchworking together elements from different participants' input. The process can help researchers gain a fuller understanding of the nature of their participants and the issues they face. If possible, it can be helpful to test any composite piece with participants to assess whether they find the piece recognisable.

Fiction often forms elements of other types of creative writing, such as poetry or plays. Kip Jones, a specialist in qualitative research, developed the concept of a 'fictive reality' when he was writing the screenplay for his research-based film *Rufus Stone*. He describes fictive reality as 'the ability to engage in imaginative and creative invention while remaining true to the remembered realities as told through the narrations of others' (Jones 2013:10). Oded Löwenheim, an autoethnographer based in Jerusalem, uses fictive reality to help protect the private information of others whose permission cannot be sought (2010:1031). The distillation of research findings into an arts-based output such as film or autoethnographic writing is in effect another layer of analytic work. Simultaneously, such a process also creates new data for ourselves or other researchers to use in future (Brkich and Barko 2013:246).

Some researchers are interested in writing fiction as part of analytic work when data is lacking (Park-Kang 2015:362). This can happen, for example, in international relations when studying a country with closed borders such as North Korea (Park-Kang 2015:371). The international relations scholar Sungju Park-Kang advocates the use of story, imagination, and empathy in research. He suggests that fiction writing can help 'to articulate sensitive and complicated problems in a more flexible and imaginative way' (Park-Kang 2015:371). Park-Kang articulates the risk that using fiction for analysis in research can lead to judgements that the resulting work lacks scholarly legitimacy (Park-Kang 2015:365). However, for him, the use of fiction is about allowing imagination to take its place in research alongside other, more conventionally accepted, qualities. Another reason for using fiction is to help engage readers' or audiences' emotions. Park-Kang makes the point that using fiction writing need not preclude other forms of analytic work, but can complement them (Park-Kang 2015:372).

Others have described this kind of fictionalisation as 'analysis in another manner, creating another layer to deepen awareness' (Caine et al 2017:217–18). It can help both researchers and participants to reach different, fuller understandings of their experiences and relationships (Caine et al 2017:218). As for Park-Kang, Vera Caine and colleagues see imagination as an integral part of this process (Caine et al 2017).

It is also worth considering not only what fictionalisation can *do* in research but what it might be *for*. We have already seen that it can be used to protect participants and 'non-consenting others' (Mannay 2016:122) and to fill gaps in data through imaginative narrative work. Caine et al (2017:217) also suggest that fictionalisation can be useful in helping researchers to 'create enough distance to perhaps see one's own experiences with new eyes, a strategy for making the familiar strange'. Drawing on the work of bell hooks they suggest that writing of one's own experience in the third person can help by 'creating an other to tell me more' (Caine et al 2017:217). (This is an interesting corollary to the option of writing about others' experiences in the first person, as we saw in Chapter 2.) These purposes are not mutually exclusive; two or all three may co-exist in the same research project. Nor are they presented here as exhaustive, as there may be many other purposes for fictionalisation in research (Caine et al 2017:219).

Poetry in data analysis

A researcher may be analysing poetic data (whether using a poetic approach or not), or taking a poetic approach to analysing non-poetic data. The latter has been called 'researcher-voiced' (from direct observation and experiences) and the former 'participant-voiced' (written by participants, or quoting them) (Prendergast 2004:74; Eshun and Madge 2016; Patrick 2016). Through what is said and the ways in which it is said – through rhythm, alliteration, rhyme and the words themselves – poetry can open windows that are otherwise closed. Lisa Patrick (2016:385) argues that 'what is known in prose might be known differently in poetry'. And, though intimidating to some, poetry is appealing to many others, and as such it has potential to reach beyond the usual audiences for academic research and writing (Eshun and Madge 2016).

Writing poetry can help researchers to develop new insights about their data (Furman et al 2007:304). One approach is to use existing words and/or phrases to create new poems. This is sometimes called 'found poetry' and can be used to present data or findings in ways that are both aesthetically pleasing and accessible for readers and audiences (Prendergast 2015:683). A sub-set of this approach is 'poetic transcription' (Ellingson 2009:63–5) which involves using participants' own words, in poetic form, to represent their views and experiences. According to Sandra Faulkner (2019:215): 'The poetry is created by paying careful attention to the line, including the use of spaces and breaks'. This method of creating poems from interview or focus group transcripts can yield different insights for researchers than other forms of analytic work (Faulkner 2019:215).

Penelope Carroll and her colleagues in Aotearoa/New Zealand used poetry as a method in their research into the experiences of people in marginal housing. They conducted 40 in-depth interviews with people living in informal dwellings, such as sheds, garages, tents and caravans, in rural and urban areas. They conducted a policy-focused thematic analysis and then reviewed the interview recordings and transcripts to reveal stories and contexts which the policy focus had concealed. They wrote down phrases and sentences which illustrated unique life events or participants' perspectives, and also noted descriptions from field notes. Then they created 34 'prose poems' (one per 'household') by arranging these into stanzas while remaining true to the flow, meaning and priorities of participants' narratives (Carroll et al 2011:628). Here's an excerpt from one of the poems.

Life In A Suburban Garage, Alison, Auckland (opening stanzas)

You live in a double garage
with children aged ten and two.
Concrete floors,
unlined ceiling and walls.
And twenty-three trips to Starship Hospital
with asthma since they were born.

In summer it's an oven,
in winter a freezer,
rain so loud on the tin roof
it scares the children.
And your ten-year-old begs you please
to say "going home",
not "back to the garage",
in front of her friends.

Carroll et al (2011) aimed for accessible, explicit poems rather than poems with literary merit. The process of creating these poems helped the researchers to reach a greater understanding of the complexities of informal housing in Aotearoa/New Zealand. This 'created empathy which allowed for a felt sense of the phenomenon and not merely a detached cognitive understanding' (Carroll et al 2011:629). Poems were shared with participants, who responded positively, describing the poems as accurate and meaningful. The poems were disseminated in written and spoken form in academic, public and policy settings. Overall Carroll et al (2011:629) found this approach to poetry to be a very useful complementary method to their conventional thematic analysis.

Another approach is to write poems using your own words. These may be in 'free verse', with no conventions about rhyming, line length, or the number or pattern of lines. Or they may be in one of the numerous 'weird and delightful' poetic forms – or even in a new form which the researcher has devised (Fry 2005:xviii). One option here is the lyric poem, which 'focuses most on aesthetics and the associations between images and feelings' (Faulkner 2020:79). It is written by the researcher using 'imagery, rhythm, sound and layout' to identify and communicate feelings (Faulkner 2019:218). Another option is the narrative poem. Narrative poems tell a story, though the distinction between lyric and narrative poetry isn't as clear as the phrases imply (Faulkner 2020:79) and may in fact be a false dichotomy (Faulkner 2020:74). Storytelling is important for researchers, and narrative poetry is particularly useful for telling stories of experience. It can also resonate strongly with readers and audiences (Faulkner 2020:70).

Longer poems and collections may also be useful for researchers to write. Long poetry forms include ballads (such as the *The Rime of the Ancient Mariner* by Coleridge) which developed from folk songs and stories, heroic verse (as used by Chaucer), and blank verse (Shakespeare). The difference between heroic and blank verse is that one rhymes and the other doesn't. Long poems can, of course, also be written in free verse.

Collections may be made up of the researcher's own poems or of poems by various people connected with the research. Some collections are published in chapbooks, the poetry equivalent of the zine (see below for more on zines). Like zines, chapbooks focus on a single theme, are usually short and are often made by hand in small quantities (Faulkner 2019:219). One particularly research-focused type of collection is known as a 'poetry cluster', that is, a set of poems on a particular theme. The poetry cluster has been described as 'a powerful way of expressing a range of subtle nuances about a topic while simultaneously producing a more general overview' (Butler-Kisber and Stewart 2009:4). Katherine Collins' contribution to this book, 'Migrants like these', is in the form of a poetry cluster.

Collaboration in poetic analysis can be done in a variety of ways. People can write poetry together, work on each other's data, or provide mentorship for one another (Faulkner 2019:220). Or they can collaborate in more elaborate forms of poetic inquiry. Rich Furman, from the University of North Carolina, worked with colleagues to inquire into adolescent identity using reflective poetry. The initial data set was a collection of poems written by Furman a few years earlier and revised using a reflective process with a two-part purpose: first, to ensure the poems expressed his views and feelings as accurately as possible; second, to ensure that they were as accessible as possible for others. To this latter end, he changed some words from those he judged to be more appropriate in poetic terms to those more likely to make his meaning clear. Then a colleague used the data set to create 'research tankas' (Furman et al 2007:305). A tanka is a Japanese short poetic form that has five lines, each with a set number of syllables in the pattern 5-7-5-7-7. This colleague used a six-step process:

1. reading and noting initial impressions;
2. reading again and identifying themes;
3. exploring dichotomies;
4. checking for words and phrases that expressed each theme;
5. organising those words and phrases into lines;
6. using those lines and the dichotomies to create tankas. (Furman et al 2007:306)

A third colleague used an interpretive technique, drawn from grounded theory and incorporating constant comparison, to analyse both the original data set and the tankas. That colleague, with a fourth colleague, then created poems responding to both the original data set and the results of the analysis.

Furman and his colleagues note, as a limitation of their approach, that while it is systematic, it also necessarily involves 'the idiosyncratic associations, reflections, and personal meanings' of the researchers (Furman et al 2007:312). We disagree that this is a limitation. We argue it applies to all data analysis in social research, because we are all social beings who cannot leave our idiosyncratic associations, reflections and personal meanings out of any decision we make. Furman et al's goal was to 'create a layered, emotionally resonant representation of the struggles of establishing adolescent identity' and, in our judgement, they have done that well. As Paiva (2020:1) asserts, 'poetry can be a resonant method when the [researcher] is attuned to the way in which thinking and feeling are intertwined'.

Here is another example of elaborate arts-based data analysis including poems. Jennifer Lapum and her colleagues from Ryerson University in Toronto investigated patients' experiences of open-heart surgery. Lapum had already collected interview and journal data from 16 people who had gone through open-heart surgery, and initial analysis highlighted the requirement for a more humanistic, patient-focused approach to healthcare. She put together a cross-disciplinary research team for further analysis which included five people:

1. an associate professor, poet, nurse, and arts-based researcher (Lapum herself);
2. a design strategist and multi-disciplinary artist;
3. a researcher and disability activist;
4. a cardiovascular surgeon and professor;
5. an assistant professor in fashion.

The team also consulted with 'knowledge users', that is, people who had experience of heart surgery and cardiovascular health practitioners (Lapum et al 2012:103). They began by immersing themselves in patients' stories as told in the original interviews and journal entries, which helped them to imagine patients' embodied experiences. They used the temporal construction of patients' stories as an organising framework. They attended to participants' vocal qualities and the characteristics of their speech and writing, such as metaphor and repetition. From this, they documented and categorised particular words, phrases and key ideas, within the organising framework. These were then reassembled into free verse poems. A second phase of analysis focused on these poems as part of the preparation of an art installation to help disseminate the research findings. The researchers read the poems closely and used a process of 'iterative dialogue, systematic inquiry, visualization, concept mapping, and metaphorical interpretation' (Lapum et al 2012:104) over nine months. They used discussion, drawing, and browsing books and magazines alongside writing in this analytic process. This enabled them to construct an 'overarching, interpretive lens' for their installation: 'to portray open-heart surgery and recovery as a journey deep within the human body, that is shared by patients and practitioners, and results in profound transformation for both' (Lapum et al 2012:106).

Poetic inquiry can also be used in reviewing literature. The poetic inquirer Monica Prendergast conducted an analysis of poetic inquiry up to the year 2012, which resulted in a collection of hundreds of poems. She was invited to speak about her work at the Poetic Inquiry Symposium in 2013. In preparing for that presentation, she carried out a piece of poetic inquiry into poetic inquiry. She read the hundreds of poems from the collection she had curated and highlighted sections that resonated with her. She identifies the characteristics and qualities that led to this resonance:

- aesthetic power
- imagery, metaphor
- capturing a moment
- truth-telling, bravery, vulnerability
- critical insight, often through empathy
- surprise and the unexpected (Prendergast 2015:683)

Then she pulled out all the highlighted sections into a separate document. She used differently coloured highlights to code each section, which led to her identification of the five 'poetic voices' used by researchers to:

- explore self, writing, and poetry as method (poetic voice);
- investigate inequalities and social justice (justice voice);
- consider self and/or participants' gender, race, sexual orientation etc (identity voice);
- examine patients' and/or caregivers' experience of care, nursing etc (care voice);
- study parenting, family, and/or religion (procreator voice) (Prendergast 2015:683).

Then she created 'found poems' from the sections of text to try to illustrate each of these voices.

Given the proliferation of the field since 2012, this typology continues to change. Nevertheless it is a useful way to think about poetic inquiry, with the 'voices' perhaps also performing 'functions' within research – as voices often do.

Leavy suggests, more simply, that poetry may be voiced by researchers, participants, or literature (2015:80–2). Another way to think about poetic inquiry is that it may be of use at any stage of the research process, and certainly has profound potential when we are writing, gathering and analysing data, or disseminating findings. Poetry is already being used by social researchers in disciplines across the social sciences, from psychology (Koelsch 2016) to anthropology (Kusserow 2017) and from geography (Thomas 2016) to sociology (Richardson 1997).

Prendergast doesn't state the language(s) incorporated in her work, which implies that it is English-only. The results from Google Scholar are also likely to be English-only, so this isn't a global analysis. Poetic inquiry may well be conducted in languages other than English. However, poetry is notoriously difficult to translate, and there are still around 7,000 languages spoken worldwide so the full extent of this practice is probably unknowable.

Some people find poetry daunting, thinking it must be difficult to write. It is true that some poetic forms are challenging. If you are new to poetry, or inexperienced, you are unlikely to be able to turn out a convincing sonnet or villanelle. However, other poetry is much more accessible. In fact, you don't even have to write original poetry; you can compile 'found poems' using excerpts from interview or focus group transcripts, from literature, or even from other work on poetic inquiry (Prendergast 2015:683). And if you write poems, you will find that poetry can be your teacher, your therapist, or your friend, just as much as prose.

One aspect of poetic inquiry that can be problematic is identifying when and how to use poetry in social research (Faulkner 2019:214). Poetry is 'not for every researcher or every project' (Leavy 2015:90). Prendergast's typology may function as a useful starting point for working out when to use poetry. Also, poetry seems particularly useful for topics that explicitly involve emotion as well as cognition (Prendergast et al 2009:xxii). It can demonstrate precision, or ambiguity, or both (Faulkner 2019). Perhaps for these reasons, it can be particularly good at evoking emotion in the reader or the listener. So another time to use poetry could be when there is a good reason to aim to engage people's emotions.

The use of poetry can also be an ethical stance. Adrie Kusserow argues that in at least some forms of social research, such as studies of conflict and forced migration, the researcher has 'an ethical responsibility not to numb, but to move the reader' (2017:80). As we have seen, poetry can be a way to achieve that emotional connection. For Frances Rapport and Graham Hartill, the ethical aspects of poetry are based on the way it enables 'a new way of knowing' by allowing for complexity, ambiguity and multiple perspectives – and so, they aver, potentially including 'the whole experience of life, with all its weaknesses and fractures' (2016:224). And poetic inquirer Monica Prendergast says that: 'In all cases, the writing process itself is an act of critical theorizing: reflexive, contemplative, embodied, hesitant, resistant' (2015:683).

CREATIVE WRITING IN PRACTICE

Migrants like these *by Katherine Collins*[1]

Katherine Collins is a Leverhulme Early Career Fellow at Oxford's Department of Education, currently writing a comparative critical biography of Paulo Freire, Orlando Fals-Borda, and Muhammad Anisur Rahman. She teaches life-writing and qualitative research methods and is a Fellow of the Oxford Centre for Life-Writing. Here she shares 'found poems' that she has created from interview transcripts from her research into migration and national identity. She explains, "I have been thinking about Annie Dillard's statement about found poetry in the author's note to her collection *Mornings Like This* (1995): 'By entering a found text as a poem, the poet doubles its context. The original meaning remains intact, but now it swings between two poles.'"

Just one tiny incident in Avignon

People who retire in England
get dug in, fossilise. We didn't
want
that. We lost our fathers; our
mothers getting older. We're free
agents. We wanted excitement.
I'm not anti-British but, young
people in Britain, they're just
ruder. Boys kicking footballs
into the side of the house, you
go out and say, 'look,
please don't do that.' You're
sworn at. Walking through
Avignon, there's a square
outside the Papal Palace. It
was early
evening, boys playing. The ball
was kicked, and it rolled
into my wife's legs. The boy
was apoplectic with apology,
'Oh madame, desolé.' We
thought, this is a place

Figure 4.1: Inspiration doll by Alke Gröppel-Wegener, created in response to this piece by Katherine Collins. Inspiration dolls comment on and play with genres of creative writing.

---

[1] This contribution should be cited as follows: Collins, K. (2021) 'Migrants like these'. In Phillips, R. and Kara, H. *Creative Writing for Social Research*. Bristol: Policy Press.

for us. In England she would have been sworn at, for being in
the way. We like the atmosphere, and the countryside;
Tarn-et-Garonne and Lot-et-Garonne, and the Lot. We didn't want
Dordogne, there's too many British there.

Metanastis
all of these words: immigrant, migrant, ex-pat, refugee.
Anybody who goes from one country to another is metanastis.

It's neutral; it's just that's what you are, if you go
from one country to another; I can't see why

you'd differentiate. And I do see among British ex-pats,
as they like to call themselves. This word,

ex-pats. It affects the way people think.
It's not used for a Nigerian who comes to Britain.

I don't see why that's funny
How can I pretend to be loyal to Ireland?
This cultural, love to hate the English.

We've got very good Irish friends,
but they don't invite you to family events.

You watch a lot of stuff on the television,
and you think, I just don't get it;

I don't see why that's funny,
and everyone around you is laughing.

I think we're just extremely English,
and we're just very English really.

Horses in Hyde Park
In England I was positioned as Irish,
by British people.

I was responsible for the IRA killing horses
in Hyde Park.

No one asked me whether they should kill horses.
Or soldiers

or civilians or anything else. When I came to Ireland
I was positioned

as English. But this is a more generous place to live
than England.

The most extraordinary ignorance
shown by people who should know better. You might
say, 'that's 24 generations ago.' You know? But it still
matters. Bad blood. Just below the surface. The men
of violence haven't gone away. They're quiescent;
they could easily come back.

Wish you were here
I'm exactly what Mrs May called a citizen of nowhere,
of everywhere. But I would regard that as a prize,
or badge of honour. Her malign throwing
half of the world onto the bonfire.

If you'd asked me three years ago I would have
said, European first with a piece of paper that said,
British. The whole thing about nationality I dislike
so, I would have said I was European: The mass

that is the whole of Europe.
Switzerland, Norway, parts of Western Russia. Not
here. This could be Israel or Jordan or the Gulf.
This could be Syria.

Is it cultural? I suppose but it's a blend.
Of culture, of space, of being able to be with people
who seem, not so much the same because they're not, but
one is loosely thinking along the same lines.

I think of the postcards I used to send.
Remember those postcards? White on both
sides. Address on one side and instead of a pretty

picture, I just put: wish you were here.

Kalimera
We've tried, wherever we've lived,
to be a part of the community.
We've become part of the scene.

We start with kalimera. We don't
want to be Europeans. Barnier.
Smart Alec Frenchman. Boo hiss.

I hope that Theresa May finds
Margaret Thatcher's old handbag
and gives him a good clout

in the vital spot. When he doubles
over knee to chin, then we have
won. We have got to win.

All that 'we once ruled the world' thing
I was repulsed by that. I have been here so long that I feel,
people don't really think of me as English. It's 'Jesus the Brits'

then, 'Well not you'. Like I have been decontaminated.
Ireland has been good to me; I became proud

of England here, embracing it as tolerant of eccentric
people. But now I find it embarrassing, this stuff

going on. Like madness. God. I have mixed
feelings about England. I have family

who are, like, 'We don't get anything so,
yeah, we're telling them to piss off'.

The whole thing is about the English search for identity;
their 'we once ruled the world' thing, spilling out as Brexit.

Play and screenplay writing in data analysis

Play and screenplay writing has been shown to make a very useful contribution to analytic work in social research. The American research methods expert Johnny Saldaña defines theatrically written work as ethnodrama and performed work as ethnotheatre (2016:12–13). However, he also notes that there are dozens of terms relating to ethnodrama or ethnotheatre, or denoting specific variants of these techniques, so evidently the terminology here is far from fixed. The common factor is that they are all based on real-life events and interactions (Saldaña 2016:14).

Lisbeth Berbary, who is based in Canada, used screenplay writing in her analysis of data from an ethnographic study on sorority women. She began with a conventional analytic approach of creating codes and categories. However, she found this didn't sit well with her poststructuralist feminist stance, which privileged complexity and multiplicity. Berbary felt that she was 'taking moments that were overlapping, contradictory, in motion, and experienced simultaneously and attempting to categorize them ... into concrete, stationary, segregated groups' (2011:187). So she looked for a way to deconstruct her categories and to represent the complex multiplicity of her participants' experiences. She wanted 'a literary form that allowed for movement through settings, thick descriptive storytelling, the use of quotes, and the integration of my own voice' (Berbary 2011:187) and eventually chose to create an ethnographic screenplay. She made the screenplay out of quotes from interview transcripts and passages from observational field notes, and rearranged the quotes and passages to create a script. This was made up of three 'acts', each containing four scenes and addressing one of Berbary's three research questions. Each scene explored the relationships between Berbary's categories of analysis. Here is an excerpt:

Summer

I feel like I'm stuffed in this dress. I can barely breathe.

She begins to adjust the dress in the mirror, pulling it up and re-organizing her breasts.

Summer

My boobs are everywhere. I even have them in the back. Wait till I have to sit down, I'll probably explode.

Roommate S chuckles, recognizing that Summer has a good sense of humor about her size.

Roommate S

Better watch those boobs. How soon you forget your Rush debacle!

Roommate S says half joking, remembering that someone tattled on Summer for having a dress that was too revealing.

Summer

You know I really can't help it. What, do you want me to wear a sack?

Roommate C

Maybe you better. At least pull it up a bit. You don't want people to think you're trashy or that you're asking for it.

Roommate C isn't joking. Summer is a little surprised and offended. She feels the need to defend herself.

Summer

It's not like I act slutty. The problem is like a combo of dressing and behaviour. Everyone knows I'm a dead end. I don't sleep around like some people.
(Berbary 2011:192)

Screenplay writing enabled Berbary to incorporate setting, action, dialogue and 'director's comments', and to combine data from multiple sources into a single action or interaction. This helped her to convey more fully the systems, perspectives and interpretations that she perceived within her research. Her work has interesting parallels with the approaches to verbatim theatre we explore later, and with 'found poetry' (shown in 'Migrants like these' by Katherine Collins).

Researchers wanting to use ethnodrama can take simpler approaches than Berbary's. You could write a dramatic monologue based on interview data to depict an individual or composite participant (Saldaña 2016:63). Or you could write a dialogue between two or more individual or composite participants, based on data from interviews, focus groups, or observational research (Saldaña 2016:99). As in Berbary's work, this can help to reveal multiple perspectives, contradictions, tensions and interpretations.

Plays can also be written collaboratively with participants. This draws on the work of the Brazilian theatre professional and activist Ernesto Boal who pioneered methods of applied theatre. Collaborative playwriting can be time-consuming to do well. Ruth Raynor spent two years writing a fictional play with her participants (Raynor 2019:695–6) (though it can be done in a few weeks, see Nordström 2016:2–3). This approach combines thinking with doing, and can create a safe, egalitarian space which enables 'critique, intuition, and analysis' by everyone involved (Raynor 2019:704).

Dissemination

Whenever researchers work on ways to communicate findings there are always compromises to be made (Pickering and Kara 2017:299). Reports written in great detail are unlikely to find many readers. Conversely, short videos can only convey a few key points, but may reach a much wider audience. Such compromises also apply when using creative writing to help communicate findings. As always, though, the use of creative methods doesn't change the fundamental principles of good practice in research. Here that means figuring out who your audience(s) are and how you can best meet their needs.

Creative writing has many roles to play in communicating research findings. This section explores some particularly innovative communication of social research findings by reviewing engagement through stories, which underpin most forms of human communication, and through comedy, which has great potential. Creative writing even has a role to play in exploring and explaining research methods – as this book demonstrates – and in drawing conclusions about methods from research experience.

Visual methods of writing for dissemination

Visual methods of writing for dissemination include: comics and graphic novels; animations; cartoons and comic strips; and zines.

A comic may be a collection of comic strips telling different stories, or a single longer story in sequential art which, if long enough, may be called a graphic novel. These can be hand-drawn or produced digitally using software such as Comic Life. Comics and graphic novels have considerable potential for use at all stages of the research process (Weaver-Hightower 2013:265), in particular the dissemination of findings (Morris et al 2012; Priego 2016). In terms of creative writing in social research, comics are often used for dissemination (for example, Rainford 2019:x–xi), and they are also used for teaching in academia (Duncan et al 2016:42). Graphic novels cover all sorts of subjects related to academia, such as politics, history, health, society and sexuality. There are even graphic novels about how to create comics and graphic novels: the seminal *Understanding Comics* (1994) and *Making Comics* (2006) by Scott McCloud. The education researcher Nick Sousanis created his doctoral dissertation in the form of a graphic novel, *Unflattening*; this was later published by Harvard University Press (Sousanis 2015).

As with other visually creative forms of writing, discussed later in this chapter, writing comics and graphic novels has an integral visual element which makes the process different from writing forms that rely on text alone. Devices such as the lengthy interior monologue or chunks of wordy dialogue don't work too well in comics. In fact, when writing for comics, the less text the better. If you do need a section of monologue or dialogue, think about how to change the visuals – use close-ups, different angles and so on – to support the movement in the text.

If you can write and draw, or have (or can acquire) skills in using digital drawing software, then you can make comics yourself. If you can write but not draw, or vice versa, you will need to find one or more collaborators. This is normal in the world of comics: for example, the author Neil Gaiman worked with a range of artists to make his well-regarded Sandman series.

Comics and graphic novels use sequential art to tell a story. There are also graphic books which, rather than using sequential art as such, use a lot of cartoon illustrations or very short comic strips to help convey text-based information. These also have creative potential for social research. One good example is the best-selling *Queer: A Graphic History* (2016) by Meg-John Barker and Jules Scheele. It is published by Icon Books who also publish the Graphic Guides series of short books on various topics, some of which are related to social research such as ethics and feminism.

A multi-disciplinary team of researchers created a graphic novel to communicate the findings of their research into the life courses of homeless people in Stoke-on-Trent, an industrial city in the centre of England. These researchers collected life stories from over 100 homeless people (Breckenridge 2014:106). They decided to present their findings in graphic novel form as five 'life stories', which were drawn by a design graduate and published under the title *Somewhere Nowhere: Lives Without Homes* (Morris et al 2012). Lead researcher Philip Brown described the team's motivation for creating a graphic novel as being 'collectively tired of talking to the usual suspects, in the usual ways and failing to change much' (Brown 2013). The graphic novel received a very different reception, according to Brown:

> The reception to the novel has been overwhelming [sic] positive. Homeless people have complimented its production and those people who have long been embedded within the homelessness sector have been very supportive. People appear to be finding their own ways to use the material. Most talk about its use in schools to help explain homelessness and all its complexity. Others within the homelessness sector have talked about how their family members have become engaged with it which has led to new discoveries about the work they do and the issues they face. (Brown 2013)

A reviewer described it as 'a particularly effective means to facilitate greater understanding among the general public' (Breckenridge 2014:108).

Gemma Sou and Felix Aponte-Gonzalez, based in Manchester, England, created a 20-page comic of their research findings. They spent a year doing ethnographic research in Puerto Rico after Hurricane Maria, following 16 low-income families to find out how they recovered from the disaster. Rather than telling the stories of actual individuals or families, Gemma Sou fictionalised the research findings, creating a composite family and telling their story. This enabled her to create ethical and respectful representations of her research participants (Sou and Douglas 2019:1). She commissioned a local artist, John Cei Douglas, to collaborate with her on making the comic *After Maria: Everyday Recovery from Disaster*. It is free to download in English and in Spanish and easily found through an internet search.

One reason comics make these kinds of research findings more accessible is that they enable readers to share people's experiences more directly and fully than text alone. Also they enable readers to 'see' places and encounters that they might not be able to see in real life, such as family members interacting in their home or aid workers handing out supplies in a disaster zone.

Helen, one of the authors of this book, also writes comics. For her, the challenge and delight of the form is that almost anything is possible. As long as you can bring your reader with you, you can jump between planets or centuries, invent a miniature ecosystem living underneath a toenail, give voice to inanimate objects. There are no limits except the limits of imagination and comprehension. The extent to which comics writers imagine the visuals varies, but they all do provide some guidance for their artist collaborators. There is no set format for comic scripts, as there is for play and screenplay scripts, but you can find some options online. Here is part of a script Helen wrote for a short comic to support the teaching of qualitative interviewing. You can see the resulting graphic in Figure 4.2.

First panel (half page width): Owen is ringing Ella's doorbell. Thought bubble: I hope I can do this …

Second panel (half page width): Ella answers the door with a welcoming face. Owen: Hi, I'm Owen, from the college.

Third panel (full page width): Ella leads Owen into her living room. Ella: Would you like a cup of tea? And some cake?

Fifth panel (half page width): Owen sitting in an armchair. Owen: Yes please.

Sixth panel (half page width): Ella, back view, heading for the kitchen. Ella: I won't be a minute.

This comic, *Conversation With A Purpose*, was inspired by research findings disseminated through pedagogy presentations at the Research Methods Festival in Bath, England, in 2016. These presentations disclosed that researchers had found a big problem in the teaching of research methods: the gap between the classroom and practice. Helen realised immediately that comics had a potential role to play in filling that gap. She worked with Sophie Jackson, a third-year student from the Cartoon and Comic Arts BA course at Staffordshire University, who drew the comic. It depicts a student's first interview in the community and includes discussion questions. It is free to download online and is now being used by teachers of research methods around the world (Kara and Brooks 2020). This comic enables readers to 'see' a student doing an interview. As a result they can consider aspects of, and issues raised, by qualitative interviewing that would not arise in classroom practice.

As well as comics and graphic novels, researchers are using other visually creative methods from animation to zines. Animation can be a great way to disseminate

Figure 4.2: Page 5 of *Conversation With A Purpose.* **Written by Helen Kara, artwork by Sophie Jackson.**

research findings, potentially reaching a very wide audience. On the other hand, it is time-consuming and can be very expensive to create. Also, an animation can only make a small number of points, so much detail and nuance may be lost. Yet it has a lot of potential for conveying research findings to non-academic audiences.

There are many different types of animation such as hand-drawn, stop motion, and digital animation. You can animate two-dimensional or three-dimensional figures, such as drawn or cut-out paper figures, clay figures, or puppets. Also, with stop motion animation, you can animate objects of all kinds, from rocks to dolls to kitchen utensils.

Nicole Vaughn and her colleagues spent a year developing a digital animation to disseminate the results of one project within their long-term community-based participatory research (CBPR) into youth violence in Philadelphia, US. They consulted with and involved members of the community throughout the process in a range of different ways. In particular, community members first suggested that animation be used, and were involved in selecting narratives from the research data for development in the animation. A professional animator was hired to create the animation, which linked the narratives with 'evidence-based action steps that could be taken by youth, adults, and public officials to support youth and reduce violence in the community' (Vaughn et al 2013:33). The animation was shown at a community event and disseminated through Facebook. Also, the main characters from the animation were used in anti-violence advertisements for use on Philadelphia's public transport systems, reaching around one and a half million transport users per month. The researchers attributed the success of this animation project to careful listening and a focus on quality while staying true to the principles of CBPR (Vaughn et al 2013:37).

A cartoon is a single illustration, usually with a few accompanying words, designed to convey information. This enables the writer to make a complicated point more quickly and effectively than by using a written paragraph of prose. Perhaps for this reason, cartoons have been used for hundreds of years to communicate news, satire and propaganda (Duncan et al 2016:14–15). Cartoons are rarely used in research, though they have considerable potential (Bartlett 2012:214).

A comic strip is a short sequence of cartoons that tell a story, usually in three to six cartoons known as 'panels'. Comic strips are used in children's comics and adults' newspapers. Some are very long-lived and well known, such as *Peanuts* and *Doonesbury*. Comic strips are also used in a range of ways in research. They have been used to illustrate points in doctoral theses (for example, Harron 2016:95,114), to formulate cartoon abstracts for academic journal articles such as those published in a wide range of disciplines by Taylor & Francis, and in data collection (Wall et al 2017:214). Some academic comic strips are published online as webcomics, for example XKCD and PhD Comics.

'Zine' is an abbreviation of 'magazine' and zines are a form of 'citizen media' (Bold 2017:218). Zines were originally handmade self-published booklets with tiny print runs of 100 or fewer. Some scholars trace them back to the 1930s

Figure 4.3: Research findings by Arthur Horner.

Source: THES / News Licensing

(Stockburger 2015:222; Bold 2017:219). One major subset, fanzines, were produced by fans of public figures or groups, such as musicians or sports teams, and handed out to other fans at events such as gigs or matches. Another popular zine genre is the 'perzine' or personal, autobiographical zine (Bold 2017:224).

Zine publishing has expanded hugely in the last couple of decades (Barton and Olson 2019:205). These days, zines may have much larger print runs or may be digital. Zines are available on almost every subject and are studied in a range of social sciences, arts and humanities disciplines (Stockburger 2015:223). They may be produced collaboratively, or as an edited text with one or more editors and various contributors, or be sole authored. These days they are sold in bookshops, archived in libraries and distributed online for digital reading or self-printing worldwide. All kinds of zines are collected and stored by university libraries and used by researchers as data. These are often rich primary sources: many are created by marginalised people who might be difficult for researchers to reach in person (Barton and Olson 2019:206). More recently, zines are being used for other academic purposes, for example, edited collections such as the digital *So Fi* zine (sofizine.com) which publishes creative sociological writing bi-annually, or authored works such as the hard copy *Market Café Magazine* on the topic of data visualisation.

The importance of zines is that they offer 'an alternative outlet for niche topics, or writers and writing, that are ignored by mainstream media' and 'offer the opportunity for connection, community, and networking between those interested in these diverse topics' (Bold 2017:215). *So Fi* was launched in June 2017. It is produced digitally and can be read online or printed by readers. Up to mid-2019, when issue 5 was available, a new edition had been produced every six months. At the time of writing, its website describes *So Fi* as 'an indie publication for social science and arts cross-disciplinary inquiry' which includes 'short stories, cartoons, photo essays, poetry, mini zines, sketches, and other creative works'. It has featured work by some notable academics with international reputations including Les Back, Howard Becker and Raewyn Connell. And sometimes the mainstream media picks up ideas, articles, or people from the zine world. Ashleigh Watson founded *So Fi* when she was a doctoral student and later became fiction editor of *The Sociological Review*.

There is lots of scope for creating and using zines in social research, for example, as data construction with participants or for disseminating findings. There are no hard-and-fast rules about how to make a zine or what a zine should look like. However, they almost always contain a lot of text, and zine makers (or 'zinesters' (Bold 2017:219)) do a lot of writing (Stockburger 2015:224). Anyone can make or contribute to a zine (Bold 2017:227); if you want to give it a try, there is lots of advice online. Also, as ideas about the goals, form, content and quality of zines vary between zine makers (Stockburger 2015:226), you can evidently make your own decisions.

CREATIVE WRITING IN PRACTICE

Your stories are moving: animation and affect in creative research dissemination *by Stacy Bias*[2]

> **Stacy Bias** is a fat and queer activist, artist, and animator based in London, UK. In this piece she tells the stories behind her animation *Flying While Fat*. She explains how animation proved useful in deepening ethical collaboration and protecting participant anonymity while also capturing and holding public attentions in ways that bypassed reflexive stigma to open a space of empathic dialogue.

"I just want you to be comfortable," my grandmother said, wincing a sorry-not-sorry apology as she brushed past me in line and handed the boarding agent a second airplane ticket bearing my name.

Sucker punch. Rush of blood. Confusion. Then clarity.

The second ticket was for me. For the *rest* of me. For the bits of me that were *too much.*

Next to the glamour of my clean-cut, god-fearing, waif-thin extended family, my fat, tattooed, queer body had always been a tension. But in that moment, it ballooned into an awkward, galumphing alien. I lumbered onto the plane woozy with anger and humiliation and sat as far from that empty seat as I could, determined to prove I fit.

Figure 4.4: Inspiration doll by Alke Gröppel-Wegener, created in response to this piece by Stacy Bias. Inspiration dolls comment on and play with genres of creative writing.

And I did fit. But only just. The drinks cart bashed my elbow. The seatbelt required an extender. The tray table wouldn't open. My hips bumped seat backs as I travelled the aisle.

[2] This contribution should be cited as follows: Bias, S. (2021) 'Your stories are moving: animation and affect in creative research dissemination'. In Phillips, R. and Kara, H. *Creative Writing for Social Research*. Bristol: Policy Press.

Bookended by my grandmother's poorly executed good intentions and the reality of my slowly bruising thighs, I awoke to a dreadful possibility. Was I too fat to fly?

I didn't fly again for seven years.

To resume flying required a personal transformation – not bodily, but politically. Thanks to my queer, outsider identity, I stumbled across Fat Activism.[3] I came to understand my body as political and my worth as intrinsic. I learned that fatness was a complicated moral issue and mainstream ideologies of fatness ignored systemic and institutionalised inequalities limiting access to affordable, healthy foods, quality health and preventative care, adequate employment and even reliable housing. I became an organiser and soon received invitations to speak publicly. With advice from fellow activists, I accepted and slowly began to travel again – ultimately moving abroad to continue my education.

To manage my anxiety about flying as a fat passenger, I kept track of each flight I took – airplane models, routes, what worked, what didn't. By the time I moved abroad, I'd amassed a wealth of information and wrote a blog post[4] to share it with others. I also formed a Facebook group[5] to help people connect. Membership quickly grew to over 11,000, with participants asking questions, offering logistical tips, flight reviews, and sharing troubling and triumphant tales.

Through repetition, the toll that flying takes on fat passengers became glaringly obvious. For those who refused to fly: regret, grief, lost personal and economic opportunity, and barriers to participation in an increasingly global society. For those who did fly: stress, anxiety, exhaustion, physical pain and injury, added cost, dehumanisation, and sometimes humiliation. As importantly, I saw the powerful resilience and creativity modelled by those who chose to fly despite hostile conditions. Their tenacity showed that resistance comes in many forms, not least simply believing one has a right to exist in spaces where one's body has been designed out of intelligibility.

I determined the best way to continue my activism was to honour and amplify the voices of these fat passengers who were consistently working to render themselves visible and valued, not merely as consumers but as creative cultural collaborators.

---

[3] Fat Activism is a social justice movement rooted in 1970s feminism that seeks to articulate and combat discrimination based on size. Fat Activists object to terms like 'overweight', 'plus-size' and 'obesity', which imply a normative weight which some people are 'over' or in excess of. All people have fat, and societal convention decides how much is too much and who is 'obese'. Fat Activists choose the word fat as a reclamation and a denial of subjective societal judgments.

[4] http://stacybias.net/2012/01/flying–while–fat–superfat–tips–for–international–air–travel/

[5] https://www.facebook.com/groups/flyingwhilefat/

I chose Flying While Fat as the topic for my undergraduate dissertation and conducted a mixed methods survey of 795 participants, and interviews with a further 28. After I completed my degree, I reached out to Dr Bethan Evans, a Senior Lecturer in Human Geography at University of Liverpool, in hopes of collaborating to get the research published. Thankfully, Bethan agreed. And while I was thrilled at the thought of publishing academically and adding weight to criticisms of airline policy, I also realised that the voices of my fellow fat flyers needed to be heard.

According to Henri Lefebvre, '(social) space is a (social) product' (1991:26). Space is constructed not only by the requirements of its function, but according to the needs of the bodies that society deems legitimate. Fat bodies, despite much research to the contrary, are assumed to exist only as a result of sustained personal failure. That perception of failure sanctions the wilful exclusion of their access requirements. Each year, airplane seats are narrowed, pitch is shrunk, and new inventions to maximise profit (like 2018's 'standing seats' with a shocking 23 inch pitch[6]) are all implemented, each with an understanding of median body size that does not include very fat bodies (or very tall bodies, or disabled bodies, or injured bodies). Failure to comply with these shifting medians results in open hostility, often not towards the airlines, whose pursuit of profit comes at the expense of everyone's space and comfort, but towards those individuals who inevitably encroach the shrinking boundaries.

To create real change, I realised, would require not only critique of airline policy from within the legitimacy of academia, but also a groundswell of empathy and understanding in the mainstream. I could think of no better way to build empathy than by amplifying the wise and creative voices of my participants.

I pored back over the data and interviews from my dissertation, searching for inspiration. There were rich seams of experience and intellect to mine but I also found several challenges.

Moving and insightful as the interviews were, when I went back to watch the recordings, something seemed lost in translation. The static backdrop and awkwardness of the interview setting flattened the interviewees and felt tense to watch. And in the absence of other contextual shots to weave together a larger narrative about their lives, the interviewees seemed reduced to 'talking heads' rather than dynamic beings engaged in a living environment.

As well, some of the violence described by participants was subtle and visual – facial expressions, nuanced body language, or actual physical violence masquerading as easily dismissible action (for example, aggressively forcing down an armrest into the body of a fat passenger). Some of the actions taken for self-preservation by

---

[6] https://edition.cnn.com/travel/article/standing-up-airplane-seat-testing/index.html

participants were similarly symbolic – "making themselves small", hugging themselves, leaning away, or trying to "leave their bodies". These can be described verbally but lose emotional resonance without visual context.

It seemed that, in the medium of film specifically, *telling* was neither as emotionally affective nor as intellectually engaging as *showing*. I saw no promise in the interviews as they were for capturing and holding the attention of an audience who likely already held negative perceptions of the storytellers themselves. To transform understanding one must first capture attention and, once captured, hold it through to completion. As the appearance of fat individuals is the fact of their stigmatisation, the complexity of showing is multiplied by the audience's ideologically constructed unwillingness to see or to be moved.

Additionally, some of the participants were feeling nervous about sharing their experiences of stigma in public. Goffman describes stigma as having a visible or discoverable attribute that sets an individual apart in a way that can be considered negative, thus rendering the individual seemingly tainted or less valuable (Goffman 2009, ch1, section 1, para 4). My participants were expressing genuine vulnerability and some wished to remain anonymous to avoid trolls on social media.

In the end, I had a wealth of powerful and beautiful stories told on poor quality video, by participants who didn't wish to be seen, to an audience who might reject them on sight before their words had a chance to sink in. I needed a creative solution.

Figure 4.5: Still from *Flying While Fat* by Stacy Bias.

Animation seemed a perfect choice. Animating the interviews would allow me to retain the participants' words and voices – while also safeguarding their identities. Using animated characters (based as closely or loosely on the actual participant as each desired) would allow me to create visual context, body language, and symbolism. And the medium itself, by virtue of its creativity and general appeal, could possibly create a sort of emotional side door through which to guide a potentially judgemental audience past their initial reflexive dismissal and into a space where empathy might be engaged.

Bethan and I won a small pot of funding. It allowed for publishing academic papers and creating the animation in collaboration with Liverpool's DADA Fest (Deaf and Disability Arts Festival). With funding secured, I began in earnest.

As an anthropology student, I was inspired by French anthropologist Jean Rouch who, in answer to criticisms of anthropology as the 'handmaiden of colonialism', was especially devoted to collaboration, transparency, and the incorporation of informant critiques throughout the process of creation. Rouch's method, called 'shared anthropology', allowed for a more reflexive practice and a deeper ethic while also offering informants greater agency in their representation (Sjberg 2008:230–9). I was similarly inspired by Afonso and Ramos regarding the unique possibilities presented by illustration as a methodology, specifically in relation to the way detailed processes allow ongoing collaboration and offer space and time through which to ask deeper questions about spatiality, materiality, and memory (Afonso and Ramos 2004). Animation is by its nature iterative. It is necessarily tedious and progress is invariably slow. This pace naturally creates multiple stopping points that can be utilised to share progress and request feedback. As I animated each scene, I was able to check in with each participant, asking deeper questions I'd not have thought to ask in an interview setting where my mind filled in the blanks with assumption, projection and my own interpretation. The end result of this effort was a truly collaborative, ethical presentation of participants' lived experience.

After its premiere with DADA Fest and brief exhibitions at the Tate Liverpool and the Bluecoat gallery, we launched the animation for free online.[7] I anticipated it would be well received amongst the fat activists and individuals for whom the themes resonated but I was amazed to find the press also picked it up with great enthusiasm. Mainstream outlets like Buzzfeed, *Cosmopolitan*, and *People* magazine delivered surprisingly detailed and sympathetic coverage alongside more traditionally empathic mainstays. Our direct YouTube views jumped to 300,000 in less than 2 weeks, then hundreds of thousands more across embedded media platforms – ultimately reaching a viewership of over 2 million in less than 3 weeks. The end result was a powerful, emotionally resonant contribution to the public conversation around airline equality.

---

[7] http://stacybias.net/flying-while-fat-animation/

The cinematic experience opens a space beyond simple statements. It is emotional. And where emotions 'do things', where they are crucial to political formations and understandings, where they create subjects and subjectivities that form systems and hierarchies of power, any opportunity to enhance empathy and understanding is a powerful tool (Ahmed 2001:10–11). Grimshaw notes that Rouch used cinema to 'evoke a notion of expanded community' where each viewer took part in a collective ritual (Grimshaw 2001, ch 6, para 54). That transformative power also lies within animation. As a method, it can also be transformative for the relationship between researcher and participant, offering new opportunities for collaboration and ethical consideration. In the creative dissemination of research, animation is a powerful tool to create impact and understanding, to make data 'real' and resonant, accessible and emotionally intelligible.

There's no greater testament to the possibilities of this impact than the stories I've heard since the launch of the animation. My favourite comes from a former neighbour whose profession finds him flying frequently. A few weeks after the animation launched, we passed each other in the hallway.

"You know, I just flew back from LA," he said, "and I have to tell you something! I was stuck in a middle seat and I was tired and cranky and this woman sat down next to me and – I'm embarrassed to say this, especially to you – but she was, you know, bigger? And my immediate reaction was like 'Ugh. Why me?', you know?"

I narrowed my eyes but carried on listening.

"And then I remembered your animation. I started thinking about what it must be like for her. I didn't really know what to do to make it better for either of us. I mean, I couldn't move and I couldn't make the seats bigger. But I figured I could at least let her know that I wasn't mad about sharing space with her. So I just smiled and said hello, you know? And I think we both felt a lot better."

Performance for dissemination

Kay Inckle's 'Imprisoned by metrics' in Chapter 2 uses the performative literary device of monologue, a word derived from Greek words meaning 'one speaks'. Researchers have also been using dialogue to give voice to participants and others, including themselves, since the 1990s (Gergen and Gergen 2019:59). Dialogue is derived from Greek words meaning 'speaks across, speaks between'. Written dialogue is a fiction technique for depicting a conversation between two or more people. Well-crafted dialogue seems realistic despite being much more purposeful and fluent than actual speech (Bochner and Ellis 2016:115).

Researchers use dialogue in a range of ways. Arthur Bochner and Carolyn Ellis's *Evocative Autoethnography* (2016), a textbook which we discussed in the section on autoethnography in Chapter 2, begins and ends with dialogue and uses dialogue liberally throughout. This makes the writing more energetic and engaging. Twenty years earlier, Karen Fox used a form of dialogue to present some findings from her research into child sexual abuse. She follows the example of Ronai (1995) to present a 'layered account' (Fox 1996:330) by presenting dialogue in three columns: one for a male abuser, one for the woman who survived his abuse, and one for Fox herself as a researcher who is also a survivor of child sexual abuse. Fox (1996:331) asserts that this approach gives equal billing to each viewpoint and so 'draws the reader into divergent perspectives of abuse'. It is certainly compelling to read. For Fox: 'The tension created by the layered method reflects the gap that often exists between the lived experiences of survivors and the codification of those experiences by researchers' (1996:330).

Dialogue is a central feature of plays and screenplays. As we have seen, play and screenplay writing are increasingly being used in social research for analytic purposes, and they can also underpin the presentation and dissemination of findings. These techniques can be used effectively without working towards an actual production; in fact, that approach can enable more flexibility and creativity (Berbary 2011:187). There is scope for researchers to make 'experiments in drama' (Gergen and Gergen 2012:120). However, where researchers also have the requisite theatrical skills or can work with theatre professionals, dramatic presentations of findings can be very appealing for audiences (Gergen and Gergen 2012:161; Salvatore 2019:286).

A play script is for a theatrical production, typically for performance on a stage in front of an audience (though some plays are written for radio, TV and other media). This imposes constraints: all of the action has to happen in one place, or the writer has to build in time for cumbersome scene changes or find a venue with a revolving stage. Usually there are only a handful of actors and it is difficult to have them perform actions such as swimming or flying with any credibility. There are also constraints with screenplay writing, which produces the scripts for films, but they are far fewer, particularly in these days of computer-generated imagery. In a film, you can move from one continent to another in seconds, live on Mars, or include an entire shoal of mermaids. There are conventions for writing plays and screenplays which are beyond the scope of this book to describe, but the information is freely available online.

Here are two examples which were not intended for production. We have seen that Lisbeth Berbary used screenplay writing as an analytic technique in her ethnographic study of sorority women. She chose this form because it 'allowed for movement through settings, thick descriptive storytelling, the use of quotes, and the integration of my own voice' (Berbary 2011:187). It also meant she could show readers the experiences of sorority women rather than just telling about them (Berbary 2011:195). Berbary presented her writing to her participants and others. She reports that many of her participants enjoyed reading the screenplay, and non-academic readers found it surprisingly accessible. Then Jocene Vallack, a former actor and director who brought her theatre experience to social research, studied the university life of students in Tanzania. She presented her findings as a play script in the academic journal *Creative Approaches to Research*; she describes the play as 'a metastory based on interview data and autoethnographies' which forms 'a collage of narratives' (Vallack 2012:32). Vallack's work, too, is enjoyable and accessible.

Verbatim plays are those based on, or only using, the spoken words of real people. These are a form of documentary theatre, with speech recorded in some prior context and then formed into a play for actors to perform. The form originated in Stoke-on-Trent in the 1970s, where Peter Cheeseman, founding director of the city's Victoria Theatre, combined his theatrical expertise with the 'non-theatrical tradition of social observation and oral documentation' (Paget 1987:318) to create *Fight For Shelton Bar*. This verbatim play about the closure of a local steelworks was performed in the city for local people, including steelworkers. In a more recent research context, a verbatim play was produced by Michael Richardson to present some of the findings from his research into intergenerational issues with Irish men. Three of his participants were grandfather, father and son from one family, and Richardson used their words to write a play that was professionally acted and directed. The director chose to rearrange parts of the script for artistic reasons, and it was also shared with participants for feedback (Richardson 2015:625). The researcher's voice is not included, which allowed the audience to feel that they were involved in the research encounter (Richardson 2015:626). Instead, the actor spoke into a Dictaphone, which created a sense of intimacy, as if the audience were witnessing a private act.

Another option is for research data to be used to identify settings and interactions which are then presented dramatically by researchers (Sangha et al 2012:287) or by professionals (Goldstein and Wickett 2009:1553; Jenkins 2015:64) or even volunteers from the audience. Cate Watson applied scriptwriting in a conference presentation to help convey the experience of a mother whose child had been diagnosed with Attention Deficit Hyperactivity Disorder (ADHD). From the mother's perspective, the diagnosis resulted from trivial events such as the child forgetting his school tie. Watson reports that the educational, medical and psychiatric professions jointly constructed this 'deviant family' (2011:402). She fictionalised the mother's narrative, created several characters, and used satire to point out the absurdity in the situation. Then, at the conference, Watson asked members of the audience to volunteer to perform the roles from the script she had written with no rehearsal or direction. As a result of this reading, Watson later refined the script, which demonstrates the possibility of continuing to explore and interpret findings through the processes of presentation and dissemination.

There is a specific form of verbatim theatre known as 'recorded delivery' that can be used for the presentation and dissemination of research findings. The recorded delivery method was developed by theatre director and playwright Alecky Blythe, inspired by a workshop run in London by theatre practitioner Mark Wing-Davey, who set participants the task of recording real-life conversations and then re-presenting them as drama (Shah and Greer 2018:60). In its simplest form, the recorded delivery method involves transmitting the speech of research participants into the headphones of actors who reproduce that speech as closely as possible, mimicking the original speakers. The creative intervention is in the selection, editing and arrangement of material from recorded interviews to produce a dramatic composition (Shah and Greer 2018:61). Productions are carefully staged, using various theatrical devices (such as the same actor playing several characters) to demonstrate that the creators and presenters of the work are aiming for authentic rather than literal truth. Sonali Shah and Stephen Greer worked with disabled-led theatre company Birds of Paradise to use recorded delivery to dramatise the social worlds of survivors from the polio epidemic of the 1940s and 1950s. This had two positive effects. First, the actors gained a greater awareness and understanding of the lived realities of the survivors. Second, staged performance and video helped to change public perceptions of people with disabilities away from the negative representations offered by popular culture (Shah and Greer 2018:66).

It is also possible to create drama from prose text sources, even if they are long, dry, and hard to digest. *The Road to Health: A Final Report on School Safety* runs to four volumes and almost 600 pages. It contains the findings of an investigation into school safety which was commissioned by the Toronto District School Board in response to the fatal shooting of 15-year-old Jordan Manners on-school premises. These findings are undoubtedly important, but a four-volume 595-page report is not accessible.

Tara Goldstein is a 'teacher educator, playwright, and performed ethnographer' (Goldstein and Wickett 2009:1553) based in Toronto. She wanted to encourage teacher candidates and other teacher educators to discuss the investigation's findings and its key recommendations. Goldstein used her theatre skills to adapt the report into a script for a 30-minute drama performance. She did not find it easy to distil a big report into a short performance (Goldstein and Wickett 2009:1556) and made a set of decisions to help with the process. She defined the audience for whom she was writing, and decided which of several stories in the report she would tell. She included public responses to the report in the script, as well as extracts from the report itself. She chose characters, one of which was herself as narrator. This was intended to highlight the fact that the performance was just one individual's interpretation of part of a long and complex report.

Goldstein's framing of her task helped her to complete a script. She then held three readings where local educators and parents were able to give feedback. After each reading she made revisions in line with the feedback she had received, and the fourth draft of her script was performed as a 'rehearsed reading' in front of 500 teacher candidates at a conference on 'safe schools' (Goldstein and Wickett 2009:1553). Goldstein didn't use professional actors, but she did enlist the support of an MA student and theatre artist, Jocelyn Wickett, as stage director. The staging was simple, focusing on the idea that the audience should understand and value their role as active listeners (Goldstein and Wickett 2009:1563). The performance was followed by workshops on topics selected to enable the discussion of practical ways to deal with some of the issues raised by the performance.

Goldstein wrote about her process to offer 'other research-based artists' a way to work with such reports to help audiences engage with the issues they raise (Goldstein and Wickett 2009:1565). This is helpful, not least because it underlines the point that theatre is one of the more complex forms that researchers can use, and it helps if at least one person on the team has good theatre skills.

For participatory researcher Victoria Foster, it was her participants who decided they wanted to present their findings as a pantomime. Pantomime plays with cross-gender acting, jokes (often topical), songs, audience interaction, and slapstick comedy. Foster was working with parents and carers involved in a local Sure Start programme to help them collaborate in research on the programme's effectiveness (2013:37). (Sure Start was an initiative to support families with pre-school children in deprived areas of England.) At the start of Foster's doctoral research project with the programme, a drama group was set up for local families – parents, carers and children. A local amateur dramatist, Diane, ran the sessions and helped the group to script, rehearse and perform a pantomime, *Hansel and Gretel Grow Up* (Foster 2013:39). This was performed to local people including Sure Start staff, health professionals and local councillors, and was well received.

Foster then tried bringing in an expert in forum theatre to work with the group using Ernesto Boal's methods of applied theatre. However, participants didn't enjoy this; they wanted their drama activities to provide an escape rather than focusing on real-life issues. They decided to produce a second pantomime, *The Wizard of Us*, to present the findings of their research, again with help from Diane. For Foster, this was only a partial success. The performance had resonance and authenticity, and empowered local individuals and communities. However, it presented an unrealistically positive view of the Sure Start programme, glossing over some of the very real problems such as tensions between service users and programme staff (Foster 2013:46). Foster had been unable to persuade her co-researchers to reflect critically on the research findings and didn't feel able to challenge them more strongly because that would have compromised the participatory methodology. However, she concluded that, on any future occasion, she would include a discussion with the audience after the performance to enable more critical reflection on the findings (Foster 2013:48). It is already clear that Goldstein found it useful to get feedback on her script in draft form from the audiences at the readings she held, so Foster's conclusions add weight to the argument that research-based drama presentations can benefit from input from a wider group, ideally before or at the very least immediately after a performance.

The work of Mercilee Jenkins bears this out. Jenkins is an established playwright and professor of speech communication, based in San Francisco. Her play, *Spirit of Detroit*, began life as a solo performance piece and evolved through a two-hander into an ensemble play. The work is about her research into the racial, class, and gender-based divisions in Detroit over the last half-century. It starts with the 1967 riot or uprising (depending on your perspective) that followed police killings of three unarmed African Americans (Jenkins 2015:65). The first solo performance was in 2007, then the ensemble play premiered at the University of Michigan in 2013 and later played the Charles H. Wright Museum of African American History in 2014. Audience reactions were influential in Jenkins' revisions of her work between performances over these seven years. At the Wright Museum, there were not only performances but also 'talkbacks' (Jenkins 2015:65). These events brought people from around Detroit together and resulted in a later oral history project at the Museum on the 1967 riot/uprising.

Comedy in dissemination

The use of humour has great potential in the context of social research (Watson 2015:169). Some academics study humour, comedy, or laughter, but their results are usually presented in a serious style. Cate Watson asserts that '… failing to admit of the presence or utility of the humorous, the comic, the ludic, and so on in the human activity we call "research" is to undermine research itself …' (Watson 2015:1–2).

An old joke says there are two kinds of people: those who view the world as a series of oppositional binaries, and those who do not (Watson 2015:127). Yet seriousness and humour are not actually an oppositional binary: neither will work without the other (Watson 2015:144). Kate Fox coined the term 'humitas' to describe the phenomenon of humour and seriousness operating in the same moment (2018:171).

Another facet of this is that what is funny to some people is not at all amusing to others (Watson 2015:141; Grech 2019:87). In 2005, three US-based doctoral students in computer science created SCIgen, a computer program that generates nonsensical research articles including graphs, figures and citations (Bohannon 2015:18). The SCIgen website states their intention was to 'maximise amusement' as well as to assess the submission standards of academic conferences that they felt existed only to make money (Ball 2005). This caught the imagination of people around the world, such that nonsensical articles have been submitted to – and, in many cases, accepted by – academic conferences and journals. A lot of people find this hilarious, though it is likely that those who have been duped are not amused.

Some years after SCIgen was created, French computer scientist Cyril Labbé found that dozens of computer-generated articles had been published worldwide. Sixteen were in conference proceedings published by Springer, based in Germany, and over 100 were published by the Institute of Electrical and Electronic Engineers, based in New York (Van Noorden 2014). Labbé informed the publishers, who removed the articles. Springer then asked Labbé for help in identifying nonsense articles. He devised another program to automatically detect computer-generated text, called SciDetect, which is now in use at Springer. This in itself seems quite ironic given that computer-generated articles are easy for humans to detect, and in theory the publishers concerned used peer reviewers.

Social researchers are not above these kinds of pranks. In 1996, Alan Sokal was successful in getting a spoof article published in the cultural studies journal *Social Text*. The article was called 'Transgressing the boundaries: towards a transformative hermeneutics of quantum gravity'. Sokal claimed he was trying to demonstrate that academics could use scientific theories and concepts inaccurately to support their own plausible yet fallacious theories and arguments (Grech 2019:87). This became something of a cause célèbre that led to a considerable controversy with many accusations and counteraccusations.

In 2018, Sokal's hoax was duplicated by three scholars, James Lindsay, Helen Pluckrose and Peter Boghossian, who wrote 20 fake articles using fashionable jargon (Grech 2019:88). They had considerable success in getting their articles published in high-profile journals on topics such as queer studies, fat studies and gender studies. This hoax is now referred to as 'Sokal Squared'.

All of these hoaxes raise considerable ethical issues which are beyond the scope of this book to review. The point we wish to make here is that these actions are at some level based on humour, though playfulness can also be a political act (Fox 2018:173). Lindsay et al (2018) stated that all the articles they wrote 'endeavored to be humorous in at least some small way (and often, big ones)'. And, again, some people found their actions to be hilarious.

Watson (2015) distinguishes between irony, satire and parody. One problem with people finding different things funny is that some people don't recognise others' use of irony, satire or parody. Another is that humour doesn't always translate between different cultures. Perhaps for these reasons, some commentators are firmly against the use of such devices in writing for research. Irony has been described as 'a particularly troublesome violation of the conventions and expectations that are formalized and codified in the research publication guidelines of such authorities as ICMJE [International Committee of Medical Journal Editors], COPE [Committee on Publication Ethics], and individual journals' (Ronagh and Souder 2015:1544). The controversies outlined here demonstrate that deploying humour in academic contexts can have negative consequences. But does that mean all researchers should abstain from any use of humour in our writing and dissemination?

We don't think so, and fortunately we are not alone. There is a small and growing body of literature suggesting there are helpful and responsible ways to use humour in research outputs (Watson 2015; Fox 2018; Batty and Taylor 2019). Watson suggests that, if we are in any doubt about our work's likely reception, we should use fictionalisation instead of humour (Watson 2015:141). As with drama, it seems helpful for comedy in research to be used by people who are professional comedy workers, such as stand-up poet Kate Fox in the UK or comedy screenwriters Craig Batty and Stayci Taylor in Australia (Batty and Taylor 2019:377). Batty and Taylor, like Berbary (2011), find screenplay writing useful at the analytic stage of research: 'As comedy screenwriters and academics, we use our craft to question, pull apart, test and offer deeper and/or alternative modes of writing for the screen, considering aspects such as structure, theme, character, visual grammar and dialogue' (Batty and Taylor 2019:377). They provide a useful distinction between comedy and fiction as method, suggesting that in comedic writing, the protagonist is often unaware of the – or a – key issue. Conversely, in fiction, 'the protagonist is usually created to represent a conscious awareness of the questions driving the project' (Batty and Taylor 2019:389–90). This means that 'the tools of comedy can be used to draw attention to theories, ideas and contexts; to critique and offer alternative readings and positions; and to make audiences/ readers think about their own knowledge' (Batty and Taylor 2019:390). Fox puts it a little differently, drawing on the work of Watson to suggest that comedy can highlight 'the gap between how the world is and how the world should be' which is 'bread and butter for anthropologists and ethnographers' (2018:172).

Events are springing up worldwide which suggest that many scholars like a little levity with their gravitas. The global competition *Dance Your PhD*, open to natural and social scientists, was launched in 2008 with 12 contestants and grew rapidly; by 2011 there were 55, and the contest has run every year since it began. The point is to make research more accessible to non-researchers. Dances are videoed and uploaded onto YouTube for judging by a panel of academics, professional dancers and previous contest winners (Myers 2012:158). More recently some universities around the world, such as the Australian National University and the University of Southampton in the UK, have instituted annual Bake Your PhD or Bake Your Research contests. Then across the UK, some researchers are learning to present their work through stand-up comedy via the Bright Club movement (Ridley-Ellis 2014:57; Fox 2018:172). These types of initiatives are perhaps more effective and certainly more ethical than writing spoof articles. While they have a serious aim – to increase the accessibility of research – they also have a light-hearted aspect which is clearly signalled, so this is humitas in practice.

CREATIVE WRITING IN PRACTICE

A funny turn *by Kate Fox*[8]

Kate Fox is a stand-up poet and writer. In this piece, she discusses the role for humour in social research writing, and gives some practical tips for those who would like to use humour in their work.

I often introduce myself at gigs or conferences by saying that I'm a stand-up poet. Then I add: "Because if you say you're a comedian who does poems, not many people will come to see you; whereas if you say you're a poet who does comedy, still not many people will come to see you but at least you get Arts Council funding". It does a lot of work that line. It tells and shows that I will be funny and playful. It is a bit self-deprecating, so might help get an audience to like me. It accurately tells them I'm working in an art form between the commercial and the subsidised. It performs in-betweenness.

People using creative writing in social research are in between all sorts of spaces and methods. I value humour for the way it can manage that in-betweenness. It can tell you and show you two things at once. It can unite the everyday and the extraordinary – bring higher things down to earth.

Figure 4.6: Inspiration doll by Alke Gröppel-Wegener, created in response to this piece by Kate Fox. Inspiration dolls comment on and play with genres of creative writing.

It has been argued that stand-up comedians use equivalent methods to anthropologists (for example, Koziski 1984; Mintz 1985; Hemmingson 2008; Smith 2015). However, it's not necessary to be a professional humorist to do this. Most people habitually use humour in their day-to-day lives but then put it aside when it comes to doing research.

I suspect this is because people fear not being taken seriously if they use humour. For me, it's important to remember that the hierarchy of 'seriousness being more able to

---

[8] This contribution should be cited as follows: Fox, K. (2021) 'A funny turn'. In Phillips, R. and Kara, H. *Creative Writing for Social Research*. Bristol: Policy Press.

produce knowledge than humour' is contextual and historical. Mikhail Bakhtin (1984), the Russian philosopher and literary theorist, referred to a glorious period in the Middle Ages when the earthy language of folk humour mixed with that of high literature, and authors like Shakespeare and Cervantes blended them to glorious, anarchic effect.

To some extent I would argue that we're back at such a time now. Politicians like America's Barack Obama, Italy's Beppe Grillo and Iceland's Jon Gnarr use humour in their political speeches (the latter two were professional humorists before they were politicians).

In academia, there are initiatives like Bright Club in which academics turn their research into stand-up comedy. Cate Watson (2015) has written a book about humour as methodology in the social sciences. Social scientists have looked at stand-ups like Russell Kane and Russell Brand (a new Russell Group) and noted that they point out the difference between what society could be, and what it actually is, like anthropologists and ethnographers.

My own PhD was about class, gender and Northern Englishness in stand-up, and used comedy (mainly in the form of a dialogic voice) to interrupt the traditional hierarchy in which monologic, 'detached' academic discourse is the best way of showing that you are gathering and disseminating knowledge.

I popped up didn't I, to say things like not to worry, comedians won't need a PhD to go on 'Live At the Apollo' in future, though a penis might be helpful.

You did, dialogic voice, I've missed you. What you did was often to bring the body back into the text, in a similar way to that called for by feminist theorists like Kristeva and Irigaray. You also brought 'ordinary' and alternative discourses into the language of the thesis.

Not everybody liked it though did they? Do you remember the conference organiser and that woman from the newsletter? They were a bit snobby if you ask me ...

The co-organiser of a postgrad conference was honest with me that they put my proposal for a humorous presentation on the 'maybe' pile at first because they weren't sure if it was going to fit with the rest of the conference – and if it might reduce the credibility that a postgrad event strives so hard for. The editor of the arts newsletter in my (traditional) university department requested that I reword my advert for my performance because it said that there would be beer at the bar and an enjoyable time might be had. I replied to point out that the event was a direct part of my research (I was going to write about how the acts performed 'Northernness') and I couldn't see how it was different to the other seminars and soirees which were advertising 'wine and canapés'.

Yes, I can't think why you thought that class was in any way relevant to the ways in which comedy is used and received ...

Nice one dialogic voice, you're performing irony there. Saying one thing, whilst showing another. Doesn't so much research do that?

Well, enough congratulating me on how great I am, though I am obviously. We've only got a thousand words left and to be honest, I want people to start using methods which will allow them to use humour to do, or disseminate, their research. Let's give them some practical ideas. Remember how you argued that laughter is emancipatory. It frees up the body and the mind, shakes people out of their habitual assumptions. It can highlight and then undermine stereotypes.

Okay. Though the obedient scholar in me also would want to point some people at intellectual arguments to back this stuff up if they want – as we often need to justify it. Look for scholars who emphasise a dialogic and *embodied* way of learning in order to overcome internalised oppressions and power battles.

Try Paolo Freire (1996) – who actually talks about a 'pedagogy of laughter' as well as his 'Pedagogy of Oppression', Jacques Rancière (2009) who talks about emancipated spectators who encounter new possibilities by watching them in performance, and Pierre Bourdieu (2000) who talks about 'countertraining' to change ingrained bodily learning and behaviours which I have suggested could mean comedy workshops and performances in order to learn to 'laugh differently'. The idea of 'laughing differently' is also used by Emily Douglas (2015) in relation to feminism. She references Michel Foucault to look at ways women could stop laughing along with sexist jokes, and make their own humour which allows them to laugh at outdated stereotypes.

I'm not sure you need practical tips. The main thing, seems to me, stopping people using humour in social research, is not feeling they have permission. Humour arises naturally all the time. Everybody knows people love to laugh, are more likely to engage with and pay attention to something if it's funny.

I am always suspicious of words like 'naturally' and phrases like 'everybody knows'. At the same time, I think if people asked themselves not why they should use humour but why they shouldn't, they might have some very powerful realisations. Nonetheless, let's do a Ten Ways Into Comedy. Everybody knows people like a 'Top Ten Ways ...'.

Yes And
Do exercises using "Yes and". Comic improvisation rests on people saying "Yes and", that is, accepting and building on ideas offered to them. Try getting two people to have a conversation in which one person starts every sentence with "Yes and", in response to the ideas of the other. Re-run the conversation but this time one partner says "No but" to every sentence.

Smash Stereotypes

In a women's comedy workshop focusing on gender issues, I got participants to think of a stereotype that could apply to themselves which they wanted to resist (for example, a student, a Northerner, a feminist, fat) and then generate associations. They then had to write a one-liner which evoked but then challenged or overturned the stereotype. For example, one participant said that due to her size she was perceived as being a "salad-dodger" but "Actually, I like onions on my burgers". (Much stand-up performance is about transforming 'abjection' and shame, due to perceived negative characteristics, into pride and laughter.)

Set Expectations

If I want workshop participants to generate funny material then I might share a funny piece of work first. At the same time, paradoxically, I reassure people that they shouldn't *try* to be funny. Generating comic material involves a willingness to test out ideas and to produce far more than you will ever use. Similarly, if people are sharing work which will be funny, it's important to let an audience know this. Unless a context very clearly shouts 'Comedy setting' then audiences usually need to be given 'permission to laugh'.

Watch Stand-Ups

In workshops, I get participants to watch a variety of stand-up performances which are readily available on YouTube and Netflix. Despite E.B. White's oft-quoted maxim that analysing comedy is like dissecting a frog – "Nobody is interested and the frog dies", looking at how stand-ups introduce themselves and the devices they use to make particular topics funny can be useful and inspiring. As examples: I have found Katherine Ryan useful on gender, Russell Kane good on class, Wanda Sykes and Trevor Noah great on race, and Stewart Lee interesting on religion.

Find Incongruities

Incongruity is the motor of humour. A fish and a bicycle, one of my poems which puts Eminem in the court of King Henry the Eighth, Bridget Christie doing stand-up about ants doing stand-up while dressed as an ant. Joke writer and teacher Sally Holloway (2010) uses the 'Hadron Joke Collider' in which she gets people to think of two ideas they want to mash together (say, animal bonding and relationships), write mind maps full of associations for both, and then draw connections between them to find funny images and punchlines. (In which one sample using the topics above might be "They had the sex drive of an animal – unfortunately it was a panda.") The process rests on generating associations for words and ideas that take them away from their original context and find new meanings for them.

Exaggerate

Much comedy is based on exaggeration – making ideas and situations bigger until they become ridiculous. One of my favourite games to illustrate this principle of absurd inflation is to get workshop participants to play a game called "It's worse than that ...", in which somebody recounts a situation to their partner, beginning each new sentence with "It's worse than that". Monty Python's 'Four Yorkshiremen' sketch is a great example of comic exaggeration.

Punchlining

Punchlines are like poetry in their economy of words. I love getting people to complete the old Bob Monkhouse line "I'm not saying Mary is a bad cook but ..." (I change it to Martin nowadays). The original line ended, "But she uses the smoke alarm as an oven timer". A group brainstorming alternative endings – from "But he uses Yorkshire Puddings as shot puts" to "But he is" – begins to see how word order (save the funny bit to the end) and word choice (for some reason some words just sound funnier than others, see Calippo versus Fab), vividness of imagery and unexpectedness can make us laugh more.

Find the Funny

One of my favourite workshop exercises is simply to get participants to write down three things that have recently made them laugh, and three that have made them angry. We discuss the items and use the group's response, interest and feedback to pick a particularly fertile topic to start off a piece of timed free writing or a poetic monologue or piece of stand-up comedy.

Say What You're Not Supposed To Say

At a comedy workshop at a humour conference, we started by going round the circle thinking of things we weren't supposed to say in a particular situation. Somebody suggested "During a conference paper". There was a joyous anarchy in saying things like "I'm really bored now, see you later" or "You're just phoning it in" or "I disagree with everything you've said but I like your tie". Comedy is often found in simultaneously exposing and transgressing social norms.

Punch Up

One of the fears of working with comedy is that it will offend or upset people. A useful principle to introduce, which guides the work of many stand-ups, is that of 'punching up'; that is, of making jokes about people with more power than you. Here we have the comedian as the 'wise fool' who speaks truth to power and who can tell the King he wears no clothes.

Finding and telling stories; storying

We have seen a number of different ways in which social researchers are using creative writing for the analysis and dissemination of findings. Doing so, we have explored some ways of writing for analysis, and others for presentation and dissemination. We recognise that in practice many forms of creative writing are useful to both dissemination and analysis, which are underpinned by some more fundamental creative writing practices, above all the finding and telling of stories. In Chapters 2 and 3, we explored the finding of stories, through the transcription of stories in circulation and the creation of new stories by researchers and participants. But stories are also a powerful means of distilling, exploring and sharing research findings. Here, researchers do not simply capture stories that are already being told; they construct new stories for our time. Stories are an appropriate medium for researching and presenting difficult subjects because it is important for all of us to tell our stories, and for others to hear them.

Moreover, storying research is well placed to negotiate the ethical challenges associated with sensitive and difficult subjects. Storying research can do more than sidestep ethical pitfalls; it can be ethically proactive. Some ethical possibilities of storying research are illustrated in Hester Parr and Olivia Stevenson's research involving missing persons in Scotland (Parr and Stevenson 2013). This research involves stories at every stage – including inviting people to tell their stories of going missing – though here we focus on the ways in which Hester and Olivia distilled their findings into anonymised, composite stories. The ethical principles of this approach include the need to anonymise findings (Markham 2012), while ensuring that reports retain their immediacy and humanity. Here, ethics means much more than the avoidance of harm. Australian researchers Louise Phillips and Tracey Bunda (2018) identify ethical drivers of collaborative storying: giving voice to those who are silenced and marginalised; challenging hegemonic and stereotypical narratives about minorities; fostering the intergenerational transfer of knowledge; forming a bridge between the past and the present; and nourishing mind, body and soul.

The implementation of these principles is illustrated in one of the stories told by Hester and Olivia: 'Sophie's story'. This story was 'creatively recomposed from an interview transcript for reading and telling' (Parr and Stevenson 2013). In other words, the researchers fictionalised their findings, and worked with a writer to actively shape the story, drawing out its essential components. This story begins as follows:

> I suffer from depression and I was going through a really bad episode, everything was a bit much, things just got pretty over the top and I took a huge overdose and that's what made me go missing, because I sent emails out to lots of people while I was under the influence of a lot of tablets and some red wine. Like to my mum and my boss and some of my friends, my sister. When I realized I was still alive, it was

a working night, it was in the middle of the week and people were going to start to wakening up and get their emails and I thought 'I'm going to disappear', so I just sort of took my iPod and left my phone at home and just like decided I would go … that was really the reason how I ended up being reported missing because I left my phone and everything at home and I didn't show up for work. I spent a lot of time vomiting, but I was aware by four in the morning that I was still alive, and very much still alive, and people were going to start getting the letters and I had not planned to still be around, so I had to go somewhere until all the tablets did their worst and that was my thinking. I got dressed for the weather, I don't know why because if you think you're going to die why do you bother? It's just a thing you do I guess. I also wanted to be wearing dark things so I wouldn't be easy to spot and I'm blonde. I knew where I was going from when I left. (Parr and Stevenson 2013)

Sophie's story found an audience much larger than the academic paper the authors wrote about it, and it resonated among that audience, making an impression and an impact. In 'Where Sophie's story went next', which closes this chapter, Hester Parr explores the ways in which 'Sophie's story' travelled.

Stories can engage readers on an emotional level, which holds their attention and makes a deeper impact than formal writing tends to manage (Stein 1998:224). We see this in stories by Marcelo Diversi, which narrate the findings of ethnographic research with street children in Campinas, Brazil. These stories create an emotional connection between the subjects of these stories and the reader (Diversi 1998:133). Here is an excerpt:

"We didn't get much sleep last night," Dalva said, helping me up on my feet.

The post office was only a few blocks from where we were, and as we walked, Dalva began telling me how they had been on the lookout for this woman dealer who was after them. "She said she's gonna kill us if we don't pay our crack debts, and we don't have no money. It's in the night that things happen, you know. So last night, we kept on going from place to place, trying to stay awake."

Dalva told me they laid down at the doorstep of a pediatric clinic, but that after a few minutes, a police car stopped by, some policemen came out and got them up, saying they couldn't stay there. I had seen this clinic before. It had caught my attention one afternoon when I was looking for some of the kids. I remembered thinking that it was in an odd place, squeezed between small clothing shops on one side and a crumbling hotel where some young women and men took their clients, on the other side. I had stopped in front of it and read the sign with big yellow letters: WHERE WE CARE FOR THE CHILDREN OF CAMPINAS. (Diversi 1998:137)

This short excerpt arguably reveals more reality than would be possible using more conventional academic writing. In just 210 words it conveys a lot about the dangers and risks in the children's lives, the seedy urban neighbourhood, and the dreadful dissonance between the desperate needs of the children and the official 'care' provided. The author's explicit goals are to 'offer fuller representations of their lived experiences' than the local and national narratives which demonise them as 'little criminals' (Diversi 1998:132).

We end this chapter with a piece by Hester Parr and Olivia Stevenson, which draws together the themes of this brief discussion on finding and telling stories, and the broader themes of creative writing for analysis and dissemination of social research findings, which has run through this chapter.

CREATIVE WRITING IN PRACTICE

'Where Sophie's story went next': the banal afterlife of an applied cultural geography *by Hester Parr*[9]

Hester Parr is Professor of Human Geography at Glasgow University. She led a research project exploring the experiential geographies of people reported as missing. The research project included creative work with interview narratives and actors who recorded audio stories and these are on: https://geographiesofmissingpeople.org.uk/outputs/missingvoices/.

Sophie's story was a creative rendition of at least one in-depth narrative interview in an academic research project. The story comprised a 'rough around the edges' account of going missing in order to end a life. Sophie's words now exist as an online audio story (see Figure 4.8), as well as a written version, and these were initially put together for the launch of public and professional resources associated with a specific research project in 2013 (geographiesofmissingpeople.org.uk). Sophie's story is an unusual autobiography, in that it is part of a collection of stories that are created from a composite writing strategy that took elements of narrative interviews from 45 people and combined them to create a series of stories that spoke to common experiences and events. This writing strategy was intended to create a public-facing accessible resource about a common experience that was not well understood – as well as working protectively – refusing the straightforward autobiographical form in order to obscure the real-life identities of previously missing people.

Figure 4.7: Inspiration doll by Alke Gröppel-Wegener, created in response to this piece by Hester Parr. Inspiration dolls comment on and play with genres of creative writing.

[9] This contribution should be cited as follows: Parr, H. (2021) 'Where Sophie's story went next: the banal afterlife of an applied cultural geography'. In Phillips, R. and Kara, H. *Creative Writing for Social Research*. Bristol: Policy Press.

The creative writing of this and other stories was always for a particular purpose – connected ambitions of an academic research project to influence contemporary policing practices relating to missing people in the UK (Parr and Stevenson 2014). Here, I'm augmenting previous published accounts – locating Sophie's story as a trauma narrative – by analysing the *legacy* of an applied cultural geography; the afterlife of a creative experiment for social purpose (Lorimer and Parr 2014). At the time of writing Sophie's story we knew that there might be dangers and risks associated with 'writing words as trauma wounds' (after Tamas 2011). We were at the start of the story's journey and sensitive to the powerful affects evoked in its circulation with various publics – notably professional police officers amongst others.

This piece, almost 7 years later, reflects on the outcomes of this *cultural geography in practice*. Over this time, I have become more attuned to what storying words do, and because Sophie's story was comprised of suicidal memories, I have been conscious of the power of creative play with traumatic experience and attentive to how this works across different professional, public and private spaces. Working progressively and professionally through such narrative is tricky because of the common *unspeakability* of trauma. Our work with stories was always about trying to find a language for the trauma of going missing and then trying to follow what that does. What follows is an account of the legacy of academic-creative story writing.

Public geographies

After we published and launched the stories online and at a national missing persons conference, we were contacted by many journalists wanting us to speak about the stories and the wider research on radio, TV and for use in print media (Hill 2012).

Figure 4.8: Sophie's story, SoundCloud.

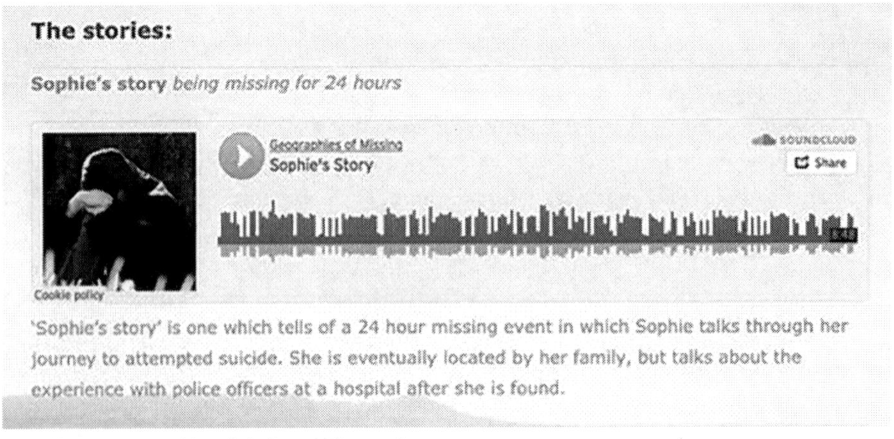

Source: www.geographiesofmissingpeople.org.uk

The stories were clearly the hook. What often occurred is that at some point, however, the journalist asked if they could speak to the person or people behind the story resources. This was a request that was always regretfully refused, with the statement that we are not ethically approved to broker for the media. I usually pointed out that the reason we created the story resources is that these are creatively produced but *verbatim* and this saves individuals the public exposure of their traumatic tales – these creative stories thus work protectively – bringing audiences close to the trauma of missing people via voice and text, but keeping the real individual at a distance – lessening the personal risk. For many journalists this renders the stories 'inauthentic', as they need their own missing persons to photograph and quote directly, perhaps alongside the story resources. The media circulation of stories has been frustrating in this way, although stories have undoubtedly been 'out there' in the public media. They have been utilised in more structured ways by other professional publics.

Theatre producers, actors and writers have been more happy to accept and work with the stories as authentic words for artful representation or generative texts for scripts on 'missing' drama, and here the stories have acquired dramaturgical resonance in which their traumatic affects have been accentuated or reworked in rehearsal and performance. The Edinburgh Fringe featured the Engineer Theatre Collective's *Missing*, for example, – a play built on verbatim interviews, using some of our materials (see Figure 4.9).

Reviewers note the 'real testimony' in this play. '*The combination of monologue, dialogue, lecture and movement results in a dramatic production which tugs at the heart, frightens and informs*' (https://broadwaybaby.com/shows/missing/27503).

Figure 4.9 Dramatising trauma stories.

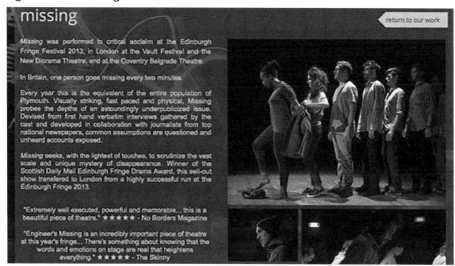

Source: https://www.engineertheatre.com/missing, © 2015 by Engineer Theatre Collective

This review picks up on our intent: that the story would not just produce an unsettling feeling in order to draw emotive attention, but that it would also engage and inform.

Moving work into professional communities

Through partnership work, we have also mobilised the stories in police training in order to intervene in rather bland training resources on missing people. In 'enlivening' training resources with creative narrative we were intending to bridge empathy gaps between police officers and missing persons, in order to counter the latter's *invisibility* as superficial or problematic subjects. This was a response that saw people – individuals – reduced to 'cases', 'incidents', 'resource problems', 'mispers' and spatial categories – with their *individual* humanity somehow threatened in processes of search. In training with specialist and experienced search officers, they reported that exposure to the storied words encouraged them to think of *people*, rather than numbers of missing persons or categories of missing or 'spatial behaviour profiles'. In turn this prompted changes in professional behaviour and styles of engagement with returning missing people. We might argue that in this way the stories were successful in mobilising trauma, in ways that brought officers 'closer in' to the experience of being missing and that this intimacy seemed to hold capacities for change:

'It personalises the missing people rather than "just one more".' (POLSA, specialist search officer)

'I have greater understanding and sympathy.' (PC, junior officer)

This shows the work of words in police training.

Creatively shaping trauma tales and enabling their mobilisation and travel in professional communities have created a legacy involving an emotive reframing of professional behaviour.

Where else do creative words do work?

The testimonial words and stories have been in public and training resources for years. The 10 creative stories in our collection now have a mostly banal life as text excerpts in policy documents or are briefly referenced in committee discussions in ways that the raw or traumatic specifics and content are not always acknowledged – the words are doing other kinds of work. For example, I sat for three years on the Scottish Government's Working Group for Missing People – a policy committee – devising a *National Strategy for Missing Persons in Scotland* (published in 2017). In these multi-disciplinary meetings the research I was there to represent was often referred to as 'the voices' or 'the stories' or 'the narratives' as shorthand. Their content was clearly coded as valuable and necessary, but they also acted like a component part that needs to be present in the state response to the problems we were discussing, rather than in terms of their specificity. This is typical in an era characterised by emotionally intelligent government. The stories were commodities, existing as a version of social and emotional capital that justified or resonated with governmental plans and action points. The voices affectively offset the banalities of the policing and administration of missing people on the page. The stories have directly influenced the content of those plans, because I came with the words and sat with them in the committees, making their content heard as much as possible. However, in the left-overs of 'feeling work' in policy spaces, the words spatialise into familiar shapes – flattened out, bubble wrapped in text boxes of 'case studies' or 'personal stories', ones we are routinely orientated to in an era of emotive governance. The stories are the same, but their editing, purpose and proximity are differently rendered on the policy page. Trauma is packaged up – often respectfully – but smoothed out into gobbet sizes and through which any editing may comprise the dangerous capacities in the words. The *textual geographies* of trauma tales like Sophie's are banal, although their placing in policy documents perhaps augments their power in other ways.

Travelling with trauma tales

This 'Creative Writing in Practice' piece relates one legacy of academic-creative stories. Sophie's words have travelled via my embodied story performances and other actor voices into large public concerts, professional meetings, conferences and training. The story has been downloaded as audio over 400 times and scattered through media articles and policy documents. The main audience for the story have been police officers and over 100,000 have been linked to it via online training. Sophie's story, the remaining 10 stories, and the trauma they speak of, is produced and reproduced through these embodied, virtual and textual spaces. Sometimes this fails to affect change and sometimes people cry and leave the room, and sometimes people really sit up and reflect and respond with new innovation and practice or policy engagement. There are, of course, limits to what storying any version of trauma can do, and that is partly a question of geography. *Where* Sophie's story is heard matters, as missing people disappear in different ways in different contexts. Simply repeating trauma tales across spaces do not mean that they automatically carry hope or potential for moving affect.

In asking 'where is Sophie's story now?' and in charting the banal travelling life of this creative research resource across public and professional events, training, policy documents and academic presentation, there are questions raised about trauma's geographies and the work of distributed traumatic words. News of Sophie's disappearance and attempted suicide has now travelled to this page. I have told a particular tale of her words and their work, but I have yet to really know how the story ends.

5

Searching and queer(ing) writing

Don't come to conclusions. Come to other things: inquiry, questions, failure, side roads, off-road. (Waite 2019:48)

In my end is my beginning. (T.S. Eliot, *Four Quartets*, 1944:27)

Introduction

Creative writing presents social researchers with challenges and opportunities. Writing – more than simply 'writing up' – is a form of enquiry in its own right, a means of searching and questioning, exploring and understanding the social world. Moreover, creative writing has radical possibilities for social research, unsettling and as we put it queering our ways of seeing and knowing. We elaborate on these two themes – searching and queer(ing) – in this final chapter. Here, we draw together threads rather than advancing firm conclusions, and we hope readers will pick up and play with these threads and ideas, as we shall continue to do ourselves.

Writing this book, we have struggled and not always agreed about our definitions of creative writing. In one of our writing meetings, Helen argued the case that all writing is creative. Richard felt the need to distinguish creative from other forms of writing, pointing to definitions of the field and practice of creative writing (for example, Harper 2019). We could each see each other's point; rather than disagreeing, we both had mixed feelings on the subject. We also remain unsure about the term creative writing. Though meaningful and alluring to us, we recognise that this term can be off-putting to some people. The latter include: those who find creativity and/or writing intimidating, seeing it as something for others; those who argue for more critical approaches to creativity (Mould 2018); and those who are suspicious and implicitly snobby towards creative writing as defined and taught in manuals and handbooks, evening classes and university courses. Some of these people may be academic supervisors, research managers, journal editors (Denzin 2010/2016:91), publishers and established authors. This can create barriers to using creative writing in research. However, the numerous examples we have given in this book suggest that there are plenty of barrier-free routes and, where barriers do exist, there may be ways to get around them.

Whether or not we see creative writing as fundamentally different from other forms of writing, we agree that the attention we have paid to this subject has helped us to become more conscious of the act of writing, the things we are

173

doing as writers, the choices we are making. As we write, we face many choices: which words to use; how to order our words into sentences; how to structure our document; which conventions to work with, and which to work against. These choices are 'simultaneously political, poetic, methodological, and theoretical' (Richardson 1997:17). This means that, however we write, and whatever way or shape of writing we choose to work with, we can become better and more creative researchers if we become more aware of our writing. Increased awareness enables us to improve our skills and expand our writing-related ambitions.

This more self-reflexive approach to writing is not simply a matter of finding a voice or developing a personal style. It is also a matter of developing sensitivity towards the social and power relations in which writing takes place, beginning with the politics of writing: of who gets to write what. Some writers have more freedom than others, more chance to be playful and experimental, to depart from expectations and conventions, and to stand by written work that is not universally applauded. Julia Molinari, who teaches academic writing to ESL (English as a Second Language) students, helping them to cope with the expectations and marking criteria in British universities, makes the point that these students are under pressure to write in particular ways, to follow conventions that some others may be freer to reject or subvert (see: 'Playing with #acwri: a play on academic writing' in Chapter 2). Similar points could be made about undergraduates, needing to pass exams and conscious of the risks of submitting unconventional writing (Blackburn and Beucher 2019). Equally, students submitting Masters or doctoral theses and dissertations, at the mercy of examiners and readers who may or may not be known to them, may not feel able to risk transgressing and playing with the conventions of writing. For all these reasons, innovations in writing for research have usually come from those with assured places in the academic establishment – scholars such as bell hooks, Laurel Richardson and Clifford Geertz – and also from those working happily outside that establishment, such as Linton Kwesi Johnson, with whom we began this book. These figures have been inspirational to us and to many others. One of our reasons for writing this book has been to continue this democratisation of creative writing for social research. When we were planning this book, we – Helen, Richard and the creators of the 15 contributions, who had gathered in Sheffield (as we explain in the Acknowledgements) – agreed that we wanted to offer some licence to researchers without the status of a hooks or a Geertz, who might want to try some form of creative writing.

Our ambition here has been to present an inclusive vision of creative writing for social research. We say this is not only for tenured professors but also for students at all levels, and for professional, practitioner and community researchers, working for a variety of clients from corporations to NGOs, with varied briefs and responsibilities (Cox and Dadas 2019). In fact, in our view, creative writing has potential for all researchers, including, demonstrably, those using quantitative methods (for example, Davis et al 2008; Harron 2016). Some researchers enjoy more freedom than others but all are constrained and enabled in a variety of ways:

academic researchers face peer review and assessment by regulators; students work within the assessment criteria; professional researchers work within client briefs; those who work for community groups are reminded of budgetary constraints and moral obligations to resist temptations towards self-indulgence. So, while we encourage creative writing in social research, we also recognise the obstacles that researchers will face in attempting this, above and beyond the challenges of writing creatively.

Searching

Social researchers often write in order to communicate what we already know, but writing can be more than this: it can be a means of finding out, a process of searching. The commonly used term 'writing up', which is sometimes used to describe the final stages of a research project, does not begin to convey the possibilities of writing for research. Indicating the synergies between creative writing and social research, the French experimental writer Georges Perec described his own writing as a form of 'questioning' (Bellos 1993:649–50). Perec distinguished four strands within his work, one of which he labelled sociological, another autobiographical: writing about others and oneself respectively; both are fundamental to social research (Phillips 2018). Writing as questioning extends through the research process: beginning with ethical considerations and extending through data collection and analysis, through the dissemination and discussion of findings.

Writing can be a way of seeing, a means of opening our eyes and ears to the world around us. Derek Neale (2006c:45) claims that: 'Writing is a process of becoming aware, of opening the senses to ways of grasping the world, ways that may previously have been blocked.' He argues that 'by de-familiarising your perceptions you will reinvigorate your writing' (Neale 2006c:46). Others have echoed this point. Wolfgang Iser (1997:4) argues that writing can make 'conceivable what would otherwise remain hidden'. Putting this in more conventionally social scientific terms, we might say that writing can enhance our observations and enrich the data we collect.

Creative writing also opens new possibilities for analysing and interpreting the data we collect, for understanding the social world. Through writing, we can 'move between the critical and the creative, the theoretical and the practical' (Waite 2017:6). Writing for research necessarily involves reading, thinking and interpretation (Waite 2017:9). According to Carolyn Ellis and Tony Adams, it 'is a way of knowing cultural experiences – a way to learn about social phenomena', which enables us to 'make sense' of the cultural and social world (Ellis and Adams 2014:263). Graeme Harper also highlights the interpretive possibilities of writing. He argues that creative writing 'is not simply about recording or presenting' (Harper 2019:40); it 'makes things, actions, and even thoughts and feelings, perceptible' (Harper 2019:42). When we write, rather than simply write up, writing can help us to think creatively as we explore and articulate our arguments (Colyar 2009:425–6).

Creative writing, as we have seen in this book, can also be a means of disseminating research findings, and thus of sharing and exploring them with audiences that may include non-specialists, who might be less likely to read formal research outputs. Means of exploration and articulation, which we explored in Chapter 4, include visual media such as zines and comics, and performance writing such as play scripts and stand-up comedy routines.

In each of these stages and spheres of research – from data collection through dissemination – creative writing can be useful, but it continues to work on other levels too. The joys of writing are suggested by the proliferation of 'writing for pleasure' classes in community adult education centres, and also in the acknowledgements and prefaces of research monographs, whose authors admit to the allure of the keyboard and the writing desk (Zuss 2012:v). For others, creative writing may be a source of profit, a livelihood. For still others, it may be a demon, an irresistible and even a destructive force in their lives. So, though it may be useful and enjoyable, creative writing is not necessarily either of these things, and it can be challenging. When social researchers explore creative writing, we cannot simply extract the useful bits; we open Pandora's box of possibilities and dangers.

Fundamentally, creative writing opens new possibilities for ethically driven social research (Kara 2018). From enhanced self-reflexivity to heightened sensitivity towards the representation of others, creative writing raises new ethical considerations, and offers solutions to ethical problems. Some scholars have argued that writing creatively in research can in itself be an ethical stance. They claim that this is because writing creatively helps researchers to break free from the fetters of 'power, institutions and the apparatus of the state', and to exercise our freedom of expression (Rhodes 2009:662). Others have argued that a creative approach can solve ethical problems, such as the use of composite or fictionalised accounts to preserve the anonymity of individual participants (Markham 2012). Alternatively, writing creatively can remove the primacy of the authorial voice and allow for the inclusion of multiple viewpoints (Markham 2012), thereby reflecting real-world complexity more fully and accurately than a single passive voice.

Searching is risky; we never know where curiosity will lead us, and what we will find (Phillips 2016). Searching writing enables theories and ideas to be 'illuminated, tested out and, in some cases, transgressed' (Batty and Taylor 2019:377). The transgressive possibilities of creative writing are signalled in a term that we have been using and exploring in this book: queer.

Queer(ing) writing

With many different voices and styles of writing, this book is polyvocal and polygraphical. As such, it has a messiness (Law 2004), which we have been careful to respect and to preserve. Ruth Raynor makes this explicit in 'Writing the end(s) ...' later in this chapter, holding on to loose ends and contradictions, resisting the temptation to tidy these away. This strategic scruffiness underpins our broader project, which revolves around queer writing and the queering of writing for social research. Messiness, we think, is something to hold on to, to tolerate and celebrate, as it is fundamentally queer. Queer, in this sense, means to trouble, to unsettle, to destabilise, to see afresh. It is to 'fail' to produce a tidy or coherent picture of the world (Halberstam 2011). To queer our writing is to trouble and to unsettle the ways in which we write and, through this writing, the ways in which we see: playfully, critically, transgressively, insightfully. Hillery Glasby, a professor of queer rhetoric, expresses this succinctly and provocatively (Glasby 2019:24): 'Mostly, I like to use my writing to fuck shit up.'

We have argued throughout this book that, when social researchers work with creative writing, we maintain a dual focus: on process and product, writing as verb and as noun. This means that, while we may sometimes produce beautiful, polished pieces of writing, we should not be seduced by them, or brush less refined or accomplished works away. Queer writing, rough and provisional as it is, is naturally attentive to process, which premature polish and editorial interference might obscure. Glasby observes that 'Finished, clean drafts are intended to conceal and erase the messy processes behind themselves', but cautions us from become seduced by 'tidy endpoints' because 'messy processes' are 'what writing and composition are about in the first place' (Glasby 2019:25; see also McRuer 2006). There is space, in writing workshops without tangible outputs, in 'bad' poetry, and in unfinished stories, for 'momentary and fleeting' glimpses of the 'norms and assumptions' that underpin and often constrain the ways in which we write (Takayoshi 2019:xii). In these scraps and glimpses, we find insights into our writing, as it is and as it might be.

In the term 'strategic scruffiness', we distinguish between productive messiness and merely sloppy writing. The difference between the two is not always obvious. Mollie Blackburn and Becky Beucher, championing queer teaching and learning in the United States, argue that educators should relax their habitual fixations on formal measures of good writing such as grammar and punctuation in order to recognise what students are really trying to say. They point out that some students may be struggling with the limits of language, and perhaps with their limited technical proficiency as writers, so assessors must try to see through these superficial flaws: 'One can easily imagine a sort of assessment in which a teacher points out run-on sentences, fragments, typographical errors, and failures to indent the first line of paragraphs. One can imagine inserting punctuation and capitalization where it is needed' (Blackburn and Beucher 2019:32).

This fixation with technical proficiency and writerly polish is not restricted to conventional academic writing. Here, Blackburn and Beucher are commenting on how teachers might assess a short story, written for a fiction class in a US high school. They remind us that the teaching and assessment of creative writing can be as mechanical and restrictive as that of any other form of writing (Blackburn and Beucher 2019:32): 'One can also imagine commending [the writer of a short story] for her use of dialogue, foreshadowing, metaphor, line breaks, and repeated use of words that convey meaning implicitly.' And, in this assessment and feedback, the imagined teachers might miss the real point of the story, which revolves around bullying and homophobia, experienced by a teenager a bit like the writer. Effectively, Blackburn and Beucher are advising us to overlook a lack of writerly polish in order to see the real point of a story.

In some other writing, rough edges in written English are not simply minor flaws, which an assessor might choose to overlook; they are more strategic and productive. Writers may subvert the conventions of received English, which are not simply neutral rules, but expressions of a cultural order and its concomitant power relations. By writing within dialect, in whatever spelling and through whatever grammar that requires, writers may challenge the dominance of Received Standard English and advance englishes – plural and seriously irreverent – in its place (Ashcroft et al 2003). We saw an example of this in Chapter 2, in the extract quoted from the novel *Incendiary* (2009) by Chris Cleave. Similarly, by actively transgressing rather than simply failing to conform not only to hegemonic English but also to the conventions of creative writing, writers may queer their words and the worlds they explore.

As we have said, this strategic scruffiness is not to be confused with a lack of polish or care. As we discussed in Chapter 3, with reference to Claire Chambers' work with young British Muslim writers, most writers aspire to write better, to develop their skills and find their voices. Our goal, in accommodating rough edges, is that these should be productive and purposeful: meaningfully queer.

Queer is a noun, an adjective and a verb. The latter – to queer – is fundamental to critical social science because it means unsettling orthodoxies, troubling certainties, challenging the intellectual order and power relations of the status quo, thereby opening new ways of seeing and new possibilities for understanding (Butler 1990; de Lauretis 1991; Fuss 2013). Queer reading means reading texts against the grain, reading in order to challenge orthodox and hegemonic categories and constructs such as hegemonic masculinity, heterosexuality and homosexuality, and creating space for something more fluid and liberating (Dollimore 1991; Sinfield 2005). At this point, queer politics reach beyond the subversive 'shattering of the illusory structures of subjectivity and meaning' (Bradway 2017:v) and reach towards what queer theorist and literary critic Tyler Bradway calls '*a creative experiment in relationality*' (Bradway 2017:vi, original emphasis). Developing this point, Bradway (2017:v) asks: 'How do the affective relations of a text "queer" its readers and the social relations of reading itself?'

Queer reading connects materiality, emotion and lived experience (de Castell and Jenson 2007; Rooke 2016:26), queer *writing* works in similar ways. Queer(ing) writing, we unsettle the seemingly immovable words on a page or a screen, words that can make phenomena seem permanent and knowable when they are nothing of the kind (Waite 2017:39). Unsettling and denaturalising binary and categorical representations, through queer theory and practice, we work to illuminate and contest the power relations in which those words and worldviews are embedded

(Barker and Scheele 2016:31). Through queer writing, we explore social worlds that are multiple and always in flux (Barker and Scheele 2016:61; Waite 2019:43). When we queer our writing, we begin to see how 'categories which seem to be both necessary and steady are actually always-already collapsing – merging into each other, sliding away into something else' (Sinfield 2005:ix–x). So, though a more creative approach to writing may help us to ask more of the words we use, it can also help us to know their limits. This leads towards an ambivalent relationship with words, in which we ask more of our writing, but remember not to trust it, and remain alert to what Canadian essayist and poet Robert Kroetsch called the 'lovely treachery of words' (Kroetsch 1989).

So, we do not simply tolerate seemingly rough edges in this book; we embrace and celebrate them. As we have explained, we do so selectively. We have tried to make this book a space for repetitions and silences, inconclusiveness, inequalities and multiplicities. The purposes, which we prioritise in all this, are those of critical social research: questioning; finding out; collecting and analysing data; analysing and sharing findings; advancing understandings. Moreover, in accommodating some 'bad' writing, we work in parallel with queer theorists and literary critics who have turned conventional literary aesthetics upside down. They explore the possibilities of 'bad reading' (Bradway 2017) and seemingly shallow and unsophisticated aesthetics, which unsettle the dominant – hierarchical and asymmetrical – relationships between writers and readers, words and the worlds they depict. Queer writing does not have a monopoly over any of this. Other forms of writing – creative writing in particular – can bring new and different 'things, actions, and even thoughts and feelings' (Harper 2019:42) into our field of view. But, while other forms of writing may *sometimes* attempt or achieve these things, queer writing revolves around them. In this book, queer has come into its own: in work that is troublesome, transgressive, sometimes abrasive, often mischievous, never conservative, often delightful, insightful and generative.

CREATIVE WRITING IN PRACTICE

Writing the end(s) ... *by Ruth Raynor*[1]

Ruth Raynor is a Lecturer in Urban Planning at Newcastle University. Her piece uses prose and an excerpt from a play script to focus on endings. She explains that creative writing for social research offers an opportunity to experiment with forms of ending as they are lived.

The ending: a threshold between absent and present, known and unknown, life and death. ... It is the line that gives form to the shape. Endings orientate us towards our limits; they are sites of exposure to the impossible or the unthinkable. So how do we research ending(s) in the social sciences? And how might creative writing position our thinking towards the ends of lives, and worlds, and ways of living? In this short piece I think these questions through my own work on everyday life and austerity in the UK.[2] Endings are everywhere in austerity. They are found in public and third sector closures, and in lives that are lost as social security falls apart. The engineers of austerity have been concerned with hiding, suppressing, and justifying these endings: the activists contesting austerity have become concerned with making them present.

Figure 5.1: Inspiration doll by Alke Gröppel-Wegener, created in response to this piece by Ruth Raynor. Inspiration dolls comment on and play with genres of creative writing.

In order to think more about endings that are written and endings that are lived, I reflect here on a piece of theatre for social research. This was developed with a group of economically marginalised women who were living the sharp end of austerity. These women were single mothers, out of paid work or in low paid, temporary and precarious employment. They faced a raft of different cuts and withdrawals. We met

---

[1] This contribution should be cited as follows: Raynor, R. (2021) 'Writing the end(s) ...'. In Phillips, R. and Kara, H. *Creative Writing for Social Research*. Bristol: Policy Press.

[2] 'Austerity' refers both to a series of budgetary reforms and cuts in the UK following the financial crisis of 2008, and to a social and cultural event, whereby austerity becomes known as and in relation to a whole range of texts, processes and lived experiences.

weekly at a family support group which itself was under threat, and now has ended. Theatre enabled us to explore different *forms* of experience in everyday life, focusing on ends. Breaking through the surface of their experiences – revealing what was underneath – the hidden, lost, or missing, and making an impression of absence, was enabled in particular ways by our approach to storying the end.

Lesley:	Listen Sandra, there's something I need to talk to you about ...
Sandra:	What, *(beat)* we're not doing yoga again are we?
Lesley:	No, no it's not the yoga,
Sandra:	Downward Dog and all that shite, I couldn't walk for a week after the last session.
Lesley:	No, don't worry I've not booked any more yoga,
Sandra:	Good cos all that breathing stresses me out.
Lesley:	It's nothing to do with that. Look, Sandra (pause) there's something I need to tell you.
Sandra:	Right. *(Pause)* Well come on then Lesley. Spit it out. *(Lesley hesitates then instead of telling the truth – that the centre is going to close – she picks up a book on the desk)*
Lesley:	Em ... Well, what it is, is ... Have you read this book?
Sandra:	Cosmic Ways to Change Your Life?
Lesley:	You should read it Sandra.
Sandra:	What, so this is what you wanted to tell iz?
Lesley:	Erm, yes. Yes, it is.
Sandra:	Noel Edmonds? *(Beat)*
Lesley:	He's a very clever man. It's changed my life this book. I mean Noel ... he was in the gutter. He lost everything didn't he?

(Excerpt from the play: *Diehard Gateshead*, written by Ruth Raynor, first staged in 2015)

The play was built around the lives of 5 women attending a third sector, local authority-funded family support centre. In the fragment above, group-leader Lesley attempts to tell one of the members, Sandra, that, as a result of cuts to core local authority funding, the centre is going to close. However this moment of bravery is disrupted by the allure of 'Noel'. Noel is a novelty jumper-wearing Saturday night UK TV star of the early 1990s. His career blossomed and died alongside yellow/pink spotted side-kick 'Mr Blobby'. After ditching Blobby and a period of insolvency, Edmonds re-birthed in 2005 via popular quiz show *Deal or no Deal*. He attributes his success to the forces of 'positive thinking' underpinning somewhat mystical (and for him, lucrative) 'cosmic ordering'. Noel recovered from his decline: he was re-birthed, and in being so evokes a model of individual and community resilience that is a quality of the neoliberal austerity agenda. 'Positive thinking' is a genre for everyday living that closes down space for dissent, and facilitates senses of autonomous agency amidst decline. Through Lesley's relation with 'cosmic ordering' we see social and cultural *mediations* of cruel optimism that emerge in response to the disbelieved reality of an ending, and to the structural conditions of decline. This strategy renders Lesley alone, feeling emotionally and practically responsible for preventing a loss that she cannot prevent.

Through the form of the play we could *attempt* (fail and fail better) to narrate the impact of service and welfare withdrawal on women's relationships with themselves, with each other, friends and family, their places and their worlds. And we could notice the forms of denial that played out amidst this end. The play makes visible conditions of violence that accompany the individuation of responsibility in austerity – until nothing but a hopeless hope feels possible.

And so through the form of the play, we could capture a feeling of the time. We could explore and evoke women's own experiences of loss and living-on through shattered presents. Through countless rewrites we kept hold of Lesley's positive attitude towards the future of the group, and her failure to address the reality of its closure even as she began to tidy things away. Lesley maintained an (obviously ludicrous) attachment to the promise of cosmic ordering (to the promise that she – with the backing of the cosmos – could fix this problem) until the end of the story. She embodied future possibility through a range of feelings, including enthusiasm, positivity, anxiety and desperation. A pragmatic relation with circumstance became subservient to the promise of positive affect.

We could write and perform emotions, moods, and conditions lived by women in austerity at the end of their support group. This spoke to other endings that women lived in austerity. The character of Lesley made present a feeling of dissonance in austerity, which resonated with audiences: this enacted a form of affective exposure that became its own fragment in the shifting of the austerity genre. The play gave shape to that which is lost, and to the challenge that accompanied fighting on or 'letting go'. Everyday endings became present in all their emotional and practical multiplicities, and this gave form to the changes that women experienced in everyday life.

The play we made together gave a particular form to the endings and withdrawals in austerity. It created a speculative bridge between absent and present, known and unknown. It created a line (not *the* line) that gave shape to *an* austerity informed by women's actual experiences. There is opportunity for thinking more and deeply with the ends of worlds, and lives, and ways of life in and through creative writing for social science, for example by exploring – how does our writing end? What does our writing end? What does this do to make meaning? Where are the limits and the boundaries in our creative practice, and what does this reveal? Creative writing for social research offers an opportunity then, for thinking with *form*: forms and mediations of experience in everyday life. And as we come to the end of this book, we might only reach out into the unknown and imagine: what next? What experiments between creative writing and social research might follow?

References

Adorno, T.W. (1984) 'The essay as form', translated by Hullot-Kentor, B. and Will, F., *New German Critique*, 32: 151–71.

Afonso, A.I. and Ramos, I.M.J. (2004) 'New graphics for old stories', in Pink, S., Kürti, L. and Afonso, A.I. (eds) *Working Images: Visual Research and Representation in Ethnography*, London: Routledge: pp 77–89.

Ahearn, A. (2006) 'Engineering writing: replacing writing classes with a writing imperative', in Ganobcsik-Williams, L. (ed) *Teaching Academic Writing in UK Higher Education*, Basingstoke: Palgrave Macmillan: pp 110–23.

Ahmed, S. (2001) 'Communities that feel: intensities, difference and attachment', in *Conference Proceedings for Affective Encounters: Rethinking Embodiment in Feminist Media Studies*, Turku, Finland: University of Turku.

Ahmed, S. (2004) *The Cultural Politics of Emotion*, Edinburgh: Edinburgh University Press.

Alaszewski, A. (2006) *Using Diaries for Social Research*, London: Sage.

Amis, M. (2001) 'Battling banality', *The Guardian*, 24 March: https://www.theguardian.com/books/2001/mar/24/artsandhumanities.highereducation.

Anderson, L. (ed) (2006) *Creative Writing: A Workbook with Readings*, Abingdon: Routledge.

Andrews, R., Borg, E., Davis Boyd, S., Domingo, M. and England, J. (eds) (2012) *Sage Handbook of Digital Dissertations and Theses*, London: Sage.

Armstrong, J. (2015) 'Empiritexts: mapping attention and invention in post-1980 French literature', *French Forum*, 40(1): 93–108.

Ashcroft, B., Griffiths, G. and Tiffin, H. (2003) *The Empire Writes Back: Theory and Practice in Post-Colonial Literatures*, London: Routledge.

Askins, K. and Pain, R. (2011) 'Contact zones: participation, materiality, and the messiness of interaction', *Environment and Planning D: Society and Space*, 29(5): 803–21.

Atkinson, R. (1998) *The Life Story Interview*, London: Sage.

Back, L. (2016) *Academic Diary: Or Why Higher Education Still Matters*, London: Goldsmiths Press.

Bakhtin, M.M. (1984) *Rabelais and His World*, Bloomington: Wiley.

Baldick, C. (2015) *Oxford Dictionary of Literary Terms*, Oxford: Oxford University Press.

Ball, P. (2005) 'Computer conference welcomes gobbledegook paper', *Nature*, 434: 946.

Banks, A. and Banks, S.P. (eds) (1998) *Fiction and Social Research: By Ice or Fire*, Lanham: AltaMira.

Barker, M.J. and Scheele, J. (2016) *Queer: A Graphic History*, London: Icon.

Barnes, T.J. and Duncan, J.S. (2013) [1992] *Writing Worlds: Discourse, Text and Metaphor in the Representation of Landscape* (second edition), London: Routledge.

Barnett, R. (2013) *Imagining the University*, London: Routledge.

Barone, T. and Eisner, E. (2012) *Arts Based Research*, Thousand Oaks: Sage.

Barrett, M. (1992) 'Words and things: materialism and method in contemporary feminist analysis', in Barrett, M. and Phillips, A. (eds) *Destabilising Theory*, Cambridge: Polity: pp 201–19.

Bartlett, R. (2012) 'Playing with meaning: using cartoons to disseminate research findings', *Qualitative Research*, 13(2): 214–27.

Barton, J. and Olson, P. (2019) 'Cite first, ask questions later?' *Papers of the Bibliographical Society of America*, 113(2): 205–16.

Batty, C. and Taylor, S. (2019) 'Comedy writing as method: reflections on screenwriting in creative practice research', *New Writing*, 16(3): 374–92.

BBC (2018) 'Free Thinking: Linton Kwesi Johnson', London: BBC Radio3: http://www.bbc.co.uk/programmes/m0001jrs.

Beck, H. (ed) (2012) *Teaching Creative Writing*, Basingstoke: Palgrave Macmillan.

Beck, J., Belliveau, G., Lea, G. and Wager, A. (2011) 'Delineating a spectrum of research-based theatre', *Qualitative Inquiry*, 17(8): 687–700.

Becker, H. (1976) 'Art as collective action', *American Sociological Review*, 39(6): 767–76.

Becker, H. (2001) 'Georges Perec's experiments in social description', *Ethnography*, 2(1): 63–76.

Bellos, D. (1993) *Georges Perec: A Life in Words*, London: Harvill.

Berbary, L. (2011) 'Post-structural writerly representation: screenplay as creative analytic practice', *Qualitative Inquiry*, 17(2): 186–96.

Berger, J. (1972) *Ways of Seeing*, Harmondsworth: Penguin.

Besley, T. and Peters, M. (2013) *Re-imagining the Creative University for the 21st Century*, Rotterdam: Sense.

Blackburn, M.V. and Beucher, B. (2019) 'Productive tensions in assessment: troubling socio-critical theories towards an advancement of queer pedagogy', in Mayo, C. and Rodriguez, N.M. (eds) *Queer Pedagogies: Theory, Praxis, Politics*, Cham: Springer: pp 23–40.

Blackshaw, T. (2002) 'Interview with Zygmunt Bauman', *Network: Newsletter of the British Sociological Association*, 83: 1–3.

Bochner, A.P. and Ellis, C. (2016) *Evocative Autoethnography: Writing Lives and Telling Stories*, New York: Routledge.

Bochner, A.P., Ellis, C. and Tillmann-Healy, L.M. (1997) 'Relationships as stories', in Duck, S. (ed) *Handbook of Personal Relationships*, New York: Wiley: pp 307–24.

Bohannon, J. (2015) 'Hoax-detecting software spots fake papers: Springer jumps into sham submissions arms race', *Science*, 348(6230): 18–19.

Bold, M.R. (2017) 'Why diverse zines matter: a case study of the people of color zines project', *Publishing Research Quarterly*, 33(3): 215–28.

Boniface, K. (2018) *Round About Town*, Axminster: Uniformbooks.

Boniface, K. (2019) 'When nothing happens in Huddersfield', in Forsdick, C., Leak, A. and Phillips, R. (eds) *Georges Perec's Geographies*, London: UCL Press: pp 236–54.

Bourdieu, P. (2000) *Pascalian Meditations*, Cambridge: Polity.

Bradway, T. (2017) *Queer Experimental Literature: The Affective Politics of Bad Reading*, New York: Palgrave Macmillan.

Breckenridge, J. (2014) 'Somewhere nowhere: lives without homes', *Rocky Mountain Review*, 68(1): 106–8.

Brewster, S., Duncan, N., Emira, M. and Clifford, A. (2017) 'Personal sacrifice and corporate cultures: career progression for disabled staff in higher education', *Disability & Society*, 32(7): 1027–42.

Brickell, K. and Garrett, B. (2015) 'Storytelling domestic violence: feminist politics of participatory video in Cambodia', ACME, 14(3): 928–53.

Brien, D.L. (2013) 'Non-fiction writing research', in Kroll, J. and Harper, G. (eds), *Research Methods in Creative Writing*, Basingstoke: Palgrave Macmillan: pp 34–55.

Brinkmann, S. (2009) 'Literature as qualitative inquiry: the novelist as researcher', *Qualitative Inquiry*, 15(8): 1376–94.

Brkich, C. and Barko, T. (2013) 'Fictive reality: troubling our notions of truth and data in iambic pentameter', *Cultural Studies – Critical Methodologies*, 13(4): 246–51.

Brown, P. (2013) 'Graphic novel: the superhero of research dissemination?' LSE blog: https://blogs.lse.ac.uk/socialcareevidenceinpractice/2013/11/12/graphic-novel-the-superhero-of-research-dissemination/.

Brown, R.H. (1977) *A Poetic for Sociology: Toward a Logic of Discovery for the Human Sciences*, Cambridge: Cambridge University Press.

Brown, N. and Leigh, J. (2018) 'Ableism in academia: where are the disabled and ill academics?' *Disability & Society*, 33(6): 985–9.

Bruce, T. (2016) *Terra Ludus*, Rotterdam: Sense.

Butler, J. (1990) *Gender Trouble: Feminism and the Subversion of Identity*, London: Routledge.

Butler-Kisber, L. and Stewart, M. (2009) 'The use of poetry clusters in poetic inquiry', in Prendergast, M., Leggo, C. and Sameshima, P. (eds) *Poetic Inquiry: Vibrant Voices in the Social Sciences*, Rotterdam: Sense: pp 3–12.

Byatt, A.S. (2001) *The Biographer's Tale*, London: Vintage.

Caine, V., Murphy, S., Estefan, A., Clandinin, J., Steeves, P. and Huber, J. (2017) 'Exploring the purposes of fictionalisation in narrative inquiry', *Qualitative Inquiry*, 23(3): 215–21.

Cameron, E. (2012) 'New geographies of story and storytelling', *Progress in Human Geography*, 36(5): 573–92.

Campbell, E., Pahl, K., Pente, E. and Rasool, Z. (eds) (2017) *Re-imagining Contested Communities: Connecting Rotherham through Research*, Bristol: Policy Press.

Carless, D. and Douglas, K. (2010) 'Performance ethnography as an approach to health-related education', *Educational Action Research*, 18(3): 373–88.

Carrigan, M. (2020) *Social Media for Academics*, London: Sage.

Carroll, P., Dew, K. and Howden-Chapman, P. (2011) 'The heart of the matter: using poetry as a method of ethnographic inquiry to represent and present experiences of the informally housed in Aotearoa/New Zealand', *Qualitative Inquiry*, 17(7): 623–30.

Castleden, H., Morgan, V.S. and Lamb, C. (2012) '"I spent the first year drinking tea": Exploring Canadian university researchers' perspectives on community-based participatory research involving Indigenous peoples', *The Canadian Geographer/Le Géographe canadien*, 56(2): 160–79.

Chambers, B. (2015) *The Long Way to a Small, Angry Planet*, London: Hodder & Stoughton.

Chambers, C., Phillips, R., Ali, N., Hopkins, P. and Pande, R. (2019) '"Sexual misery" or "happy British Muslims"? Contemporary depictions of Muslim sexuality', *Ethnicities*, 19(1): 66–94.

Chatwin, B. (1987) *The Songlines*, London: Franklin Press.

Chilton, G. and Leavy, P. (2014) 'Arts-based research practice: merging social research and the creative art', in Leavy, P. (ed) *The Oxford Handbook of Qualitative Research*, New York: Oxford University Press: pp 403–22.

Cioffi, F. (2005) *The Imaginative Argument: A Practical Manifesto for Writers*, Princeton: Princeton University Press.

Clance, R. and Imes, S. (1978) 'The imposter phenomenon in high achieving women: dynamics and therapeutic intervention', *Psychotherapy Theory, Research and Practice*, 15(3): 1–9.

Cleave, C. (2009) *Incendiary*, London: Sceptre.

Collier, A. (1994) *Critical Realism: An Introduction to Roy Bhaskar's Philosophy*, London: Verso.

Colyar, J. (2009) 'Becoming writing, becoming writers', *Qualitative Inquiry*, 15(2): 421–36.

Connolly, P., Bacon, N., Wass, V., Hoque, K. and Jones, M. (2016) '"Ahead of the Arc" – a contribution to halving the disability employment gap', London: The All Party Parliamentary Group on Disability.

Cook, J. (2012) 'Creative writing and PhD research', in Beck, H. (ed) *Teaching Creative Writing*, Basingstoke: Palgrave: pp 99–103.

Cottom, T. (2019) *Thick and other Essays*, New York, NY: The New Press.

Cowie, P. (2017) 'Performing planning: understanding community participation in planning through theatre', *Town Planning Review*, 88(4): 401–21.

Cox, M.B. and Dadas, C. (eds) (2019) *Re/Orienting Writing Studies: Queer Methods, Queer Projects*, Boulder: University Press of Colorado.

Crawley, S.L. and Broad, K.L. (2004) '"Be your (real lesbian) self": mobilizing sexual formula stories through personal (and political) storytelling', *Journal of Contemporary Ethnography*, 33(1): 39–71.

Davis, C., Senechal, M. and Zwicky, J. (eds) (2008) *The Shape of Content: Creative Writing in Mathematics and Science*, Boca Raton, Florida: CRC Press.

Day, J. (2015) *Cyclogeography: Journeys of a London Bicycle Courier*, Honiton: Notting Hill Editions.

de Castell, S. and Jenson, J. (2007) 'No place like home: sexuality, community and identity among street-involved queer and questioning youth', in Blackburn, M.V. and Clark, C.T. (eds) *Literacy Research for Political Action and Social Change*, New York: Peter Lang: pp 131–52.

de Freitas, E. (2003) 'Contested positions: how fiction informs empathic research', *International Journal of Education and the Arts*, 4(7): 4.

Delamont, S. (2004) 'Ethnography and participant observation', *Qualitative Research Practice*, 217: 206–7.

de Lauretis, T. (1991) *Queer Theory: Lesbian and Gay Sexualities*, Bloomington: Indiana University Press.

de Leeuw, S., Parkes, M.W., Morgan, V.S., Christensen, J., Lindsay, N., Mitchell-Foster, K. and Russell Jozkow, J. (2017) 'Going unscripted: a call to critically engage storytelling methods and methodologies in geography and the medical-health sciences', *The Canadian Geographer/Le Géographe canadien*, 61(2): 152–64.

DeLyser, D. and Sui, D. (2014) 'Crossing the qualitative-quantitative chasm III: enduring methods, open geography, participatory research, and the fourth paradigm', *Progress in Human Geography*, 38(2): 294–307.

Denzin, N. (2003) *Performance Ethnography*, Thousand Oaks: Sage.

Denzin, N. (2010/2016) *The Qualitative Manifesto: A Call to Arms*, Walnut Creek, CA: Left Coast Press/Abingdon, Routledge.

Dillard, A. (1995) *Mornings Like This: Found Poems*, New York: Harper-Collins.

Diprose, K. (2017) 'Lighthouse Keeper', in Farren, M. (ed) *Un/Forced: An Anthology of Poetry and Fiction from Rhubarb*, Shipley: Ings Poetry.

Diprose, K., Valentine, G., Vanderbeck, R., Liu, C. and McQuaid, K. (2019) *Climate Change, Consumption and Intergenerational Justice: Lived Experiences from China, Uganda and the UK*, Bristol: Bristol University Press.

Diversi, M. (1998) 'Glimpses of street life: representing lived experience through short stories', *Qualitative Inquiry*, 4(2): 131–47.

Djohari, N., Pyndiah, G. and Arnone, A. (2018) 'Rethinking "safe spaces" in children's geographies', *Children's Geographies*, 16(4): 351–5.

Dollimore, J. (1991) *Sexual Dissidence*, Oxford: Oxford University Press.

Douglas, E.R. (2015) 'Foucault, laughter, and gendered normalization', *Foucault Studies*, 20: 142–54.

Douglas, K. (2012) 'Signals and signs', *Qualitative Inquiry*, 18(6): 525–32.

Dresser, R. (2015) 'What subjects teach: the everyday ethics of human research', *Wake Forest Law Review*, 50: 301–41.

Duncan, R., Taylor, M. and Stoddard, D. (2016) *Creating Comics as Journalism, Memoir and Nonfiction*, New York: Routledge.

Eggers, D. (2007) *What is the What*, London: Hamish Hamilton.

Elbow, P. (1998) *Writing with Power: Techniques for Mastering the Writing Process*, New York: Oxford University Press.

Elbow, P. (2000) *Everyone Can Write: Essays Toward a Hopeful Theory of Writing and Teaching Writing*, New York: Oxford University Press.

Eliot, T.S. (1944) *Four Quartets*, Norwich: Jarrold & Sons Ltd.

Ellingson, L. (2009) *Engaging Crystallization in Qualitative Research: An Introduction*, Thousand Oaks: Sage.

Ellis, C. and Bochner, A. (2000) 'Autoethnography, personal narrative, reflexivity: researcher as subject', in Denzin, N.K. and Lincoln, Y.S. (eds) *Handbook of Qualitative Research* (second edition), Thousand Oaks: Sage: pp 733–68.

Ellis, C. and Adams, T.E. (2014) 'The purposes, practices and principles of autoethnographic research', in Leavy, P. (ed) *The Oxford Handbook of Qualitative Research*, New York: Oxford University Press: pp 254–76.

England, K.V. (1994) 'Getting personal: reflexivity, positionality, and feminist research', *The Professional Geographer*, 46(1): 80–9.

Eshun, G. and Madge, C. (2012) '"Now let me share this with you": exploring poetry as a method for postcolonial geography research', *Antipode*, 44(4): 1395–428.

Eshun, G. and Madge, C. (2016) 'Poetic world-writing in a pluriversal world: a provocation to the creative (re) turn in geography', *Social & Cultural Geography*, 17(6): 778–85.

Evans, M., Moore, S. and Johnstone, H. (2018) *Detecting the Social: Order and Disorder in Post-1970s Detective Fiction*, Basingstoke: Palgrave Macmillan.

Farrant, F. (2014) 'Unconcealment: what happens when we tell stories', *Qualitative Inquiry*, 20(4): 461–70.

Faulkner, S. (2019) 'Poetic inquiry: poetry as/in/for social research', in Leavy, P. (ed) *Handbook of Arts-Based Research*, New York: Guilford: pp 208–30.

Faulkner, S. (2020) *Poetic Inquiry: Craft, Method and Practice*, Abingdon: Routledge.

Finley, S. (2019) 'Multimethod arts-based research', in Leavy, P. (ed) *Handbook of Arts-Based Research,* New York: Guilford: pp 477–90.

Finnegan, R. (2007) *The Hidden Musicians*, Middleton: Wesleyan University Press.

Fish, S.E. (1980) *Is there a Text in this Class? The Authority of Interpretive Communities*, Cambridge: Harvard University Press.

Forsdick, C. and Stafford, A. (eds) (2006) *The Modern Essay in French*, Bern: Peter Lang.

Forster, E. (1974 [1927]) *Aspects of the Novel*, London: Edward Arnold.

Foss, S. and Waters, W. (2016) *Destination Dissertation*, Lanham: Rowman & Littlefield.

Foster, D. (2007) 'Legal obligation or personal lottery? Employee experiences of disability and the negotiation of adjustments in the public sector workplace', *Work, Employment & Society*, 21(1): 67–84.

Foster, V. (2013) 'Pantomime and politics: the story of a performance ethnography', *Qualitative Research*, 13(1): 36–52.

Fox, K. (1996) 'Silent voices', in Ellis, C. and Bochner, A. (eds) *Composing Ethnography: Alternative Forms of Qualitative Writing*, Walnut Creek: AltaMira: pp 330–56.

Fox, K. (2018) 'Standing up to false binaries in humour and autism: a dialogue', in Davies, H. and Ilott, S. (eds) *Comedy and the Politics of Representation*, New York: Palgrave Macmillan: pp 171–88.

Freire, P. (1996) *Pedagogy of the Oppressed*, London: Penguin.

Fry, S. (2005) *The Ode Less Travelled: Unlocking the Poet Within*, London: Arrow Books.

Furman, R., Langer, C., Davis, C., Gallardo, H. and Kulkarni, S. (2007) 'Expressive, research and reflective poetry as qualitative inquiry: a study of adolescent identity', *Qualitative Research*, 7(3): 301–15.

Fuss, D. (2013) *Inside/Out: Lesbian Theories, Gay Theories* (second edition), London and New York: Routledge.

Gabriel, Y. (2000) *Storytelling in Organizations: Facts, Fictions, and Fantasies*, Oxford: Oxford University Press.

Gabriel, Y. and Connell, N.A.D. (2010) 'Co-creating stories: collaborative experiments in storytelling', *Management Learning*, 41(5): 507–23.

Gandolfo, D. and Ochoa, T. (2017) 'Ethnographic excess', in Pandian, A. and McLean, S. (eds) *Crumpled Paper Boat*, Durham, NC: Duke University Press: pp 185–8.

Gembus, M.P. (2018) 'The safe spaces "in-between" – plays, performance and identity among young "second generation" Somalis in London', *Children's Geographies*, 16(4): 432–43.

Gergen, K. and Gergen, M. (2019) 'The performative movement in social science', in Leavy, P. (ed) *Handbook of Arts-Based Research*, New York: Guilford: pp 54–67.

Gergen, M. and Gergen, K. (2012) *Playing with Purpose: Adventures in Performative Social Science*, Walnut Creek: Left Coast Press.

Gerver, M. (2013) 'Exceptions to blanket anonymity for the publication of interviews with refugees: African refugees in Israel as a case study', *Research Ethics*, 9(3): 121–39.

Glasby, H. (2019) 'Making it queer, not clear', in Banks, W.P., Cox, M.B. and Dadas, C. (eds) *Re/Orienting Writing Studies: Queer Methods, Queer Projects*, Boulder: University Press of Colorado: pp 24–41.

Goffman, E. (2009) *Stigma: Notes on the Management of Spoiled Identity*, New York: Simon & Schuster.

Goldberg, N. (1991) *Wild Mind: Living the Writer's Life*, London: Random House.

Goldstein, T. and Wickett, J. (2009) 'Zero tolerance: a stage adaptation of an investigative report on school safety', *Qualitative Inquiry*, 15(10): 1552–68.

Goodson, P. (2017) *Becoming an Academic Writer: 50 Exercises for Paced, Productive and Powerful Writing*, Thousand Oaks: SAGE.

Grech, V. (2019) 'Write a scientific paper (WASP): academic hoax and fraud', *Early Human Development*, 129: 87–9.

Grimshaw, A. (2001) *The Ethnographer's Eye: Ways of Seeing in Anthropology*, Cambridge: Cambridge University Press.

Guidi, P. (2003) 'Guatemalan Mayan Women and participatory visual media', in White, S.A. (ed) *Participatory Video: Images that Transform and Empower*, London: Sage: pp 252–70.

Gullion, J.S. (2014) *October Birds*, Rotterdam: Sense.

Halberstam, J. (2011) *The Queer Art of Failure*, Durham: Duke University Press.

Halperin, D.M. (1990) *One Hundred Years of Homosexuality*, Abingdon: Routledge.

Hamid, T. (2017) 'Islamic Tinder', in Mahfouz, S. (ed) *The Things I Would Tell You: British Muslim Women Write*, London: Saqi: pp 81–4.

Hannam-Swain, S. (2018) 'The additional labour of a disabled PhD student', *Disability & Society*, 33(1): 138–42.

Harley, A. and Langdon, J. (2018) 'Ethics and power in visual research methods', in Iphofen, R. and Tolich, M. (eds) *The SAGE Handbook of Qualitative Research Ethics*, London: SAGE: pp 188–202.

Harper, G. (2013) 'The generations of creative writing research', in Kroll, J. and Harper, G. (eds) *Research Methods in Creative Writing*, Basingstoke: Palgrave Macmillan: pp 133–54.

Harper, G. (2019) *Critical Approaches to Creative Writing*, Abingdon: Routledge.

Harron, P. (2016) *The Equidistribution of Lattice Shapes of Rings of Integers of Cubic, Quartic and Quintic Number Fields: An Artist's Rendering*, Doctoral dissertation: Ann Arbor.

Haslam, S. (2006a) 'Life writing', in Anderson, L. (ed) *Creative Writing: A Workbook with Readings*, Abingdon: Routledge: pp 270–80.

Haslam, S. (2006b) 'Editing', in Anderson, L. (ed) *Creative Writing: A Workbook with Readings*, Abingdon: Routledge: pp 372–82.

Hawkins, H. (2015) 'Creative geographic methods: knowing, representing, intervening. On composing place and page', *Cultural Geographies*, 22(2): 247–68.

Hawkins, H. (2017) *Creativity*, Abingdon: Routledge.

Hawkins, H. (2018) 'Geography's creative (re)turn: toward a critical framework', *Progress in Human Geography*, 43(6): 963–84.

Hemmingson, M. (2008) 'Make them giggle: auto/ethnography as stand-up comedy – a response to Denzin's call to performance', *Creative Approaches to Research*, 1(2): 9–22.

Henderson, D. and Taimina, D. (2001) 'Crocheting the hyperbolic plane', *The Mathematical Intelligencer*, 23(2): 17–28.

Heron, J. and Reason, P. (2005) 'The practice of co-operative inquiry: research with rather than on people', in Reason, P. and Bradbury, H. (eds) *Handbook of Action Research*, London: Sage: pp 144–54.

Hill, A. (2012) 'Campaign to unlock secrets of people who go missing', *The Guardian*, 16 September. Source: https://www.theguardian.com/uk/2012/sep/16/campaign-unlock-secrets-missing-persons.

Holland, S., Butt, M., Harper, G. and Wandor, M. (eds) (2003) *Creative Writing: A Good Practice Guide*, London: English Subject Centre, Royal Holloway University of London.

Holloway, S. (2010) *The Serious Guide to Joke Writing: How to Say Something Funny about Anything*, Gorleston: Bookshaker.

hooks, b. (1991) 'Theory as liberatory practice', *Yale Journal of Law and Feminism*, 4: 1–12.

hooks, b. (2009) *Belonging: A Culture of Place*, New York: Routledge.

Hughes, R. (1991) *The Shock of the New*, London: Thames & Hudson.

Hume-Cook, G., Curtis, T., Potaka, J., Tangaroa Wagner, A., Woods, K. and Kindon, S. (2007) 'Uniting people with place through participatory video: a Ngaati Hauiti journey', in Kindon, S., Pain, R. and Kesby, M. (eds) *Participatory Action Research Approaches and Methods*, Abingdon: Routledge: pp 160–9.

Hunter, M.A. (2008) 'Cultivating the art of safe space', *Research in Drama Education: the Journal of Applied Theatre and Performance*, 13(1): 5–21.

Inckle, K. (2014) 'Strong and silent: men, masculinity and self-injury', *Men & Masculinities*, 17(1): 3–21.

Inckle, K. (2015) 'Debilitating times: compulsory ablebodiedness and white privilege in theory and practice', *Feminist Review*, 111(1): 42–58.

Inckle, K. (2018a) 'Unreasonable adjustments: the additional unpaid labour of academics with disabilities', *Disability & Society*, 33(8): 1372–6.

Inckle, K. (2018b) 'Irrational perspectives and untenable positions: sociology, madness and "disability"', in Holland, S. and Spracklen, K. (eds) *Subcultures, Bodies and Spaces: Essays on Alternativity and Marginalization*, Bingley: Emerald: pp 169–90.

Iser, W. (1997) 'The significance of fictionalizing', *Anthropoetics*, 3(2): 1–9.

Jack, K.F. and Tetley, J. (2016) 'Using poems to explore the meaning of compassion to undergraduate nursing students', *International Practice Development Journal*, 6(1): 1–13.

Jackson, M. (2017) 'After the fact: the question of fidelity in ethnographic writing', in Pandian, A. and McLean, S. (eds) *Crumpled Paper Boat*, Durham: Duke University Press: pp 48–67.

Jackson, P. (2013), *Food Words: Essays in Culinary Culture*, London: Bloomsbury.

Jacobsen, M.H. and Marshman, S. (2008) 'Bauman's metaphors: the poetic imagination in sociology', *Current Sociology*, 56(5): 798–18.

Jarman, D. (1992) *Modern Nature*, London: Vintage.

Jenkins, M. (2015) 'Artist's statement: the politics of performing place in *Spirit of Detroit*', *Text and Performance Quarterly*, 35(1): 62–75.

Jennings, L.E. and McLean, K.C. (2013) 'Storying away self-doubt', *Journal of Research in Personality*, 47(4): 317–29.

Jervis, J. (2015) *Sensational Subjects*, London: Bloomsbury.

Jones, K. (2013) 'Infusing biography with the personal: writing Rufus Stone', *Creative Approaches to Research*, 6(2): 4–21.

Jones, K. and Leavy, P. (2014) 'A conversation between Kip Jones and Patricia Leavy: arts-based research, performative social science and working on the margins', *The Qualitative Report*, 19(38): 1–7.

Josselson, R. (2011) '"Bet you think this song is about you": whose narrative is it in narrative research?', *Narrative Works*, 1(1): 33–51.

Kara, H. (2017) *Research and Evaluation for Busy Students and Practitioners: A Time-Saving Guide*, (second edition), Bristol: Policy Press.

Kara, H. (2018) *Research Ethics in the Real World: Euro-Western and Indigenous Perspectives*, Bristol: Policy Press.

Kara, H. (2020) *Creative Research Methods: A Practical Guide* (second edition), Bristol: Policy Press.

Kara, H. and Brooks, J. (2020) 'The potential role of comics in teaching qualitative research methods', *The Qualitative Report*, 25(7): 1754–65.

Kearney, K.S. and Hyle, A.E. (2004) 'Drawing out emotions: the use of participant-produced drawings in qualitative inquiry', *Qualitative Research*, 4(3): 361–82.

Keegan, M. (2012) 'The opposite of loneliness', *Yale News*, 27 May: https://yaledailynews.com/blog/2012/05/27/keegan-the-opposite-of-loneliness/.

Keegan, M. (2014) *The Opposite of Loneliness: Essays and Stories*, New York: Simon and Schuster.

Kersting, K. (2003) 'What exactly is creativity?' *American Psychological Association*, 34(10): 1–40.

Kidd, L.I. and Tusaie, K.R. (2004) 'Disconfirming beliefs: the use of poetry to know the lived experience of student nurses', *Issues in Mental Health Nursing*, 25(4): 403–14.

Kindon, S., Pain, R. and Kesby, M. (eds) (2007) *Participatory Action Research Approaches and Methods*, Abingdon: Routledge.

King, S. (2000) *On Writing*, London: Hodder and Stoughton.

King, D. and Wyndham, F. (eds) (1993) *Bruce Chatwin: Photographs and Notebooks*, London: Jonathan Cape.

Koelsch, L. (2016) 'The use of I poems to better understand complex subjectivities', in Galvin, K. and Prendergast, M. (eds) *Poetic Inquiry II – Seeing, Caring, Understanding: Using Poetry as and for Inquiry*, Rotterdam: Sense: pp 169–79.

Koziski, S. (1984) 'The standup comedian as anthropologist: intentional culture critic', *Journal of Popular Culture*, 18(2): 57–76.

Kroetsch, R. (1989) *The Lovely Treachery of Words: Essays Selected and New*, Ontario: Oxford University Press Canada.

Kroll, J. and Harper, G. (eds) (2013) *Research Methods in Creative Writing*, Basingstoke: Palgrave Macmillan.

Kuhn, T. (1962) *The Structure of Scientific Revolutions*, Chicago: Chicago University Press.

Kusserow, A. (2017) 'Anthropoetry', in Pandian, A. and McLean, S. (eds) *Crumpled Paper Boat*, Durham: Duke University Press: pp 71–90.

Lakoff, G. (1987) *Women, Fire and Dangerous Things: What Categories Reveal about the Mind*, Chicago: University of Chicago Press.

Lapum, J., Ruttonsha, P., Church, K., Yau, T. and David, A. (2012) 'Employing the arts in research as an analytical tool and dissemination method', *Qualitative Inquiry*, 18(1): 100–15.

Law, J. (2004) *After Method: Mess in Social Science Research*, London: Routledge.

Leak, A. (2001) 'Paris created and destroyed', *AA Files*, 45/46: 25–31.

Leavy, P. (2015) *Method Meets Art: Arts-Based Research Practice*, New York: Guilford.

Leavy, P. (ed) (2019) *Handbook of Arts-Based Research* (Paperback edition), New York: Guilford.

Lefebvre, H. (1991) *The Production of Space*, translated by Nicholson-Smith, D., Oxford: Blackwell.

Le Ha, P. (2009) 'Strategic, passionate, but academic: am I allowed in my writing?', *Journal of English for Academic Purposes*, 8(2): 134–46.

Lewis, P.J. (2011) 'Storytelling as research/research as storytelling', *Qualitative Inquiry*, 17(6): 505–10.

Lindsay, J.A., Boghossian, P. and Pluckrose, H. (2018) 'Academic grievance studies and the corruption of scholarship', *Areo Magazine*, 2 October: https://areomagazine.com/2018/10/02/academic-grievance-studies-and-the-corruption-of-scholarship/.

Lorde, A. (2017) *Your Silence Will Not Protect You*, London: Silver.

Lorimer, H. and Parr, H. (2014) 'Excursions: telling stories and journeys', *Cultural Geographies*, 21: 543–7.

Löwenheim, O. (2010) 'The "I" in IR: an autoethnographic account', *Review of International Studies*, 36: 1023–45.

Luey, B. (2010) *Handbook for Academic Authors*, New York: Cambridge University Press.

Macfarlane, A. (1978) *The Origins of English Individualism*, Oxford: Oxford University Press.

Maciel, M.E. (2006) 'The unclassifiable', *Theory, Culture & Society*, 23: 47–50.

Magné, B. (2004) 'Georges Perec on the index', *Yale French Studies*, 105: 72–88.

Mahoney, D. (2007) 'Constructing reflexive fieldwork relationships: narrating my collaborative storytelling methodology', *Qualitative Inquiry*, 13(4): 573–94.

Mannay, D. (2016) *Visual, Narrative and Creative Research Methods: Application, Reflection and Ethics*, Abingdon: Routledge.

Manzo, L.C. and Brightbill, N. (2007) 'Towards a participatory ethics', in Kindon, S., Pain, R. and Kesby, M. (eds) *Participatory Action Research Approaches and Methods*, Abingdon: Routledge: pp 33–40.

Markham, A. (2012) 'Fabrication as ethical practice: qualitative inquiry in ambiguous internet contexts', *Information, Communication & Society*, 15(3): 334–53.

Martin, D. (2019) 'Endotic Englishness: Meades, Perec and the everyday curiosities of place', in Forsdick, C., Leak, A. and Phillips, R. (eds) *Georges Perec's Geographies*, London: UCL Press: pp 186–99.

Martin, N. (2017) *Encouraging Disabled Leaders in Higher Education: Recognising Hidden Talents*, London: Leadership Foundation.

Massey, D. (1991) 'A global sense of place', *Marxism Today*, June: 25–9.

Massey, D. (2003) 'Encounters', in Tate (ed) *The Weather Project Catalogue*, London: Tate.

Massey, D. (2004) 'Geographies of responsibility', *Geografiska Annaler: Human Geography*, 86(1): 5–18.

Matless, D. (2015) *The Regional Book*, Axminster: Uniformbooks.

Matless, D. (2019) 'Seeing more flatly: *The Regional Book*', in Forsdick, C., Leak, A. and Phillips, R. (eds) *Georges Perec's Geographies*, London: UCL Press: pp 170–84.

Mattingly, D. (2001) 'Place, teenagers and representations: lessons from a community theatre project', *Social & Cultural Geography*, 2(4): 445–59.

Maugham, W.S. (1951) 'Mayhew', in *Collected Short Stories, Volume 4*, Harmondsworth: Penguin: pp 173–5.

McCloud, S. (1994) *Understanding Comics: The Invisible Art*, New York: HarperPerennial.

McCloud, S. (2006) *Making Comics: Storytelling Secrets of Comics, Manga and Graphic Novels*, New York: William Morrow/HarperCollins.

McCulliss, D. (2013) 'Poetic inquiry and multidisciplinary qualitative research', *Journal of Poetry Therapy*, 26(2): 83–114.

McFarlane, H. and Hansen, N.E. (2007) 'Inclusive methodologies: including disabled people in participatory action research in Scotland and Canada', in Kindon, S., Pain, R. and Kesby, M. (eds) *Participatory Action Research Approaches and Methods*, Abingdon: Routledge: pp 114–20.

McKee, R. (1999) *Story: Substance, Structure, Style, and the Principles of Screenwriting*, London: Methuen.

McNally, D. (2018) 'Collaboration as acknowledged co-production: a site-based approach to Tribe', *Cultural Geographies*, 25(2): 339–59.

McNicol, S. (2019) 'Using participant-created comics as a research method', *Qualitative Research Journal*, 19(3): 236–47.

McRuer, R. (2006) *Crip Theory: Cultural Signs of Queerness and Disability, Volume 9*, New York: NYU Press.

Meades, J. (2014) *An Encyclopaedia of Myself*, London: Fourth Estate.

Merleau-Ponty, M. (2002) *Phenomenology of Perception*, London: Routledge.

Mintz, L. (1985) 'Standup comedy as social and cultural mediation', *American Quarterly*, 37(1): 71–80.

Mohan, G. (2001) 'Beyond participation: strategies for deeper empowerment', in Cooke, B. and Kothari, U. (eds) *Participation: The New Tyranny?*, London: Zed: pp 153–67.

Moran, J. (2019) *First You Write a Sentence*, London: Penguin Random House.

Morgan, E. (2000) 'Transgression in Glasgow: a poet coming to terms', in Phillips, R., Watt, D. and Shuttleton, D. (eds) *De-centring Sexualities: Politics and Representations Beyond the Metropolis*, London: Routledge: pp 278–91.

Morgan, N. (2011) *Write to be Published*, Oxford: Snowbooks.

Morley, D. and Worpole, K. (eds) (1982) *The Republic of Letters*, London: Minority Press.

Morris, G., Dahl, S., Brown, P., Scullion, L. and Somerville, P. (2012) *Somewhere Nowhere: Lives without Homes*, Salford: University of Salford Housing and Urban Studies Unit.

Mort, G. (2013) 'Transcultural writing and research', in Kroll, J. and Harper, G. (eds) *Research Methods in Creative Writing*, Basingstoke: Palgrave Macmillan: pp 201–22.

Mould, O. (2018) *Against Creativity*, London: Verso.

Murray, D.M. (1972) 'Teach writing as a process not product', reprinted in Villanueva, V. and Arola, K.L. (eds) (2003) *Cross-Talk in Comp Theory*, Urbana: National Council of Teachers of English.

Murray, R. (2009) *Writing for Academic Journals*, Maidenhead: Open University Press.

Murray, R. (2014) *Writing in Social Spaces: A Social Processes Approach to Academic Writing*, Abingdon: Routledge.

Myers, N. (2012) 'Dance your PhD: embodied animations, body experiments, and the affective entanglements of life science research', *Body & Society*, 18: 151–89.

Nagar, R. and Ali, F. (2003) 'Collaboration across borders: moving beyond positionality', *Singapore Journal of Tropical Geography*, 24(3): 356–72.

Neale, D. (2006a) 'Writing what you come to know', in Anderson, L. (ed) *Creative Writing: A Workbook with Readings*, Abingdon: Routledge: pp 56–69.

Neale, D. (2006b) 'Showing and telling', in Anderson, L. (ed) *Creative Writing: A Workbook with Readings*, Abingdon: Routledge: pp 127–39.

Neale, D. (2006c) 'Writing what you know', in Anderson, L. (ed) *Creative Writing: A Workbook with Readings*, Abingdon: Routledge: pp 44–55.

Neale, D. (2006d) 'Versions of a life', in Anderson, L. (ed) *Creative Writing: A Workbook with Readings*, Abingdon: Routledge: pp 330–42.

Neale, D. (2009) 'Voices in fiction', in Neale, D. (ed) *A Creative Writing Handbook: Developing Dramatic Technique, Individual Style and Voice*, London: A&C Black.

Newman, J.H., Landow, G.P., Newman, J.E., Turner, F.M., Garland, M.M. and Castro-Klaren, S. (1996) *The Idea of a University*, New Haven: Yale University Press.

Ní Laoire, C. (2007) 'To name or not to name: reflections on the use of anonymity in an oral archive of migrant life narratives', *Social & Cultural Geography*, 8(3): 373–90.

Nicholson, H. (1997) 'In amateur hands … home movies', *History Workshop Journal*, 43: 198–213.

Nordström, P. (2016) 'The creative landscape of theatre-research co-operation: a case from Turku, Finland', *Geografiska Annaler: Human Geography*, 98(1): 1–17.

Nygaard, L. (2015) *Writing for Scholars: A Practical Guide to Making Sense and Being Heard*, London: Sage.

Orwell, G. (2013) *Politics and the English Language*. Penguin Classics edition (first published 1946), London: Penguin.

Paget, D. (1987) 'Verbatim theatre: oral history and documentary techniques', *New Theatre Quarterly*, 3(12): 317–36.

Paiva, D. (2020) 'Poetry as a resonant method for multi-sensory research', *Emotion, Space and Society*, 34: Article number 100655.

Pandian, A. and McLean, S. (eds) (2017) *Crumpled Paper Boat: Experiments in Ethnographic Writing*, Durham: Duke University Press.

Paré, A. (2019) 'Re-writing the doctorate: new contexts, identities, and genres', *Journal of Second Language Writing*, 43: 80–4.

Parfitt, E. (2019) *Young People, Learning and Storytelling*, Cham: Palgrave Macmillan.

Park-Kang, S. (2015) 'Fictional IR and imagination: advancing narrative approaches', *Review of International Studies*, 41: 361–81.

Parr, H. (2007) 'Collaborative film-making as process, method and text in mental health research', *Cultural Geographies*, 14(1): 114–38.

Parr, H. and Stevenson, O. (2013) *Missing People, Missing Voices*, www.geographiesofmissingpeople.org.uk.

Parr, H. and Stevenson, O. (2014) 'Sophie's story: writing missing journeys', *Cultural Geographies*, 21(4): 565–82.

Patrick, L.D. (2016) 'Found poetry: creating space for imaginative arts-based literacy research writing', *Literacy Research*, 65(1): 384–403.

Peacock, J.L. and Holland, D.C. (1993) 'The narrated self: life stories in process', *Ethos*, 21(4): 367–83.

Pelias, R.J. (2019) *The Creative Qualitative Researcher*, Abingdon: Routledge.

Perec, G. (1997) *Species of Spaces and Other Pieces*, translated by Sturrock, J., London: Penguin.

Phillips, A. (2012) 'List', in Lury, C. and Wakeford, N. (eds) *Inventive Methods: The Happening of the Social*, Abingdon: Routledge: pp 96–109.

Phillips, L.G. and Bunda, T. (2018) *Research Through, With and As Storying*, Abingdon: Routledge.

Phillips, R. (2010) 'The impact agenda and geographies of curiosity', *Transactions of the Institute of British Geographers*, 35(4): 447–52.

Phillips, R. (2016) 'Curious about others: relational and empathetic curiosity for diverse societies', *New Formations*, 88: 123–42.

Phillips, R. (2018) 'Georges Perec's experimental fieldwork: Perecquian fieldwork', *Social & Cultural Geography*, 19(2): 171–91.

Phillips, R. and Johns, J. (2012), *Fieldwork for Human Geography*, London: Sage.

Phillips, R., Ali, N. and Chambers, C. (2020) 'Critical collaborative storying: making an animated film about halal dating', *Cultural Geographies*, 27(1): 37–54.

Phillips, R., Chambers, C., Ali, N., Diprose, K. and Karmakar, I. (2021) *Storying Relationships: Young British Muslims Speak and Write about Sex and Love*, London: Zed/Bloomsbury.

Pickering, L. (2018) 'Paternalism and the ethics of researching with people who use drugs', in Iphofen, R. and Tolich, M. (eds) *The Sage Handbook of Qualitative Research Ethics*, London: Sage: pp 411–25.

Pickering, L. and Kara, H. (2017) 'Presenting and representing others: towards an ethics of engagement', *International Journal of Social Research Methodology*, 20(3): 299–309.

Piirto, J. (2009) 'The question of quality and qualifications: writing inferior poems as qualitative research', in Prendergast, M., Leggo, C. and Sameshima, P. (eds) *Poetic Inquiry*, Rotterdam: Sense: pp 83–100.

Plummer, K. (1995) *Telling Sexual Stories*, London: Routledge.

Plummer, K. (2012) 'My multiple sick bodies', in Turner, B.S. (ed) *Routledge Handbook of Body Studies*, London: Routledge: pp 75–93.

Polkinghorne, D. (1988) *Narrative Knowing and the Human Sciences*, Albany: SUNY Press.

Pope, R. (2005) *Creativity: Theory, History, Practice*, Abingdon: Routledge.

Pratt, G. (2009) 'Circulating sadness: witnessing Filipina mothers' stories of family separation', *Gender, Place and Culture*, 16(1): 3–22.

Pratt, G. (2012) *Families Apart: Migrant Mothers and the Conflicts of Labor and Love*, Minneapolis: University of Minnesota Press.

Pratt, G. and Johnston, C. (2017) 'Crossing oceans: testimonial theatre, Filipina migrant labor, empathy, and engagement', *GeoHumanities*, 3(2): 279–91.

Prendergast, M. (2004) '"Shaped like a question mark": found poetry from Herbert Blau's *The Audience*', *Research in Drama Education*, 9(1): 73–92.

Prendergast, M. (2015) 'Poetic inquiry, 2007–2012: a surrender and catch found poem', *Qualitative Inquiry*, 21(8): 678–85.

Prendergast, M., Leggo, C. and Sameshima, P. (eds) (2009) *Poetic Inquiry: Vibrant Voices in the Social Sciences*, Rotterdam: Sense.

Priego, E. (2016) 'Comics as research, comics for impact: the case of higher fees, higher debts', *The Comics Grid: Journal of Comics Scholarship*, 6: 16.

Pring, J. (2018a) 'Union leads call for action on "silent massacre" of disabled staff and students', *Disability News Service*, 22 November: https://www.disabilitynewsservice.com/union-leads-call-for-action-on-silent-massacre-of-disabled-staff-and-students/.

Pring, J. (2018b) 'Union backs claims of widespread discrimination by "hostile" university', *Disability News Service*, 16 August: https://www.disabilitynewsservice.com/union-backs-claims-of-widespread-discrimination-by-hostile-university/.

Rainford, J. (2019) *Equal Practices? A Comparative Study of Widening Participation*, Staffordshire University: PhD Thesis.

Rancière, J. (2009) *The Emancipated Spectator*, London: Verso.

Rapport, F. and Hartill, C. (2016) 'Making the case for poetic inquiry in health services research', in Galvin, K. and Prendergast, M. (eds) *Poetic Inquiry II – Seeing, Caring, Understanding: Using Poetry as and for Inquiry*, Rotterdam: Sense: pp 211–26.

Raynor, R. (2016) *Holding Things Together (And What Falls Apart …)*, University of Durham University: PhD Thesis.

Raynor, R. (2017) 'Dramatising austerity: holding a story together (and why it falls apart …)', *Cultural Geographies*, 24(2): 193–212.

Raynor, R. (2019) 'Speaking, feeling, mattering: theatre as method and model for practice-based, collaborative, research', *Progress in Human Geography*, 43(4): 691–710.

Reisman, M. (2011) 'Integrating fantasy and reality in Jeanette Winterson's *Oranges Are Not the Only Fruit*', *Rocky Mountain Review*, 65(1): 11–35.

Rendell, R. (1977) *A Judgement in Stone*, London: Hutchinson.

Reuter, M.E. (2015) *Creativity: A Sociological Approach*, Basingstoke: Palgrave Macmillan.

Rhodes, C. (2009) 'After reflexivity: ethics, freedom and the writing of organization studies', *Organization Studies*, 30(6): 653–72.

Richards, R. (2007) *Everyday Creativity and New Views of Human Nature*, Greenwich: Ablex.

Richardson, L. (1997) *Fields of Play: Constructing an Academic Life*, New Brunswick: Rutgers University Press.

Richardson, M.J. (2015) 'Theatre as safe space? Performing intergenerational narratives with men of Irish descent', *Social & Cultural Geography*, 16(6): 615–33.

Rico, G.L. (1983) *Writing the Natural Way*, Los Angeles: Tarcher.

Ridley-Ellis, D. (2014) 'Stand-up comedy for researchers', in Daly, I. and Brophy Haney, A. (eds) *53 Interesting Ways to Communicate Your Research*, Newmarket: Professional and Higher Partnership: pp 57–8.

Ronagh, M. and Souder, L. (2015) 'The ethics of ironic science in its search for spoof', *Science and Engineering Ethics*, 21: 1537–49.

Ronai, C.R. (1995) 'Multiple reflections of child sex abuse: an argument for a layered account', *Journal of Contemporary Ethnography*, 23(4): 395–426.

Rooke, A. (2016) 'Queer in the field: on emotions, temporality and performativity in ethnography', in Browne, K. and Nash, C. (eds) *Queer Methods and Methodologies: Intersecting Queer Theories and Social Science Research*, Abingdon: Routledge: pp 25–40.

Rose, G. (1997) 'Situating knowledges: positionality, reflexivities and other tactics', *Progress in Human Geography*, 21(3): 305–20.

Rose, M. (2016) 'A place for other stories: authorship and evidence in experimental times', *GeoHumanities*, 2(1): 132–48.

Runco, M. and Jaeger, G. (2012) 'The standard definition of creativity', *Creativity Research Journal*, 24(1): 92–6.

Saldaña, J. (2016) *Ethnotheatre: Research from Page to Stage*, Abingdon: Routledge.

Saldaña, J. and Omasta, M. (2018) *Qualitative Research: Analysing Life*, Thousand Oaks: Sage.

Salvatore, J. (2019) 'Ethnodrama and ethnotheatre', in Leavy, P. (ed) *Handbook of Arts-Based Research*, New York: Guilford: pp 267–87.

Sandelowski, M. (1991) 'Telling stories: narrative approaches in qualitative research', *Image: Journal of Nursing Scholarship*, 23(3): 161–6.

Sandercock, L. (2003) 'Out of the closet: the importance of stories and storytelling in planning practice', *Planning Theory and Practice*, 4(1): 11–28.

Sangha, J., Slade, B., Mirchandani, K., Maitra, S. and Shan, H. (2012) 'Ethnodrama on work-related learning in precarious jobs: racialization and resistance', *Qualitative Inquiry*, 18: 286–96.

Sawyer, R.K. (2010) 'Individual and group creativity', in Kaufman, J.C. and Sternberg, R.J. (eds), *Cambridge Handbook of Creativity*, Cambridge: Cambridge University Press: pp 366–80.

Sennett, R. and Cobb, J. (1972) *The Hidden Injuries of Class*, New York: Knopf.

Shah, S. and Greer, S. (2018) 'Polio monologues: translating ethnographic text into verbatim theatre', *Qualitative Research*, 18(1): 53–69.

Sheringham, M. (2000) 'Attending to the everyday: Blanchot, Lefebvre, Certeau, Perec', *French Studies*, LIV: 187–99.

Sinclair, I. (2008) 'The Olympics scam', *London Review of Books*, 30(12): https://www.lrb.co.uk/v30/n12/iain-sinclair/the-olympics-scam.

Sinfield, A. (2005) *Cultural Politics – Queer Reading* (second edition), London: Routledge.

Sjberg, J. (2008) 'Ethnofiction: drama as a creative research practice in ethnographic film', *Journal of Media Practice*, 9(3): 229–42.

Slotnick, R. and Janesick, V. (2011) 'Conversations on method: deconstructing policy through the researcher reflective journal', *The Qualitative Report*, 16(5): 1352–60.

Smith, D. (2015) 'Self-heckle: Russell Kane's stand-up comedy as an example of "comedic sociology"', *Ephemera*, 15(3): 561–80.

Solnit, R. (2006) *A Field Guide to Getting Lost*, Edinburgh: Canongate.

Somers, M.R. (1994) 'The narrative constitution of identity', *Theory and Society*, 23(5): 605–49.

Sou, G. and Douglas, J. (2019) *After Maria: Everyday Recovery from Disaster: A Graphic Novella*, Manchester: University of Manchester.

Sousanis, N. (2015), *Unflattening*, Cambridge, Massachusetts : Harvard University Press.

Sparkes, A.C. (2000) 'Autoethnography and narratives of self', *Sociology of Sport Journal*, 17(1): 21–43.

Stein, S. (1998) *Solutions for Writers: Practical Craft Techniques for Fiction and Non-Fiction*, London: Souvenir.

Stockburger, I. (2015) 'Stancetaking and the joint construction of zine producer identities in a research interview', *Journal of Sociolinguistics*, 19(2): 222–40.

Sword, H. (2012) *Stylish Academic Writing*, Cambridge, MA: Harvard University Press.

Sword, H. (2017) *Air & Light, Time & Space: How Successful Academics Write*, Cambridge, MA: Harvard University Press.

Takayoshi, P. (2019) 'Foreword', in Banks, W.P., Cox, M.B. and Dadas, C. (eds) *Re/Orienting Writing Studies: Queer Methods, Queer Projects*, Boulder: University Press of Colorado: pp xi–xv.

Tamas, S. (2011) 'Biting the tongue that speaks you: (re) writing survivor narratives', *International Review of Qualitative Research*, 4: 431–59.

Tan, C. (2017) 'A Confucian conception of critical thinking', *Journal of Philosophy of Education*, 51(1): 331–43.

Thackeray, W.M. (1848) *Vanity Fair: A Novel without a Hero*, London: Blackie.

Theobald, M. (2016) 'Achieving competence: the interactional features of children's storytelling', *Childhood*, 23(1): 87−104.

Thomas, S. (2016) 'Geopoetics: an opening of the world', in Galvin, K. and Prendergast, M. (eds) *Poetic Inquiry II − Seeing, Caring, Understanding: Using Poetry as and for Inquiry*, Rotterdam: Sense: pp 191–204.

Thompson-Lee, C. (2017) *Heteronormativity in a Rural School Community*, Rotterdam: Sense.

Thomson, P. and Kamler, B. (2016) *Detox Your Writing: Strategies for Doctoral Researchers*, Abingdon: Routledge.

Todd, S. (2014) *People: The Rise and Fall of the Working Class*, London: John Murray.

Tolia-Kelly, D.P. (2007) 'Participatory art: capturing spatial vocabularies in a collaborative visual methodology', in Kindon, S., Pain, R. and Kesby, M. (eds) *Participatory Action Research Approaches and Methods*, Abingdon: Routledge: pp 132–40.

Tracy, S. (2010) 'Qualitative quality: eight "Big-Tent" criteria for excellent qualitative research', *Qualitative Inquiry*, 16(10): 837–51.

Vallack, J. (2012) 'News from Dodoma: a play about research in Tanzania', *Creative Approaches to Research*, 5(1): 32–49.

Van Noorden, R. (2014) 'Publishers withdraw more than 120 gibberish papers', *Nature*, 24 February: https://www.nature.com/news/publishers-withdraw-more-than-120-gibberish-papers-1.14763.

Varley, A. (2008) 'A place like this? Stories of dementia, home, and the self', *Environment and Planning D: Society and Space*, 26(1): 47–67.

Vaughn, N., Jacoby, S., Williams, T., Guerra, T., Thomas, N. and Richmond, T. (2013) 'Digital animation as a method to disseminate research findings to the community using a community-based participatory approach', *American Journal of Community Psychology*, 51(1–2): 30–42.

Waite, S. (2017) *Teaching Queer: Radical Possibilities for Writing and Knowing*, Pittsburgh: University of Pittsburgh Press.

Waite, S. (2019) 'How, and why, to write queer: a failing, impossible, contradictory instruction manual for scholars of writing studies', in Banks, W., Cox, M. and Dadas, C. (eds) *Re/orienting Writing Studies: Queer Methods, Queer Projects*, Louisville, CO: University Press of Colorado: pp 42–53.

Wall, S. (2008) 'Easier said than done: writing an autoethnography', *International Journal of Qualitative Methods*, 7(1): 38–53.

Wall, K., Higgins, S. and Smith, H. (2005) 'The visual helps me understand the complicated things', *British Journal of Educational Technology*, 36(5): 851–67.

Wall, K., Higgins, S., Hall, E. and Gascoine, L. (2017) 'What does learning look like?' in Emme, M. and Kirova, A. (eds) *Good Question: Arts-Based Approaches to Collaborative Research with Children and Youth*, Victoria, BC: Canadian Society for Education through Art: pp 211–27.

Walsh, E., Anders, K. and Hancock, S. (2013) 'Understanding, attitude and environment: the essentials for developing creativity in STEM researchers', *International Journal for Researcher Development*, 4(1): 19–38.

Walzer, C. (2008) *Out of Exile: Narratives from the Abducted and Displaced People of Sudan*, San Francisco: McSweeney's Books.

Wandor, M. (2012) 'The creative writing workshop: a survival guide', in Beck, H. (ed) *Teaching Creative Writing*, Basingstoke: Palgrave Macmillan: pp 51–9.

Warner, M. (2012) *Stranger Magic: Charmed States and the Arabian Nights*, London: Vintage.

Watson, C. (2011) 'Staking a small claim for fictional narratives in social and educational research', *Qualitative Research*, 11(4): 395–408.

Watson, C. (2015) *Comedy and Social Science: Towards a Methodology of Funny*, Abingdon: Routledge.

Weaver-Hightower, M. (2013) 'Sequential art for qualitative research', in Syma, C. and Weiner, R. (eds) *Graphic Novels and Comics in the Classroom*, Jefferson: Mcfarland: pp 260–73.

Wegener, C. (2014) 'Writing with Phineas: how a fictional character from A.S. Byatt helped me turn my ethnographic data into research texts', *Cultural Studies – Critical Methodologies*, 14(4): 351–60.

Weiner, R. and Syma, C. (2013) 'Introduction', in Syma, C. and Weiner, R. (eds) *Graphic Novels and Comics in the Classroom*, Jefferson: Mcfarland: pp 1–11.

Winterson, J. (1985) *Oranges Are Not the Only Fruit*, New York: Atlantic Monthly Press.

Winterson, J. (2005) *Lighthousekeeping*, London: Harper Perennial.

Woodrow, N. (2016) *The Geography of Welcome: Refugee Storytelling, Cultural Translation and Co-performing Activism*, PhD Thesis, Queensland University of Technology.

Young, L. and Barrett, H. (2001) 'Adapting visual methods: action research with Kampala street children', *Area*, 33: 141–52.

Zundel, M., Holt, R. and Cornelissen, J. (2013) 'Institutional work in *The Wire*: an ethological investigation of flexibility in organisational adaptation', *Journal of Management Inquiry*, 22(1): 102–20.

Zuss, M. (2012) *The Practice of Theoretical Curiosity*, New York: Springer.

Index